IMPRESSIONS THAT REMAINED

VOLUME II

IMPRESSIONS
THAT REMAINED

MEMOIRS

BY

ETHEL SMYTH

D.B.E.; Mus. Doc.

IN TWO VOLUMES—VOL. II

PART II—(*continued*)
GERMANY AND TWO WINTERS IN ITALY
(1880 TO 1885)

PART III
IN THE DESERT
(1885 TO 1891)

NEW EDITION

LONGMANS, GREEN, AND CO.
39, PATERNOSTER ROW, LONDON
NEW YORK, TORONTO
BOMBAY, CALCUTTA, AND MADRAS

1923

PREFACE[1]

WHEN it was suggested that a Preface to this new Edition of *Impressions that Remained* and *Streaks of Life* would not be amiss, no proposal could have seemed more bewildering to the author. How does one set about giving a new send-off to an old book?

Then came the reflection that every unknown writer who suddenly puts forth into print will often be asked if this was really a maiden effort? Or, in cases like mine, the question may run: ' What made you think of writing your memoirs '? And probably nine times out of ten such enquiries are only a matter of polite ritual. Yet some of these kind questioners may really wish for an answer; if so, this is obviously the moment to say that up to Christmas 1917 I had never attempted anything more ambitious than articles on the Suffrage, and further that the inception of ' Impressions ' was due to a not infrequent combination of ill-luck and happy chance.

I was in Paris, blending war-work with daily visits to a celebrated aurist, and at that time had reason to believe that to listen to music, or think in terms of music, would always be as intolerable to me as it was then. Twice a week I dined alone with a very dear friend, Count Joachim Clary, one of ' les enfants de la maison ' at the Empress Eugénie's English home. I had first known Clary as a clever, good-looking, active, rather spoilt youth; now, though still a young man, he was a cripple, scarcely able to move hand or foot, his

limbs twisted and gnarled with arthritis, in constant pain
day and night, and totally blind. Yet his originality, his
culture, his unconquerable sense of humour and, above all,
his superb courage, made our friendship one of the assets of
my life.

One evening, when I had been recounting some absurd
childish adventures, he said: ' It's a queer thing; we know
each other so well, yet of your life before we met I know
nothing.' And he went on to suggest that these early
experiences, so typically English and already so remote,
would be well worth writing down, and exactly the sort of
thing to read to an invalid after dinner.

I at once set to work and wrote a few chapters, which
Clary approved. Whereupon I showed them to another
friend of mine, Madame Bulteau, who, under the
pseudonym ' Jacques Vontade,' had written a remarkable
book called 'L'Âme des Anglais.' We all called her
' Toche,' and I never knew what Christian name this
symbol stood for; but to me and many, many others she
was what some old Greek has called ' the theatre of my
actions.'

Some day no doubt a literary monument will be raised to
the memory of this wonderful woman. In touch with
some of the most brilliant spirits of France and other
countries, surrounded by a faithful band of privileged intimates, she was, I truly believe, one of the most passionately
adored people that can ever have existed on this planet—the
life, the hope, the support, the inspiration of everyone, male
or female, who came into her orbit. I know of two English
friends of hers besides myself, who, when the time comes,
will have a hand in the upraising of that monument, Edmund
Gosse and Maurice Baring, the latter of whom wrote to me
last autumn when she died: ' Have you read the O. Henry
book, and do you remember what he said about his fits
of depression, how there were days on which he " wouldn't

bet on himself.'' ?   What she did was to make you bet on yourself.'   Nothing could more perfectly describe the chief action of that noble, generous spirit; and I ask myself what greater service one mortal can render another.

Madame Bulteau's opinion of my early chapters coinciding with Clary's, I submitted them to Maurice, who had come from the front to spend a few terribly busy days in Paris, and his verdict was the same as the others.   Soon afterwards I went back to England and was setting to work in real earnest when news came of Clary's wholly unexpected death.   Just before I left he had remarked one day that his life might well drag on for years, and I had replied that in the somewhat similar case of my brother Johnny the same thing had been said, yet the end came suddenly and painlessly.   (I repeated this conversation to the Empress, whose views on how to talk to sick people are described in *Streaks of Life*, and her caustic comment was : ' Alors c'est comme cela que vous consolez vos amis !')   One could only be thankful, of course, that Clary's sufferings were over, yet I often wish he had lived to see the book finished.

Thus it was that ' Impressions that Remained ' and its mainly autobiographical successor came to be written ; thus was the writer mercifully tided over a dark time when it looked as if constructive work on another field would have to be abandoned for ever.

One more thing I should like to say.   In writing what I have hitherto written—and future efforts, if any, will be in the same case—it has been my ardent hope and belief that many readers would say to themselves : ' I am not an artist, nor, so far as I am aware, have I ever attempted to hit any difficult mark ; yet this woman's experiences are curiously like my own !'

If the issue of a new edition may be taken as a proof that this was no vain hope, nothing could make me happier as a musician. For I hold that the permanent quality of an artist's work depends in some mystical manner on the genuineness and multiplicity of his points of contact with life. More than this is needful, of course; the not wholly negligeable matter of talent, for instance; also the gift of self-expression and adequate technical equipment. But the indispensable foundation—in my opinion at least—is a very close touch with reality; a touch, moreover, that has to be constantly tested and readjusted as the years roll on.

Finally, to conclude in the old French manner with a *moralité*, it seems to me that if one can but grow wisdom and determination enough to keep up this difficult process to the very end, aided and abetted by the one sense that grows stronger with advancing years, the sense of humour, then, I venture to think, no one need be afraid of growing old.

1923.

CONTENTS

OF

THE SECOND VOLUME

(PART II.—*Continued.*)

CHAPTER XXVII (Summer 1880 to Summer 1881)

APPENDIX III

CHAPTER XXVIII (Autumn 1881 to Autumn 1882)

CHAPTER XXIX (Autumn 1882 to Christmas 1882)

PART III. IN THE DESERT

CONTENTS

CHAPTER XLV (Epilogue)

APPENDIX VI

MUSICAL QUOTATIONS IN THE SECOND VOLUME

PART II.—*Continued*

GERMANY AND TWO WINTERS IN ITALY

CHAPTER XXVII

SUMMER 1880 TO SUMMER 1881

WHILE travelling with my mother I had been told about a charming newcomer in our neighbourhood whom she had as yet seen little of, but who was said to be very musical and looking forward to meeting the Leipzig daughter. Knowing what ' very musical ' amounts to in England expectation did not run high, but on the day she had been asked to lunch I sat down at the piano, just for fun, as her dogcart drew up at the door, and began playing ' Im Freien '—a Schubert song I was wild about just then. Presently a very nice-looking woman of the smart sporting type was ushered in who cheerfully uttered the words : ' Ah ! dear old Chopsticks !' . . .

The drawback of this anecdote is that probably few serious musicians know ' Chopsticks,' and the sort of people who know ' Chopsticks ' are still less likely to know ' Im Freien.' I shall therefore give a few bars of each, and to simplify matters will transpose ' Chopsticks ' for the first time in its life into the key of the other—five flats.

Chopsticks.

(Bars 4 to 8).   Im Freien

Fortunately there was one person present worthy this moment—my mother.

On the other hand, during these holidays I was destined to meet a being in whose existence I did not believe—an Englishwoman of my own type, that is one not born to the profession, with whom I could associate musically on equal terms; and as she lived only ten miles off it became my habit to fly over to see her whenever I could, generally with a roll of music paper tied on to my saddle. Thus began the friendship between me and Adela Wodehouse (wife of Mr. Edmund Wodehouse, M.P. for Bath), a friendship which was the chief musical stimulus of my life in England, and which has lasted to this day—unchanged but for the *patina* that all things real, solid, and delicate acquire with years.

That summer I sang enough Schubert to satisfy even my mother. Papa, though wholly unmusical, liked soft music after dinner, and there was one song we christened ' Papa's Surprise ' for he never recognised it. Each time it began he would say : ' Now I like that,' and gradually his *Times* would sink on to his knees and his eyes close. The song is Schubert's ' Du bist die Ruh '—for two verses the gentlest strain ever penned; but in the third, at the words (I translate literally) ' This canopy of thine eyes, by thy brilliance . . . ALONE . . . LIGHTED ' ! it suddenly surges, and very quickly too, to a crash on a high note . . . after which there is a pause. At this point again and again Papa would wake up with a start and say : ' Hullo !—is that the gun? '

During these holidays a case of mis-interpreted symptoms occurred which I cite as a warning to mothers and aunts. Mary Hunter's second baby, Phyllis, a very pretty child with big blue eyes, showed such an extraordinary sensibility to music—straining out of her nurse's arms till her head almost touched the keyboard—that we concluded, much to her father's horror, she must be a musical genius. But she turned out to be merely an exceptionally highly strung child; and though in after years she bore the infliction of a musical aunt with heroism, she rather dislikes music than otherwise.

      .   .   .   .   .

And now, on the eve of chronicling yet another great friendship, the moment has come to express regret that unlike other women-writers of memoirs, such as Sophie Kowalewski, George Sand, and Marie Bashkirtseff—if for a moment I may class myself with such as these—I have so far no orthodox love affairs to relate, neither soulful sentiment for musician of genius, nor perilous passion conceived among the reeds of the Crostewitz lake for proud Prussian guardsman. In my letters to Lisl, where all the secrets of my heart stand revealed, I again and again express a conviction it is foolish to insist upon, so obvious is it, that the most perfect relation of all must be the love between man and woman, but this seemed to me, given my life and outlook, probably an unachievable thing. Where should be found the man whose existence could blend with mine without loss of quality on either side? My work must, and would always, be the first consideration, and as I said elsewhere, the idea that men might think one wanted to catch them checked incipient romance. For a space I had imagined myself in love with the husband of one of my friends, *not* Aloysius by the by !— a ridiculous fancy at once confessed to his wife, who was

rather gratified and not at all alarmed. This fleeting sentiment was mastered and consigned to limbo without its object
being any the wiser; and all the time I was more or less
aware that had this individual been eligible such an idea
would never have entered my head. As in the case of my
own admirers, immunity from consequences favoured the
tender illusion of a hopeless attachment. What Fate had in
reserve for me as regards the supremest relation of all who
could say? . . . meanwhile, as my mother wrote in a letter
to a friend, the desire to be looked after, helped, and loved
was as imperative as the instinct of independence that seemed
predominant. And as, in order to receive you must give
. . . give I did! But only to women.

Let me say here, that all my life, even when after years
had brought me the seemingly unattainable, I have found in
women's affection a peculiar understanding, mothering
quality that is a thing apart. Perhaps too I had a fore-
knowledge of the difficulties that in a world arranged by man
for man's convenience beset the woman who leaves the
traditional path to compete for bread and butter, honours
and emoluments—difficulties honest men are more aware of,
perhaps, than she of the sheltered life. I had no theories
about it then but I think I guessed it. Even among the con-
formists I saw good, brave women obliged because of their
sex to give way before dullness, foolishness, or brutality;
and in natures inclined to side with the handicapped these
things kindle sympathy and admiration. And further it is a
fact, as H. B. once remarked, that the people who have
helped me most at difficult moments of my musical career,
beginning with my own sister Mary, have been members of
my own sex. Thus it comes to pass that my relations with
certain women, all exceptional personalities I think, are
shining threads in my life.

In one of her letters Jane Austen remarks that so and so
is ' too apt to like people '—a tendency which is possibly a
sign of a generous temperament, as one would like to
believe, but which also implies lack of self-control, and sometimes a wilful drugging of one's critical faculties. Owing to

this weakness I often made mistakes, yet only one bad one—
a misfortune mentioned from honesty, as it happened long
after the date at which these Memoirs close. And I may
add that if the world is inclined to scoff or speak ill of
women's friendships, this is one of those cheap generalities
which will pass muster only as long as women let men do
their thinking for them, and which moreover are given the
lie to by the experience of many who hand them round, did
they but choose to testify. Having said this I will now pass
on to the next on my list of great friendships.

Barbara Hamley had often spoken to me of Agnes and
Rhoda Garrett, who were among the first women in England
to start business on their own account and by that time were
well-known house decorators of the Morris school. Agnes
was sister to Mrs. Fawcett and Dr. Garrett Anderson—
Rhoda, their cousin, rather older than Agnes, daughter of a
clergyman whose second wife appeared to consider herself
exonerate from responsibility as regards her predecessor's
children. Late in the autumn Barbara introduced me to
these great friends of hers, and during the next two years
their house became the focus of my English life owing to the
friendship that sprang up between Rhoda and me. Both
women were a good deal older than I, how much I never
knew—nor wished to know, for Rhoda and I agreed that
age and income are relative things concerning which
statistics are tiresome and misleading.

How shall one describe that magic personality of hers, at
once elusive and clear-cut, shy and audacious—a dark cloud
with a burning heart—something that smoulders in repose
and bursts into flame at a touch! Though the most alive,
amusing, and amused of people, to me at least the sombre
background was always there—perhaps because the shell
was so obviously too frail for the spirit. One knew of the
terrible struggle in the past to support herself and the young
brothers and sisters; that she had been dogged by ill-health
as well as poverty—heroic, inflinching through all. Agnes
once said to me : ' Rhoda has had more pain in her life than

was good for her,' but no one guessed that like her brother Edmund—champion of Rhodes, youthful collaborator with Lord Milner, cut off at the zenith of his powers—she carried in her the seeds of tubercular disease.   And yet when the end came there was little of surprise in one's grief; thus again and again had one seen falling stars burn out.

I spoke of her humour; on the whole I think she was more amusing than anyone I have ever met—a wit half-scornful, always surprising, as unlike everyone else's as was her person . . . a slim, lithe being, very dark, with deep-set burning eyes that I once made her laugh by saying reminded me of a cat in a coal scuttle.   Yet cat's eyes are never tender, and hers could be the tenderest in the world.

I always think the feel of a hand as it grasps yours is a determining factor in human relationships, and all her friends must well remember Rhoda's—the soft, soft skin that only dark people have, the firm, wiry, delicate fingers. My reason tells me she was almost plain, but one looked at no one else when she was in a room.   There was an enigmatic quality in her witchery behind which the grand lines, the purity and nobility of her soul, stood out like the bone in some enchanted landscape.   No one had a more subtle hold on the imagination of her friends, and when she died it was as if laughter, astonishment, warmth, light, mystery, had been cut off at the source.   The beauty of the relation between the cousins, and of that home life in Gower Street, remains with us who knew them as certain musical phrases haunt the melomaniac, and but for Agnes, who stood as far as was possible between her and the slings and arrows which are the reward of pioneers, no doubt Rhoda's life would have spent itself earlier.   Her every burden, human and otherwise, was shouldered by Agnes, and both had a way of discovering waifs and strays of art more or less worsted by life whose sanctuary their house henceforth became.

Soon after making their acquaintance I went back to Leipzig with a new interest to look forward to for my next stay in England.

.   .   .   .

There is not much to relate about that autumn and winter in Germany. The various musical events, sonatas and quartetts hopefully composed and privately performed, though enthralling incidents at the time, are of no interest in after years to anyone—not even to the composer herself. But March 1881 I well remember, for a stray reference shows it was then that I paid my first visit to a princely castle—a real castle this time.

There was a certain young Prince Reuss cramming under Wach for his law degree who was a very gifted composer and might have gone far but for his high estate. This youth, too delicate to propose it himself (for Herzogenberg only taught me as a special favour) implored me to persuade Aloysius to give him lessons, which Aloysius who had a strange passion for teaching consented to do. And often did he complain, both before Reuss and behind his back, of the new pupil's ' durchlauchtige Schlamperei ' (Serene-Highness-like slovenliness). I thus saw a great deal of this young man who was very attentive, so much so that Brahms's joke of the moment was to call me ' die durchlauchtige Miss. ' Frau Livia, too, thought well to remind me that the alliances of these princelings are as carefully regulated as those of the Hohenzollerns themselves—a warning that half amused, half infuriated me. Frau Livia never could understand that from my point of view Reuss was no more a possible husband than a chimney sweep—in fact less so, for I might have ridden rough-shod over the sweep but never over the traditions of a mediatised princeling. Yet it rather provoked me, and Lisl too, that safely entrenched in the Almanach de Gotha, Reuss seemed to think he could flirt with an ineligible young woman as much as he pleased— King Cophetua miraculously inoculated against possible complications with the beggar-maid.

The Reusses, as may be gathered from bewildering reference to them in contemporaneous history, are all named Heinrich and numbered, the numbers running up to 60 and then starting afresh. The reigning Reuss-Köstritz, our Heinrich's father, was rather a nice old man almost as musical as his son, and there were two very friendly daughters a little older than I, one of whom married the King of Bulgaria. They once told me comically and truly that they were ' langweilig aber herzvoll ' (dull but full of heart). Their brother, Heinrich XXIV, was saved from commonplaceness by an abounding sense of humour which now and again stopped dead at unexpected places—as often happens with German princes.

To the castle of these potentates, when it became impossible for the home-loving Herzogenbergs to go on refusing repeated invitations, did we repair. The manner of life seemed curious to me but was I believe typical; a mixture of formality and unbending, of lavishness and pettifogging economy not without humorous charm. Certain features of it horrified my democratic fellow guests. For instance the fare of the singing mistress, a Leipzig gentlewoman treated by them as family friend, was included in her yearly fee on a second-class basis, which was quite reasonable since it is a German saying that only princes, English people, and fools travel first-class. But if by chance they travelled together, which sometimes happened, as the princesses often shopped in Leipzig, they would converse with this lady amicably on the platform and then stalk into their own first-class com-partment, never dreaming of asking her to join them. From start to finish of our stay music was made, and it was the same when a few days later I went to Weimar to visit a connection, Cecilia Wodehouse, who had married a certain Baron von Liliencron, cousin of Herzogenberg and an admir-able 'cellist. What has always seemed to me the only thing that counts, being a matter that boom and fashion cannot affect, is the general level of musical intelligence in a country, including the part played by art in domestic life; and certainly at that time Germany was ideal in that respect.

That year the fury of the Germans raged over the South African war, and I then fully realised a fact of which incidents such as the scene with the musical stationer had given me an inkling; namely that, unutterably kind as every-one was to me personally—and let me say once for all that

forty volumes of Memoirs would not exhaust that theme—
England had become an object of jealous detestation to the
coming race of political thinkers in Germany. Unfortunately
every male German seemed to be a politician, and I was
assailed on all sides, cross-questioned, and bullied about our
South African muddles till at last I wrote to my father asking for a few good arguments.   As there were none no
wonder his replies were unconvincing.

That spring someone lent me a well-bred little mare, and
remembering the Fiedler incident carefully informed me she
could not jump.   But one day I met an hilarious party driving a wagon full gallop in a field lane, and when I pressed
her up against some stout rails to make room, she suddenly
leapt them sideways in a style only an accomplished fencer
could manage without coming to grief.   Put at them in
orthodox fashion her performance was so brilliant that I
persuaded the owner to let me ride her in a ' Schnitzel Jagd '
—mild steeplechases got up periodically by the Leipzig young
men.   If I had won I should certainly remember, and still
more certainly record the fact !

.   .   .   .   .   .

When the time came round again for leaving Leipzig, love
of ' Faust,' and curiosity to see old German architecture took
me home *viâ* the Harz, Brunswick, and Hildesheim.   The
Brocken, viewed at midday in the wrong light, looked so
insignificant and hideous that I wished I had never gone
there, but the old towns made up for it; also Bremen, where
as a special favour, and in spite of the South African war, I
was allowed to taste the famous century-old wine kept in a
vat as big as a small house.   It was like stale gooseberry
wine only nastier.   These journeys were conducted on such
economical lines that they cost less, all told, than a through
ticket to England.   Herzogenberg once said, after we had
been on a joint excursion somewhere, that at every place
I came to I made for the most villainous looking hotel I
could find and asked for a ' Kutscher Zimmer ' (a cabman's
room), which was more or less true.   But what matter ; who
cares about comfort in early life?   At Hildesheim I saw a

gigantic rose-tree, said to be 500 years old, that almost hid the church tower it clambered over, and when I told our gardener Allen about it he said : ' Dear me, that's quite a novelty.' Allen, like most old gardeners, was a character, but all I will say about him is that he constantly used a fine terse expression I have clung to all my life—the sort of expression you never hear in drawing-rooms—*making a job* of a thing. No weakening adjective; not a good job . . . just *a job.*

.   .   .   .   .   .

That summer, when not at Frimhurst or visiting Alice and Mary in the North, I of course spent all my time with the Garretts, and seeing that for nine months of the year I was in Germany this pained my mother. They rented an old thatched cottage at Rustington of which they had made the most perfect of habitations, and the summer holidays and any odd days they could snatch from business were spent there. Rustington was then quite an unfrequented spot— a few straggling old cottages and farmhouses, a fine Norman church, sometimes flicked by spray when S.W. gales blew, and an almost deserted beach.

I think I have never been happier in my life than there. An exhausting fight against the stream of prejudice, such as the Garretts had waged for many years, was not to be my portion till later ; still we were all three hard-working women, and if circumstances are propitious no one can be more happily lazy than workers. Of course both cousins and all their friends were ardent Suffragists, and I wonder now at the patience with which they supported my total indifference on the subject—an indifference I was to make up for thirty years later.

Their great friends the Parrys had a house close by, and besides helping me with invaluable musical criticism and advice Hubert Parry lent me a canoe, in which on very calm days, cautiously dressed in bathing costume, I put out to sea. There too I got to know the Fawcetts, and saw how that living monument of courage, the blind Postmaster-General, impressed the country people as he strode up and down the hills in the company of his wife. I thought Mrs. Fawcett rather cold, but an incident that happened the summer after the death of Rhoda, to whom she was devoted, taught me otherwise. One day when I was singing an Irish melody I had often sung at Rustington—' At the mid hour of night ' —I suddenly noticed that tears were rolling down her cheeks, and presently she got up and quietly left the room. After that for many years I never saw her. Then came the acute Suffrage struggle, during which the gulf that separated Militants from National Unionists belched forth flames, but through all those years, remembering that incident, I always thought of Mrs. Fawcett with affection. . . .

The beach at Rustington is connected in my mind with one of the oddest manifestations of the tender passion I ever heard of. A certain man we knew, not a bachelor, was secretly beloved—only it wasn't quite a secret—by a maiden of gentle birth. The man, a strong swimmer, was in the habit of seeking out desolate places on the shore, depositing his garments in a bundle among the brushwood, and swimming out miles and miles to sea. One day when he returned he found a little bunch of flowers on the bundle and thought it was a joke of some passing stranger . . . but next day the same thing happened. Much perturbed, he varied his jumping-off place, but without success, for the hour of high tide is no secret and he was marked down by this infatuated maiden again and again. Just as I was leaving Rustington his much amused wife told us he talked of giving up bathing

.　　.　　.　　.　　.　　.

My mother's trips to Homburg had now become an annual necessity—the one welcome result in her eyes of her growing infirmities—but whoever took her there that year I fear it was not I. Nina was out now, and Violet just emerging, and it became an institution that during mother's absences from home, whether abroad or on visits to Alice and Mary, Aunt Judy should install herself at Frimhurst as chaperone. As I have said, the whole family adored her, and their affection was warmly reciprocated, but I fancy that finding herself once more within reach of Aldershot and the homage of the R.E.'s was the supreme delight of these visits.

Of course they flocked to see her, and there were many little expeditions to the camp—tea with old friends, or at the R.E. mess, regimental sports, and so on. Nothing if not feminine, Aunt Judy would often insist on her nervousness, but I always think it argued great courage on the part of an invalid to drive about the country in our carriages, for owing to rising prices my father's bargains in horseflesh were becoming ever younger and less well-mannered, and our fantastic reputation for accidents was growing. Driving to balls in winter was really no joke, for two great belts of fog rising from the Canal and the Blackwater (of vegetable-marrow fame) lay across the road to almost anywhere, and at such spots Papa would spend the time head out of window, exhorting the coachman in Anglo-Indian phraseology to ' keep on the track.' And a legend had reached Aunt Judy in the far North that, ever hopeful, he had once continued these admonitions, with emphatic reinforcement, while the carriage was in the very act of slowly turning over into the ditch. But fortunately for her most of her chaperone visits took place in the summer when at least the fog danger was in abeyance.

I think she thoroughly enjoyed supervising her charges' little flirtations, and certainly took a touching interest in them as some of her letters to be given later will show.[1] At first I meant to eliminate where possible the poor spine, the feather bed, the wretched head, etc., etc., referred to elsewhere, but her literary style twines so gracefully among these unlovely themes, like dog-roses among old brambles, that I thought better of it. In a letter not appended there is trenchant allusion to my preoccupation with my new friends; ' the General's portrait of Ethel flying hither and thither after successive deities of her imagination—tho' I regard these attachments as so much froth and foam on the top of a deep affection for her own people—is very vivid, and sounds

---

[1] Appendix III., p. 41, No. 2 et seq.

anything but soothing to tired and sensitive nerves. However I suppose one must pay for bringing a pocket Niagara into the world! But she is not in the first uproar of youthful flightiness now and I do wish she were more considerate of you.' I re-echo that wish with all my heart, but cannot help thinking that if dear Aunt Judy had herself been No. 1, as in days of yore, she might have been more lenient!

During the particular summer I am writing about she arrived as usual a few days before my mother's departure for the North, and learned that this time her flock was to include a certain Miss H.—one of mother's treasures picked up in Homburg who was about to pay us a first visit, and whose dramatic arrival next day she had the luck to witness. A new cook being expected by the same train, the tax-cart had been sent to the station as well as the brougham, and in due course the horrified party assembled on the lawn saw the cart pull up at the front door with a stout person in it clad in bright blue velvet (it was a hot summer's day) and covered with chains and brooches. My mother rose and made at a relatively rapid pace for the porch, prepared to send this audacious lady back whence she came with a month's wages, but lo and behold! it was her new friend, who having asked for the Frimhurst conveyance, and finding only the tax-cart, had, like a sensible woman, got in, the groom taking her of course for the cook. As Papa was a magistrate, policemen were often about the place, and a handy constable, despatched at once to find out what had become of the brougham, returned in five minutes to report that a fly was in the canal with a lady inside.

The lady turned out to be the new cook; the lost brougham came home two or three hours later, and the very simple explanation of the whole affair was that our then coachman was yet another old soldier, and that between Frimhurst and the station there were no fewer than seven public-houses. . . . Miss H. informed us that the groom's face when bidden to take her to the front door was a study, and added that if we knew all she had learned about the family during that drive we should never hold up our heads again!

Before starting next day my mother had specially begged Aunt Judy to send an account of her impressions of the new guest, and the impressions were not favourable.[1] A cheery, bouncing Canadian, not in her first youth, she was the last person to appeal to Mrs. Ewing's taste, but the real rock of offence was a determined effort to set up a flirtation with my father. As I have hinted, Aunt Judy herself was not averse to a little delicate flirting on her own lines; we all, even mother, her great friend, used to smile to ourselves when, after washing her hair, she would appear in the drawing-room, cover the hearthrug with a towel, and with a charming ' May I? ' lie down flat on her back, spreading out her long pale-golden tresses fanwise. But she was an old friend, and such tender little graces were soon put out of court by the extremely vigorous methods of the other. Papa's conduct under assault seems to have been blameless; indeed, the lady being neither young nor beautiful I can well believe that though gratified he was more bored than anything else.

And now mark how even a very clever woman will put her foot into it sometimes. In an evil hour Aunt Judy thought it her duty to report these proceedings to the absent lady of the house; the result was manifest gratitude . . . tempered by so much secret resentment, that from henceforth my mother's enthusiasm for her friend began to cool ! And this is the explanation of a thing that had puzzled me—the rather sudden petering out of the correspondence.

But if this was a case of moral zeal in the wrong place, the more I reflect, the greater waxes my admiration for Aunt Judy's physical courage. At one time we had a pair of carriage horses afflicted with nerves to such an extent, that nothing would induce them to wait at the front door. My father's solution of this difficulty was to ' keep them moving ' round and round the grass plot till what seemed a favourable moment for attempting a brief halt somewhere near the porch. Passenger No. 1 would then be hustled in, the door banged, and off went the horses again, tearing and

---

[1] Appendix III., p. 44.

plunging, till one by one the other passengers had been collected. Meanwhile Papa would stand on the steps, bellowing directions, but he always yielded courteously to Aunt Judy's entreaty that she might be first in the field, ' so that there may be room,' she said, ' to fall flat on my face.' And in that posture she was once borne round and round the grass plot at a hand-gallop for several minutes, deeming it safest on the whole to lie quite still. I am sure it need not be added that my father saw nothing peculiar in this sort of start for a quiet afternoon drive.

APPENDIX III

(a)

FROM ELISABETH VON HERZOGENBERG (LISL)

(1)

Ober Döbling : June 12, 1878.

(*In German.*) . . . What a queer desire . . . to want to hear ' one more dream ' ! well, here it is. It was the day of your departure; you were starting first, not I, and had not come to say good-bye. I was surprised at this and went to the window to see if you were not coming . . . and then suddenly there was a big piece of water—the Channel I suppose—and I saw you on the boat. I stretched out my arms towards you, you did the same, and as I ran to the

shore, I saw you making signs the result of which was that
the ship came to land.   But while we were saying good-bye
it went off again, and you said you would catch it at the next
landing-place.   I feared for your heart and said : ' Anyhow
I will go with you all the way, Ethel,' and we hurried along
arm in arm.   But I felt I couldn't keep it up and got
frightened yet didn't want to forsake you, and both of us
were in a state of strange distress and sadness; then all
became misty till the deafening noise of a mill past which we
were tearing woke me up. . . . How vividly I remember
looking out of the window, seeing you standing there, and
stretching out longing arms towards you ! . . .

(2)

July 15, 1878.

(*In German.*) . . . What you say about your multi-
farious occupations, including, it would seem, some literary
undertaking or other, fills me with apprehension.   It seems
to me you have a specific duty towards your gift for music
and should not let yourself be drawn away in other directions.   If you were not in the growing stage I would say
nothing ; why should you not develop yourself in all directions and put forth as many shoots as you please?   But
talent is a Destiny that imposes definite responsibilities . . .
and one must wholly give oneself up to it when young if it is
to bear good fruit.   You know that as well as I, but your
ambitions take you into side paths.   I am absolutely against
the one-sided education that turns people into machines—
botanical, geographical, mathematical or otherwise—and
brushes aside all human considerations as not to the purpose.
But in the case of a normal, healthily developed individual
like yourself, who has eyes and ears for everything that
merits attention, who has cultivated no one quality at the
expense of the rest, who in a word is first a human being and
then an artist, I do not think there is any danger of becoming one-sided—even though one's whole energy be focussed
by the burning glass of enthusiasm in the interests of one
specific talent, and a flame kindled that everything else must
feed.

Ethel ! you have not yet served your music for seven years,

and you think its conquest easier than is really the case—that is to say you don't think so really, but your quickly stirred nature responds to this and that call, and whatever you are doing at the moment seems to you of supreme importance . . . even lawn tennis !   And then you become deaf, or won't listen, to the soft voice of what ought to be dearer to you than everything else !   I was going to say all this before your last letter arrived in which you confess that you are idle ! . . . O wicked, lazy Virgin, who does not deserve that the precious lamp should have been put into her hand unless she takes better care of it ! . . . Ethel, beware lest it should be with you as with me. . . . I often could weep to think of the time I have lost, how badly I have husbanded my little talent.   And now here I am—for all my artist's soul in the bonds of wretched dilettantism !   If you knew what pain my conscience gives me, how it hurts as if it had an actual seat within like the heart one feels beating, you would do anything to avoid such a fate.

It is evident to me that the first step, difficult as it seemed, of winning your freedom, was nothing compared to what should follow—the daily working up of energy for a persistent diligence against which our weaknesses, big and little, are for ever in array ! . . . Poor little Ethel, no one can understand your state of mind better than I, who am far more lazy by nature than you !   And now, when I would give anything to work hard, it is too late ! . . .

Tell me how you divide up your day, how much time remains for music when you have got through your literary work, your riding, your social distractions, your dinner-parties, your lying about in the fields with Goethe under your arm?   I cannot imagine how you can get in any real work, even a little counterpoint.   I know that to work 3 *Canti firmi* carefully takes me a lot of time, and besides that there is your piano practice to be done, your reading at sight, your studying, if possible, of scores, and your Variations to be written ! . . . O Ethel how can the day be long enough for all this? and yet you long for more, cannot console yourself for renouncing your usual lawn-tennis triumphs, and are pining for balls ! . . . Ach Gott ! Ach Gott ! what a demon of life possesses you ! (la cigale ayant chanté tout l'été, etc.). . . . My beloved child, you asked for a sermon and now you've got one !   And don't talk to me about your youth ;

you are far older than your years in many ways and in some
respects have more wisdom than many a woman of 40—
therefore have no excuse.

. . . I am sorry the doctor you were all so attached to is
dead, but glad that he is no longer there to allow you to
dance !   Ethel—how can one take such trivial things so
seriously !   Look at me ! I too was young once and often
thought how good it must be to abandon oneself, undeterred
by other considerations, to the physical intoxication, the
blood-stirring, cunningly-wrought rhythms of dancing.   But
as it so came that I was not allowed to dance I never made a
hardship of it—and here are you in despair, at missing a
few balls ! !   Oh !   Oh !   Oh ! . . .

(3)

July 24, 1878.

(*In English.*) . . . Letters are such poor things (though
dear kind things) as one always says less or more than one
means.   You mustn't then take it too seriously when I
wonder at your *passion* for physical amusements.   I *can*
quite understand it, though I never had a share in these pursuits, but what I couldn't help being troubled at was the
importance you gave to half a year's sacrifice of these games,
dancing, riding, etc.   All you say about your being a doll
filled with sawdust and all that is rubbish of course, as you
very well know, and I won't have you blaspheme in that
way ; but what I clearly see is that you must have even more
musical gift than I thought till now, as it could develop itself
under so difficult circumstances.   I always fear if you once
give the devil of games your little finger, he'll take your
whole hand without that you get conscious of it, and your
physical nature will swallow your spiritual nature. . . .
About the parties your mother likes you to go to, you could
make her understand, surely, that you daren't loose your
time (oh ! what a precious thing is time !) in that shameful
way idle people do.   Say what you like, but have the energy
without which talent comes to nothing.   As Heinrich always
says, talent is above all things a gift of character, and he is
right.   (*In German.*) The other day when I gave him a
very mitigated account of your proceedings he got quite sad

and thoughtful, shaking his head and saying : ' I don't know
that our little Ethel will come to much if things go on like
that.' And he thinks so highly of you, my child ! . . .

(4)

August 14, 1878. (*In English.*) My dearest Ethel,—I
believe I left you rather long without news, but darling, only
think that at Vilden I was with a sister—my only sister that
I had not seen for two years ! How much to recapitulate,
how much discoveries to make, how much to look and hark
at, how much honey to suck, how much to pat and kiss and
what else ! We went on chattering, though that is not the
right word, the whole day and had a good time of it ! and I
have grown prouder than ever of this sister. O Ethel what
a poor earthly, dusty creature I feel near her, yet this best of
all women loves me and I feel as if this love could prevent
me of growing wicked and help me even to get better.
Darling, it's no use trying to make a picture of her ; I could
only enumerate certain qualities and particularities of her,
and you best know how very far that kind of description is of
a real characterisation. What I best would like to say of
her is what Portia says of the star, when she goes home with
Nerissa : ' So shines a good deed in a naughty world.'
Darling, you know what we mean by ' Einheit '—unity I
suppose you call it—well, I never met a person whose personality had such a unity, such a perfume of perfect harmony. And then, what makes her so beautiful in my eyes,
she has won ' the peace that passeth all understanding,' that
we, you, my Ethel, and I, aim at ; and this peace wraps
everyone in its sweet shade that approaches her ; it seems not
so unattainable as you said in that letter of yours you felt it
to be, so that I begin to hope it for myself and you. Ethel,
I do feel quite incapable of describing this sister to you yet I
should so much like to give you a ' taste ' of her, as I am
quite superstitious in respect to her, and really do believe
only a glimpse of her must work wonders. I wish you knew
her, then you would see what a doll filled with sawdust *I* am
compared to her ; and though I hope you wouldn't leave off
liking me you would *venerate* her.

Another pleasure I had in Vilden was Brahms. He lives on the other side of the lake and we spent an afternoon with him. (*In German.*) I never saw him in kindlier mood; he showed us five new songs and a Motett he wrote in memory of poor von Holstein. He is sparing of words, this remarkable man, and often gives an impression of dryness; but every genuine experience of his turns into gold within. What exquisite emotion is once more enshrined in this piece, what ripeness in the contemplation of life and death! and at the same time the whole is expressed in terms of pure music. A real, joy-giving work of art. Henry privately copied it (a secret, mind! or else woe betide us!) and I know it nearly by heart; thus we carry it about with us, safely hidden in the deepest depths of our drawers and souls, and are so happy about it. Nothing is comparable to this delight in the fine work (*im schönen Wirken*) of others—this pure, calm, admiring contemplation of beauty, detached from all personal striving; nothing is more soothing, emancipating, beneficent;[1] and that my Heinrich can do this, can so utterly get rid of himself in such moments, is one among the many things that make his worth for me. There are so many who in their ardent hunger for their own development never achieve this quiet forgetfulness of self; how much they are to be pitied! . . .

I can imagine how it amuses you studying the ' Liebeslieder ' with those automatons; it must be like striking sparks from flint. . . . It's not that there are so many faults in your counterpoint, but it sounds so awkward and as if . . . it had rather bored you! You must first learn to find it amusing work!

(5)

September 29, 1878. (*In German.*) . . . I look back upon this summer with so much happiness; being together with my splendid sister has left a warmth, a deep resonance in my soul that nothing can take away; and the good time with my mother, combined with counterpoint, and watching the dear, gentle cows browsing among the green fields . . . what sympathetic memories!

[1] ' Lösend, erlösend.'

Yesterday was the 10th anniversary of our wedding day; think how old we are, 10 years married, and thank God as full of joy in each other as we ever were! It is strange after such a lapse of time to feel so young, as though on the brink of Life in which one has already swum so far. Many things have come differently to what I hoped for; even when I was engaged my fondest dream was . . . children. I remember once in those days taking a child on to my lap with a strange feeling of emotion, and when Heinrich petted it I thought to myself how well it would be with me some day. But it was not to be, and I have learned that the happy have plenty of spare strength which they can and ought to devote to renouncing cheerfully even that which is best and most beautiful. . . .

(6)

Dresden : March 1879.

(*In English.*) . . . I know you oh! so well now, and I have the feeling as if your coming life was spread before my eyes—not in its details of course, but in its colour, its key, and as if I saw a deep sunshine and a calm, serene atmosphere reposing on it. Bless you my child. . . . (*In German.*) Yes, the doctor does give hope; after a short easy cure next summer all may yet come true! I thank you for sharing this time with me, this longing to call a child my very own. Till that happens, and for my part I dare no longer hope, tell yourself that this much you have done for me—wakened in me a mother's tenderness such as I never felt before in this world except in dreams. During those bad days, when it was given to me to comfort you and hold you to my heart and dry your tears, the moment was both sad and happy, for I thought to myself : What must it be if *that* lot should be mine, the one I long for! Yet how good is this, and how I love this other child of mine! . . .

(7)

Dresden : March 1879.

(*In German.*) . . . O my child, cheer up about it all; you repented, and God, the kind God of Love, asks no more of us! . . .

In the train I read ' Adam Bede ' (but for that the thought
of your trouble would have worried me all day) and I was in
a good mood for appreciating its beauties—that fine fellow
Adam, and the harmony in Dinah that cannot but take hold
of one even though she speaks another language than ours,
and deals in conceptions that have not our sympathy. How
beautiful harmony is, no matter from what source it springs !
. . . Once more, do not trouble your head about all that past
business. My child, in this burning love for what we think
good and right let us remain deeply linked together, as in
other things, for ever and ever. I will always warn you if
I think you need it and if you see me falter or fail you must
help me. And if that is not a lasting bond I don't know
what is. . . .

(8)

May 25, 1879. (*In German.*) I feel sometimes as if the
happiness bestowed on me were almost too great, as if I
were spoiled by Fate ; and yet when I see Julia, to whom a
second child will so soon be born, I stretch out my arms for
more happiness, have visions of that which I long for as if it
had already belonged to me, and must come back again.
But I do not feel it as a *pain,* my darling, or only sometimes ;
as a rule I even enjoy the faculty of comprehending the joys
I know not, and find compensation for what is denied me in
this intense realisation of what I miss. . . . How I thank
you for calling me Mother ; do you know you have helped
me, for since I have you I bear it more easily having no child
of my own. Thank God that there is such a thing as love on
this earth—now don't add this time ' *and hunting* ' ! . . .
Good-bye liebstes Weibliches (*untranslatable ; means ' the
one I love best of the female sex* ')—whose name is written
deep down in my heart close to Heinrich's ! . . .

(9)

Graz: June 14, 1879. (*In German.*) . . . I cannot understand why you should wish X to be *fond* of you ; if one is
really loved by the people that matter how can one care two
straws what others, however admirable and interesting, feel

for one? . . . I fear it is love of conquest! Beware, Ethel, of that trait in you. And if you are so bent on conquest, why not put your energy into conquering your little weaknesses, and when you have to do without what you want, accept the fact with a cheerful countenance? . . . I cannot understand you in this whole affair, for ' understanding ' means, surely, that one would feel or act similarly under the circumstances—and that I cannot achieve. (*In English.*) O my child . . . this tendency of yours to be influenced by what is *nearest!* . . . and I see so many pencils stretched out to write upon the blank pages of that book so dear to me called Ethel! . . . Keep fast to me, near me, in spite of them; I can never let go of you!

(10)

Graz: September 21, 1879. (*In German.*) . . . What you find ' amusing ' in the butterfly you describe, however charming, I cannot understand. Don't you see how unpleasant it is, this playing with feelings that ought to be taken seriously . . . (or possibly working oneself up into imaginary states of mind) all this misuse of good energy, of fine words, of the gentle physical expressions we call caresses? . . . One would imagine these things ought to be used sparingly; is one to find it ' amusing ' if they are carelessly, and perhaps worse than carelessly expended?

(11)

September 24. (*In German.*) . . . I wonder how you would like Julia? What you think me so rich in, instincts, she does not possess at all. In a certain sense she is lifted high above the region where children of nature have certain things in common. For instance her feeling for the baby is . . . mainly prophetic! her eye rests upon it with most affection when she has just been looking at its 5-year-old little sister, because she is saying to herself ' it will be like that some day.' The sense of deep belonging-together with the new-born child, of unconscious tenderness, the joy of feeling this little being dependent on one, all this is nothing to her; she puts it on one side in a manner not given to me. But in other directions she has acquired a freedom in loving, suffering, and understanding, before which I bow down in shame. And what a heavenly absence of egotism! you never hear her speak of herself, and every one who talks to her is persuaded of his own exquisite importance though she never uses the conventional methods of the world. But this expenditure of kindness and sympathy fatigues her, and she flies the company of others rather than seeks it. Both of them wish to live for themselves and the family only, and when they do associate with other people, it never gets beyond intellectual relations. They are kind—sympathise and awaken sympathy—but never embark on an intimacy that might fetter. What they demand above all things is . . . freedom. Intercourse with others makes Harry positively ill, but no one who has any dealings with him imagines that *he* could possibly be that person! . . .

We have had trouble about the baby; the wet-nurse, such a nice little Moravian, lost her milk and had to go. O Ethel, she flung her arms round my neck sobbing, poor little thing, and when the substitute came hung over the cradle crying; she loved that child, and had forgotten her own over it; and that is the detestable part of this wet-nurse business. . . .

(12)

Dresden.

September 25, 1879. (*In English.*) . . . What I wonder at is to hear you always judging my standard as higher than yours, and to see you still sticking to yours. In that respect, then, you have no ambition, for else how could you bear the thought of having a smaller and poorer view of some of the most important things of life? Your sister's judgment may be more sensible, founded as it is on what she thinks you are, than mine, which is only founded on hopes. (*In German.*) But if the least alive thing in nature, crystal, can bud with new crystals, why should not the most alive thing, the human being, suffer change, and suddenly—or gradually— see things in a new light? Has such a thing never happened, and may I not cling to such a possibility to quiet and comfort myself? Have you never noticed that in people otherwise thoroughly cultivated, there is sometimes one spot in heart or brain that seems untilled, where nothing, or only weeds, grow? And hard by are exquisite flowers. Do you remember, once when we were speaking of marriage, I made some such remark about you? ' You have yet to learn to *feel* on this subject,' I said, more or less; ' these views you are expressing are not real living ones, they are the superficial result of experiences you think you have made. You don't feel the coarseness (*das Rohe*) of what you say on these topics, because it isn't a question of your feeling anything at all; you are merely constructing, putting this and that together.' And I would say the same thing to you to-day, when I find myself obliged once more to go over ground I thought we had left behind us for good and all! Ethel! like Penelope I will never weary of re-doing the stitches so sadly unpicked; I will always hope and believe that you can never fall short of the only way of looking at Life that appears to me thinkable for a being like you.

> ' Möge Jeder still beglückt
>   Seiner Freude warten ;
>   Wenn die Rose selbst sich schmückt
>   Schmückt sie auch den Garten.' [1]

This childish verse is full of the deepest wisdom.

The expression ' Plan of Life ' exactly marks the difference between us. You are full of plans of a most decided character; I never have any, and it has always appeared to me that one should have none, that all one should try for is to develop one's powers to the full . . . to make all one can of oneself, to ' adorn ' oneself in the noblest sense of the word. I want to see you less preoccupied with the future, less hungering after fruit that has yet to ripen, more lovingly immersed in the beautiful, rich present hour that is yours. . . . Greet your sister. Would that she held me in less high estimation but backed me up better! What a quantity of things yet to be done! . . . what a quantity of things you always have yet to do! I wonder, and I say it without irony, how in the midst of such a turmoil you can

---

[1] ' Calmly and contentedly let each await his joy ; in adorning herself the rose adorns the garden.'

keep the power of listening to the still small voice and catching its delicate vibrations. Strange how much you experience—I how little! and yet it seems to me I have a rich, rich life. . . . Good-bye my child, on the 30th we will hold high festival. . . .

(13)

October 9, 1879. (*In German.*) . . . How can you think I wanted you to take pains to fall in love with someone! Nothing is farther from my wishes, and that you have no inclination in this direction troubles me not at all; on the contrary I look upon it as a healthy trait compared to the sentimentally-expectant state of mind of our German girls. But that you should nevertheless think of *marriage* is more than I can understand—and there was a time when you were happy at feeling that marriage on such lines would be impossible to you. How proud I was of that victory!—now It is all over and done for! That you say things out so honestly and call them by their names I love in you, but I fancy you are wrong in thinking that what one might almost call this mapped-out, all-round ambition of yours is usual and normal. To be able to follow one's instincts, unhampered by trammels of any kind, is a happiness so rare and exquisite, that I, who had neither the energy to fight for my own freedom, nor the possibility of putting that sort of thing through, could often envy you. But this field of ambition—a legitimate one since it is a question of real power, which is inseparable from ambition in a certain sense—is not enough for you, and here you are, thinking of adopting a Plan of Life that shall enable you to satisfy countless other ambitions on other fields! It is this insatiability that alarms me so and that I can't go with. Surely it is worth while pausing and asking yourself whether it would not be wiser to curb this tendency, instead of merely registering that you are thus fashioned. Ethel, you say I must not forget in associating with you that we are different, that what satisfies me would not satisfy you—or rather, as you yourself modestly put it, that you are ' not good enough for what would make me happy.' I recognise the difference of our natures so clearly that I don't really want you to marry at all, believing you to be one of those natures that require no completing, that need not lose themselves in another in order to find themselves; what is more, you are strong enough to stand alone and have a right to say you intend to mount guard over your own development and live for yourself.   Thus marriage seems to me no necessity in your case, but before I would allow that nevertheless you ought to marry, as a matter of fact merely because you haven't enough money, I should have to give up my best faith in you, and I can't do that yet awhile ! . . .

One last word I must say.   You are cleverer than I in many ways, but I have one advantage over you—that I have been in existence 11 years longer, and have looked on at life for 11 more years than you.   And this experience I have made in myself; that as you grow older the number of things which impress you, which you know in the depths of your heart to be worth striving after, grows less and less ; and that on the other hand the passion and respect for what has retained its value increases.   This experience I shall see you making some day ! . . . I believe it, because I desire it. . . . (*In English.*)   Trust me, trust me, my child; I can but love you better every day that good love becomes older ; when I speak the hardest I feel the softest, believe me, and am fondest of you when I scold you ! . . .

(14)

December 30, 1879.   (*In English.*) . . . There you are, perfectly happy in the house of the excellent Fiedlers who carried you off after knowing you just 3 days ! and though I am pleased I marvel again how that all rushed so quickly upon you, you little steamboat.   What a talent to make friends you have, and to jump into relations which to assimilate myself to I should want months !   I didn't tell it you yesterday because really it is too childish, but I do feel jealous about the gladness and comfort you have in that house and which I can give you, things being as they are, so rarely in that opulent form which is so becoming to your health, my poor child !   I seldom envy rich people but I do envy Fiedlers in this case . . . and I had nothing to give my child but my poor love—*no,* my rich, rich love—and a little sadness to accompany it ! I would like to have you near me, telling me that you feel happiest of all with

Your old Mother.

You made I suppose the acquaintance of that nasty S—— ; I wonder how he pleased you. Can you understand that Joachims allow such a man to be intimate with them? What a pity that dear Joachim is so weak, so feeble ! . . .

(15)

Jannary 6, 1880. (*In English.*) . . . O darling, if I could only make you understand that I do not grudge you the affection you feel for that kind Mary Fiedler and her for you; if it seemed so, make those ' damned ' letters responsible for it, please ! only that for one like me, faithful and heavy to a perhaps exaggerated degree, who always had difficulty of giving a newcomer the place in her heart that was held by an old friend, it seems hard to see *the* friend, the most cherished of all, so easy in giving and accepting affection, and apparently always craving for more—for only where a need is does its satisfaction come so very easily. . . .

(16)

February 4, 1880. (*In English.*). . . . Of course I forgive you my child. I know that in the same moment you do or speak wrong, the repentance springs up in your heart, so how could I not forgive? But I wish, I wish you could learn to subdue your rather wild nature so that the good and mild sides would not come out only at second thoughts ! . . . The things I went through yesterday were hard to bear and I am wearied and sore of heart. If Henry were not such an angel what a poor creature I would feel; he is my blessing and my rest. My poor mother is in such a state of irritation, full of the old torturing King Lear feelings; she thinks herself loved less than formerly, and this is mixed up with so much old suppressed sorrow that one must have the greatest pity and forbearance. When she is as she is now she cannot support the sight of other people intimate with us

—can't realise and understand it. That's why I ask you not to come, darling, till perhaps Monday. . . .

(*Evening*) It will comfort you to hear things go better now; poor old King Lear is quieted again, and feels she tortured herself unnecessarily; still, as I know her too well, I still think it better not to come before Monday, my poor little one! The pity I felt for her yesterday and to-day is indescribable. Many things in her biography help to explain what else would nearly seem symptoms of madness, so utterly beside herself can she get. . . . I suffered tortures!

Oh. . . !¹

(17)

March 1880. (*In German.*) . . . My father goes away to-morrow . . . he is too old to educate, and as I can't force him to be nicer to you, and also think it more dignified in you not to expose yourself to his unfriendliness, don't come till the evening, darling. Besides which he is here for such a short time that I ought to devote myself entirely to him. If I hold back and am different to you under such circumstances, can I possibly help it? Come at 7! such a good meal will I give you! (*in English*) and bring your violin, and we'll make a good fight against all the blue devils of this world. Come into the garden, maid—come into my parlour and right into my heart, where there is love enough, if that can help. Come and be welcome to a little nice ham, and omelette, and a new volume of Bach, and an old

LISL.

(18)

Würzburg: March, 1880.

(*In English.*) . . . If you knew how it distressed me once more to see my old mother unkind, unjust and unreasoning, just with *you*, my Ethel, of all people in the world, and to go

¹ The groan in Brahms's Ballad ' Eduard.'

off on this journey with her was no comfort just then! We slept in the train, but once I woke up in terror, as I feared I had shrieked 'Ethel' in a horrible dream in which, entering our little dining room, I saw my mother and you on two chairs, she almost swooning and you bathed in tears! But as so often happens it was only my heart that had shrieked. I feel it working away at every new little shock and hope I shall have quiet and peace here. . . . [*N.B.—She was at Würzburg, consulting an obstetrician.*] . . . It is curious to think of this everlasting battle with sterile Nature, trying with art and cunning to force from her what she will not give of her own free will—she who is otherwise such a spend-thrift! My old mother wishes me good as hard as she can; if she could give me a child in bringing it into the world herself, I think, old and worn as she is, that she would do it. Yet I never can open my heart to her, never tell her how I yearn for a baby. I shrink to speak of all that with her, which is an ingratitude, but we differ too much in our way of naming and feeling and 'taxing' things. If I lived with her I should be lonely, yet I love her and thus I suffer. . . . Go and see after my lonely husband! Thursday I have thee again my darling. . . .

(*Later.*) The doctor was there, says I can be helped, and I come back in the spring. My heart is light; I learn to hope again.

(19)

Verona : April 10, 1880.

(*In German.*) . . . I won't dwell longer on this wonderful place lest I sadden you, poor little Tannhäuser! But listen my child; to-day I said and swore to myself that you *shall* see it all! we will not always dissuade you from letting your thirsty eyes and soul drink in all this beauty; and believe me, one loses nothing by waiting; on the contrary one is storing up receptivity.

My child, I am so thankful, so grateful that things are as they are between us, and at the thought that nothing can ever change this wonderful sense of belonging together. Well for us that we have each other! Though you some-times distress me, and I you, down in the depths the essential is so safe, so real—and like all real things can never pass

away. . . . (*Later.*)   Your second letter has just come;
Ethel! as if you do not always belong to me wherever I may
happen to be!—you, who have so great a part in me—you,
my child, my friend, my comrade! . . .

(20)

Florence, April 17, 1880.   (*In German.*) . . . I met Frau
Hildebrand to-day at Julia's.   Nothing is less favourable for
purposes of observation than being surrounded by members
of your own family—old friends of the person in question—
while you yourself have known and been known by that person in effigy for ever so long.   Animals when first they meet
sniff each other a little and at once find out all that is necessary; we humans put out cautious feelers, think this and
fancy that to ourselves, and are no wiser than before.   When
I say ' we ' I except you, little seven-league-booted one, but
now don't go and imagine I say this in wicked irony—I who
talk about you to Julia at her special request nearly all day!
Send your Cello Sonata quick, quick; she wants to hear
something of yours. . . .

(21)

Florence : April 20, 1880.

(*In English.*) . . . Your last letter made me sad, not only
because of your seediness, but because of your depression, so
different from what I hoped and believed.   (*In German.*)
My child, what has become of the calm, steady mood of your
first letters, the sense that we are together though separated,
the all-round steadfastness?   Is what is best and strongest
in you to take the form of words only? Am I to wait for ever
for the pedal-point—' the note that sounds so softly, but can
always be heard by those who listen for it in secret '?   Is it
always to be thus with you : ' revelling high as heaven,
saddened unto death '?   From one year to another I look to
see you getting older, but, O wild little stag, the horns I
keep hoping you have rubbed off once for all grow again and
again, and vainly I seek for traces of the true wisdom you
have so much platonic affection for! . . . My mother, so
Julia says, regrets her Leipzig aberrations and puts it down

to the fragmentary, idle life she leads when with us. She is
very dear and kind to me, but we never refer to that time—
it is best not to. . . .

(22)

Florence, May 2, 1880. (*In German.*) . . . Hildebrand
is doing a profile relief of me which takes up a lot of my
time, but of course I am delighted and as proud as a pea-
cock. The best part of it, however, is the intercourse with
the delightful man himself. What with great cleverness and
fineness, simple direct manners, and natural charm of intelligence, he is one of the most attractive of men. As for her,
one can sum it up thus : that though she is a *dilettante* in
many ways I imagine her a great artist in loving. . . . X
has sent me a horrible sketch of you; it was kindly meant,
and touched me greatly, but . . . God in His wrath made
him take to drawing ! By the by if you see my fat brother
in Dresden don't let him know how often I write to you ; the
poor fellow is a martyr to jealousy. Tell me if you like his
boy . . . and the rest of the family. . . .

I am thankful when there is a day of rest at home; not
that we see so very much, but that little is too much for me ;
I get tired of enjoying when I only feel and don't understand. But I am making progress in an amateurish way
and getting to know whether I am really admiring a thing
myself or merely standing before something admirable ; if
the latter I steal away quickly. . . . Of all this however
you, extraordinary being that you are, forbid me to speak,
but it is permitted I hope to mention Hildebrand's new
group, for whenever I think of it a sort of shining joy floods
my soul. You know how I have always admired his work,
specially the Sleeping Shepherd-Boy, but this group fills one
with the sort of religious reverence that only perfect works of
art inspire. You have no idea of the beauty of the young
Bacchus—the languid perfection of the body, supported by a
comfortable-looking, not at all revolting old Satyr—beauty
that makes one think of one's best possessions, the C Major
Symphony of Mozart for instance. Surely Hildebrand must
soon win round his last opponents ; can anyone dare to go on
picking holes after this, or deny that here is an irresistible

art-force before which one must do homage—in a word a master? . . .

Please construct for me a suitable message to Frau —; I can't think of one myself but you'll hit on something . . . (it's quite a speciality of yours). . . . I am glad I did not come to Italy sooner; that much one may say, mayn't one, without raising a storm? . . .

(23)

Berchtesgaden : July 30, 1880.

(*In German.*) . . . We are having a difficult time with poor M—, and perhaps, being with us is not what I hoped it would be for her. I had fancied that seeing people as absolutely happy as we two are with our work, our beloved music, might show her that this way lies salvation for stricken souls such as hers; but now I wonder whether on the contrary the spectacle does not depress her, for her talent is a poor bird with crippled wings that has forgotten how to sing, and I sometimes fear will never learn it again. The few hours I have to myself I ravenously devote to Bach's Choral Preludes; and sometimes, when the unutterable peace comes over me that the contemplation of beauty, the losing oneself in the soul of an artist like Bach, brings with it, I am almost frightened to think in what vast measure this highest of all joys has been given me compared to poor M— thirsting in the desert! My life is so strangely happy that I even question whether I have the right to help one so unhappy—whether I can call forth in myself what is necessary to the comprehension of so much suffering. Often and often I feel thus when with M—. There is the whistle of the train that brings Brahms and Frau Schumann . . . goodbye !

(24)

September 22, 1880. . . . After untold suffering L— brought her baby into the world . . . to see it die at once ! How terrible that must be, Ethel, and yet . . . I still long and long—nevertheless !

(b)

FROM MYSELF TO MY MOTHER

(1)

Salomonstr. : October 19, 1878.

. . . On Thursday (the next Gewandhaus concert) *such* an event takes place—the 50th anniversary of the day Frau Schumann made her debût (as a child of 8) in the Gewandhaus ! She is going to play nothing but his things of course, and it will be very glorious. The whole place is to be decorated, the floor one mass of flowers, etc. She, poor woman, is naturally in an awful state of mind about it, wrote such a touching letter to Frau v. Herzogenberg saying : ' You understand how painful it will be on such an occasion as this to be the object of general attention ' ! ! After this is a party, at Frau Frege's, where she, Joachim and his wife, perhaps Brahms, Madame Schwabe and others will be. I am looking forward to it much and wonder if Frau Schumann will remember me, though on such a night I shall of course not put myself forward in any way. For Frau Schumann's sake I shall be heartily glad when it is all over —if she can bear it is very doubtful—and do think it's cruelty to animals, and yet one couldn't do less. . . .

FROM SAME TO SAME

(2)

October, 1878.

. . . This has been a great week on account of the Frau Schumann festival. It went off most gloriously. The woman surely never played as she did last Wednesday at the rehearsal, and above all last Thursday in the concert. Thanks to the death of the Concertmeister's wife's uncle, I got a ticket just under the piano. The Saal was beautifully decorated, with trophies, and all round the room laurel wreaths with 1828-1878 therein, really very pretty. One most successful idea was selling little bouquets on the stairs, to be thrown at Frau S. as soon as she appeared. When she entered, from every corner of the room showered flowers.

She did not in the least expect it; whichever way she looked she was smothered in them. I never saw anyone look so delighted in my life; round about the piano they lay a foot thick and she and Reinecke really had to dig a pathway and a clear space round the stool. She played too exquisitely, such fire and pathos, and looked so beautiful at the same time in dark red velvet with a long satin train. The two Miss Schumann's sat behind me and remembered me very well. I was so pleased and then—great moment—just as the symphony was beginning, in came Frau S. from the artists' room and sat next me!! I was too shy to remind her of my own existence just then, but love to think I sat near her on that great night. After the concert Lisl came down to meet me in the Saal (she had sat in the gallery) and fairly took my breath away with her loveliness. I had never seen her really ' dressed up ' before, and simply say I never saw anything like her in my life. She was in dark red striped velvet and satin with (*pro tem.*) an ermine tippet round her neck; her hair seemed *strahlend* [1] and she wore a slender wreath of some flower—single-leaved, white and striped with dark red; in German they are called Vatermoerder!! [2] Such a painful piece of Teutonic realism. I wore my light green, and created, as you may imagine—at least the dress did—a tremendous sensation at Frau Frege's, whither a happy few repaired. Frau Schumann is staying there, and soon after we arrived she appeared, radiant. The love she bears for the happy Lisl is so touching. What is it in Lisl that none can resist, old, young, rich or poor? The old nurse who nursed me during my illness seemed to love ' die gnädige Frau ' much in the way Frau Schumann loves her! Late in the evening when most of the guests had retired I went up to dear Frau Schumann and had a blissful conversation with her. I don't fancy she much remembered me at first, though she was so sweet and kind, but when I, knowing Lisl had told her of me, said I was Ethel Smyth she brightened all over and said : ' Ich gratulire ! da sind Sie in gute Hände gekommen.' [3] At this minute up came Lisl and put her arm round me and said, ' Dieses ist mein Pflegekind ! ' [4] Frau S. said, ' Wir waren Nachbarn im Concert

---

[1] Giving out light. [2] Parricides.
[3] ' I congratulate you ! You have got into good hands !'
[4] 'This is my adopted child.'

aber da wollten Sie gar nichts von mir wissen.' Lisl said,
' Sagen Sie das ja nicht! Ethel war viel zu bescheiden Sie
dort anzusprechen.' [1] Frau S. was so dear, said she hoped
she would see me again, and I kissed her hand, feeling rather
like the page-boy in Rohtraut—' Ihr tausend Blätter im
Walde wisst ich habe schön Rohtraut's Mund geküsst!'[2]
When Brahms comes in January I hope to see more of that
grand woman. I do envy Lisl her love—no I don't. One
can't envy Lisl anything, she deserves all the love a mortal
can give her. . . .

FROM MYSELF TO MY FATHER

(3)

April, 1879.

. . . I still have two more of my Xmas-present rides
before me, and during the last I obtained an insight into German notions of sport I shall never forget. I rode as usual
with my two cavaliers (this is proper in Germany!) to the
race-course, which is a great open grassy place about as big
as the parade ground in front of Colonel Cooke's house, the
course being round it, and not very plentifully bestrewed
with fences that even the keen filly would walk over. I
noticed a small concourse of horsemen in elaborate get-ups
(or gets-up!) at one side, and a hare quietly cropping the
grass in the distance. In fearful excitement this object is
pointed out to me by the gentlemen with, ' There is a hunt
to-day!' I also was much excited though I didn't quite see
how it was going to be managed. ' Where are the hounds?'
I ask. They stare at me in blank astonishment and proceed
to explain that there are none, and eventually I gather that
two tame hares are kept on the premises and let out about
once a week; the sport is that one of the riders shall ride
after the hare, halloing and cracking a long driving whip.
The hare of course moves slowly on, and the object is for the
other riders to tear about preventing her from getting off the

---

[1] ' We were neighbours in the concert, but she wouldn't have anything to do with me!'—' Don't say that! Ethel was far too modest to
speak to you *there*!'
[2] ' The thousand leaves in the forest know I have kissed beautiful
Rohtraut's mouth!'

grass plot into the woods at the side ! ! ! ! ! ' If she does get into the woods,' say I, ' what then? ' ' O then we go home, and towards evening she comes back and of her own accord goes into her hutch where she is shut up again.' Did you ever hear of anything so absurd? I laughed till I nearly fell from my steed and my cavaliers were rather hurt in their feelings! However, it is possible, though not probable, that if one had never known the other thing this sort of ' sport ' might be entertaining. . . .

(c)

From Juliana Horatia Ewing (' Aunt Judy ') to My Mother

(1)

Exeter : May 7, 1879.

My dear Mrs. Smyth,—I got here very successfully, having had a good deal in the way of travelling companions—a large party of Churchills and then a Colonel Cardew who was amazingly chatty both about the war and agriculture, and temperance *v.* teetotalism, and the good results of giving tea and coffee to his haymakers, and money instead of cider. He was followed by a nurse and baby, and by Baby's Mamma and Aunt, who mopped and mowed before it as if it were Mumbo Jumbo.

That one day was lovely, but to-day it is as cold and cheerless as ever. Mind you take care of yourself, and get change of air and exercise—' carriage exercise ' in the *close* carriage ! It is not fit for you to play any tricks. I must say I was struck with your needing care and told the girls so, as they will probably tell you. It is by *little cossetings* (each of which alone might be done without, but the sum of which does what no medicine can) that health slowly returns after severe illness. Jenner once said to me : ' Try and think of your own health for the next seven months, will you? ' and sometimes it is the least selfish plan one can pursue; for it *is* an effort (especially in a large family where everybody else is in normal health) to trouble for what one knows would do one good. One feels inclined to crawl into a hole and stop there. But one can't recover by that process.

I got such a bright chatty letter from Captain Patten with some most flattering accounts of the P.M.O. in Cyprus shedding tears over ' Jan of the Windmill '; a very nice pat of butter. I hope to enclose your Pot-Pourri receipt to-day; I haven't yet got at anything for Ethel except Col. Durnford's pamphlet on Iswandala, but I don't think she would care for it. I think I must send her a letter I got from Mrs. Durnford with some facts.

Dear Mrs. Smyth, I do not know how to thank you and the General and your children for the home you give me at Frimhurst. I am not ungrateful, only ' unaccustomed to public speaking ' in the giving of thanks! It has added a great pleasure to the visit to see your young ones growing up nicer and nicer. I do like your children . . . I am reduced to the classic language of the day . . . *awfully*! Give them my best love, and all that is proper to send to the General.

Yours very affectionately,

J. H. EWING.

(2)

[*Note.—This was one of the letters written when the writer was acting as chaperone. All the people mentioned in it were in, or connected with, the R.E., and the young men either were, or were supposed to be, admirers of my sister Nina. ' Rex,' i.e. Mr. Ewing, had been posted to Ceylon, and though he and Aunt Judy were very fond of each other, he did not in the least desire the presence of an invalid wife in that far-off spot, nor had she the faintest wish to leave England.*]

Frimhurst : May 5, 1881.

Dearest Mrs. Smyth,—Thank you very much for your kind message. I did not at all like going without seeing you, but I wanted to catch Mrs. Jelf who is only to be quite a short time in England, and this was taking me up to town on the 11th. But your hospitable and kind General, who had most amiably pressed me to stay on a bit before your letter came, has smoothed out my plans by allowing me to ask Mrs. Jelf to come down here and see me for a couple of nights.

Now I must report on *my nieces* ! Don't you think I must feel like a hen with a brood of adventurous ducklings when they offer me tandem-drives and saloon-pistol practice? That is chaff. They are very good indeed, and I even induced Violet to take care of her cold which was rather bad but is now pretty well gone.

Now I must tell you that Mr. Hippisley [1] had to go away on duty, so Mr. Foster came and brought Mr. Godsell, which deprived me of my little confidential chat with Mr. Hippisley. The General was in town that day but he left me with permission to ask Mr. Foster to dinner (!). Mr. F. could not stay however. But he invited ME to tea with him to see the alterations in the R.E. mess and the honourable place they have given to the pictures Rex and I presented the Mess with, . . . but with such an appealing glance of those fine eyes of his towards the young ladies that I accepted *for the party,* on condition that the General would consent and let us have the carriage. I can hardly help laughing to think how guilty I looked and how shaky I felt when I petitioned the General on his return, but he gave consent at once.

I must tell you, for you will be amused, that I am sure the General suspects that you and I are in *mysterious* correspondence ! ! He has made several leading remarks, but I have kept your counsel inviolate; still I think he and I have now a *tacit* understanding. *Par exemple,* he has planned a little dinner party for me (by your wish I believe) and when we had confabbed about the married guests and the dinner, he proceeded to the question of bachelor guests and suggested Mr. St. Lawrence. I agreed and with a most guileless countenance, I trust, suggested Mr. Foster. To which the General replied, ' No ! we mustn't have the Rivals together ! '

(*Saturday.*) I could not go on with this yesterday, my spine and head were so troublesome all day. At one time I feared we should have to give up our expedition, but a dose of Sal Volatile and Soda water got the worst edge off my headache, and with air cushions and a hot bottle (!) I got

---

[1] Later on he married my sister Violet.

through very well, and enjoyed it very much. The air here now is something divine and feels like tonic and balm in one.

Well. We drove to the familiar I Lines and Mr. Foster came out to meet us followed by Mr. Godsell and they took us over the new mess improvements and showed us our pictures in places of high honour ; and told us, to my keen delight, that they had just expelled the *World* by vote from the mess, and showed us all the things that have been presented since I was there. Then we adjourned to Mr. Foster's rooms and had tea, and I must say his surroundings confirm my impressions about him. A very choice little collection of books and such nice pictures, and most beautiful eastern curios in the brass and pottery and carpet line. Violet (though she was not the right one !) exploded when he left us into : ' There is a man with something in him ! ' and it is very true. There is a pretty water-colour of his father's place over his bed, but I came no nearer to any of the practical information you are wisely desirous to get. But I may soon for—wasn't it an odd and delightful accident?— Mrs. Jelf was in the Camp and Mr. Godsell brought her in to see me ! It seemed so odd that we should meet again for the first time in an R.E. hut, in the old Lines we both loved so well. . . .

Now about our little dinner to-night. Mr. St. Lawrence could not come. So the General put it to popular vote at table whom we should ask instead, and we all looked at opposite points of the compass and voted for Mr. Foster, as if he were a perfectly new and original inspiration ! ! I am sorry Mr. St. Lawrence could not come. Of course he does not attract *me* so much as the scholarly and artistic qualities of Mr. Foster do, but I liked what I saw of him the other day. I haven't a notion which Nina prefers, and as I think nothing is so offensive as chaff where there is any possibility of a serious sentiment, I need hardly say that we discuss them quite in the abstract. She complains that Mr. St. L. is so ugly. which I don't agree to, but as she seems to feel personally aggrieved that Fate has not endowed him with eagle's eyes like Mr. F. that rather scores to his account ! !

Now I think I have told you all about ' the Rivals ' ! By the by I did not answer your question as to how I liked the lady I found here. To give you a quite straight answer I was *not* prepossessed in her favour. It is indeed a sad story, and I do not wonder your pity bubbled over into kindness; but as you ask me, I'll tell you frankly that the impression she produces on me is that of a person who might become embarrassing, and even mischievous. (I know you have asked for my critical opinion for what it is worth! I hope you know I should not be uncharitable enough to express it without being asked.) Her latest *billet doux* was to Nina, saying, ' I *must* call you Nina.' Nina asked me what I thought, and I hope you won't think I was wrong in counselling her to answer the note courteously but shortly, and to take no notice of the suggestion, which I think a little impertinent. My feeling is that if she presumed with *you*, you could put her down quite effectually, but that the young things might feel it a nuisance to be involved in terms of intimacy, which there seems to be no special reason for setting up.

Don't you always feel the Academy rather a test of acquaintances? I do not quite like the mental picture of your dear Nina being ' hailed ' by her Xtian name in the Academy by Miss H., with possibly a body-guard of the cavaliers whom she seems to have presented her London address to as freely as Mrs. Tupper presented her *cartes de visite*! Don't think I am prudish about any little independent and Canadian ways she may have. Details of etiquette vary infinitely and she is not a child; but unless one's instincts deceive one her mind is not of that *bona fides*, pure, and honest cast which does lift some noble if eccentric individuals as much above the Law as St. Paul. I think my feeling is that if one has ties of duty or sentiment to a person of her type, one stands by them in spite of little ways one may not like; (in Jeremy Taylor's delightful way of putting things in his prayers : ' My friends and *my father's friends* let me never ungratefully despise or neglect ')—but when there is no tie, I always feel it wise to think *how one would like a person in London*! . . . and I don't fancy her with your chicks in London.

What an unmitigated brute I do feel to sit here enjoying your hospitality, and backbite a young lady who wants to be intimate with you! And you know I may be quite wrong. But my impression is that she lacks the two great elements of qualification for satisfactory friendship—*genuineness* and *mental delicacy*. . . . (Don't let me in for a libel case ! !)

My back aches so I must stop. It is the sweetest day to-day, and this place does look so lovely. Every breath one draws is a delight. Certainly if it is a torment to be so constitutionally, hopelessly, neuralgically, barometrically susceptible to climatic influences when they are against one, it is an extra sense to revel in heather breezes and pine odours and dry air, and feel the pains in one's bones, as old women say, vanish like bad dreams.

Tell Alice her father's solicitude breaks out every morning with : ' Well. I quite expect we shall hear some news of an arrival in Edinburgh *to-day*.' He has said this for days past, and we all look a *little* embarrassed and very hopeful !

By the bye I have not said a word of our two sad departures this week. We groan daily ! Bob must have great individuality, one does miss him so. It is so unnatural not to see him warming his hands at the drawing-room fire after dinner ! I think the intense hugging he gave me at the last moment was somewhat vicarious—for lack of you !

My best love to ' Alice ' (she will think I am the unrighteous chastising the ungodly to object to Miss H. calling Nina ' Nina ' !) and thank her for telling me I could not live in Ceylon. As I *may* not, it is well to know there is a good reason. Rex has been so comforting. He sent me a very nice bit of butter the other day by saying it was such a blessing ' *in Emergencies* ' to have a *wise wife* ! It was very soothing. . . . Now I *will* leave off chatting !

Yours very affectiontely,
Juliana Horatia Ewing.

P.S.—I hope the General and I shall be forgiven all the bad words we use about Mr. Gladstone. What do his Scotch admirers think of matters in the Transvaal?

(3)

Frimhurst : May 13, 1881.

. . . Oh, I think I must tell you of a funny scene we had the other day as result of our tension on Alice's behalf. . . .

Scene—The Drawing Room.

Costumes—Our best company manners.

Dram. Personæ—Mrs. Wickham and Mrs. Herries

(deafer than ever, poor thing) kindly calling on me, I and the girls, the General, and David (bringing in tea).

Naturally there were many enquiries for Alice and Mr. Davidson, arising out of enquiries after you, and we got through *the delicate subject* very satisfactorily considering that a gentleman was present and one of the ladies had to be bawled to. Old Mrs. Wickham was still nodding with sympathy, she and the General having drawn up knee to knee, and we all looking so exactly posed for a comedy, when re-enter David *with a telegram*. We all fluttered. Mrs. Wickham nodded herself nearly into the General's lap, *he* put his spectacles well out of the way on the top of his head (as I observe he generally does when he has anything he is anxious to see clearly). Mrs. Herries smiled and nodded at her mother as much as to say no explanations were needed, David grinned blandly, and the dear General tore and fumbled at the envelope with anxiety, and then stopped—drove his hand into his trousers pocket for a shilling and roared in stentorian tones of command to David to take it to the man then and there. Exit David looking disappointed, and the General began again at the envelope, but before he got it fairly opened he bawled again to David to stop, as there might be an answer. Then out came the telegram and he read it, and then, to our amazement, dismissed David with a vigour to which the previous words of command had been as nothing, and then fell back in his chair in convulsions of laughter. . . .

Can you imagine the situation when we learned it was a telegram from the fishmonger to say he was out of white-bait? and as the General justly said afterwards, ' He's paid a shilling and I've paid a shilling and we might have had the whitebait for 1s. 6d. ! ' . . .

. . . You must let me be a little egoistical in the process of letting you know how kindly I feel the *graciousness* of your hospitality in allowing me to lay the flattering unction to my soul that I am of use to you by staying on with your young ones. My spine is so troublesome that if I were in London I could go nowhere and see nothing. And now can you imagine an Earthly Paradise that I could wish for better suited to my helplessness and my craving for fresh air than this lovely place of yours, where I can move from your comfortable old-fashioned sofa, and in a few strides (my giant strides !) sit under pine trees?—where I can see dear Nina and Violet and their friends play tennis, and sit among them and not feel out of everything without the fatigue of ' going to a party,'—and where I can sketch day by day and hear nightingales in the evening without an expedition to reach either privilege ! . . .

(4)

Frimhurst : June 2, 1881.

(*June* 2) . . . We are all in very good case and it is very hot, but deliciously cool in your drawing-room and the sun draws out all the pine perfume all over the place. The evenings are glorious. After dinner the girls and I squeeze ourselves on to one seat (made by Nina) on the cutting and frighten away the nightingales by our unseemly yells, for Nina lives in dread of a mad dog and Violet of a cockchafer in her hair, and they respectively try to startle each other whilst I am eaten alive by gnats. . . '(' such country pleasures do we prove ').

(5)

Frimhurst : June 17, 1881.

. . . The girls *were* so good over my failing them for the dance. I would not for worlds have deprived poor Violet—so new to it—of one of those nice friends' little dances. And indeed I had quite looked forward to combining a chaperone's privileges of easy chairs and refreshment with some pleasant chats in that familiar spot, the Club House, myself. I got up and dressed and was up an hour or two—and then had to roll back ignominiously to bed ! I cannot forgive myself even now. . . . Ascot has been very good for me too ! ! mentally it has soothed my conscience for having lost them a treat, and physically I have had the only thing I am fit for just now, absolute quiet and silence with just an amusing little chat at the end of the day. But I have had a stringent parade of the children before my bed on each occasion, and they looked charming. I am sorry Violet's dress was not made with a gathered body but still it looked very nice. The pink print, which *has* a gathered body is so very becoming to her. It suits her figure and makes her look so young ! You. will laugh at this as recommendation for her but she is very easily made to look five years older than she is. Do you not think so ? I'm afraid brains, of which she has a *very* good share, always have a tendency to age people in youth, though perhaps rather otherwise when they become really old. People who think get bent brows and set lips. . . . I told Violet how Mrs. Jelf admired her (she thinks her prettier than Nina) for I have great theories that far more girls suffer from doubting their own attractiveness than from vanity, especially if they have pretty sisters.

The dress Nina got in exchange for the rather dreadful print she brought down from town is very becoming. They have certainly had three very ideal Ascot days and I think the General has enjoyed himself very much too, though they do not give a report of him such as Mrs. Byrne gave of her Colonel : ' I lose him . . . I know not where he is ! English husbands are so *sly*. I assure you Colonel Byrne . . . he is a ME-TE-OR ! ' . . .

(6)

71 Warwick Rd., Earl's Court : July 13, 1881.

. . . I know you will be glad to hear that my goods and chattels came, that the day was fine, in fact roasting, that the losses, breakages, &c., are on the whole less than one might expect, and that the shipping agents did everything, as I think, at very reasonable charge. My sitting room here (' the Sunflower room ' as it is called from its paper, which is less startling than it sounds) does look quite pretty though I say it as shouldn't. I have been living in it, sitting on the floor among my odds and ends, with a carpenter and a charwoman. The carpenter handy but sententious, the charwoman willing but absolutely unreliable—however I suppose if she'd been born with brains for a Prime Minister she would have preferred the place. But she *has* reminded me of the cook Dr. Johnson dismissed for the reason that— ' Madam, she was all wiggle-waggle. I could get nothing categorical out of her '. . . .

(7)

Sheffield : October 23, 1881.

. . . I have got to a time of life when one feels the
tragedy of ' B.A.' [1] more deeply than Nina and Violet can
do !   Life holds so much less real affection and accomplished
desire than one hopes when one is young.   But B.A.'s have
a terrible touch of the comic at times !   Dot[2] has bolted from
a most unexpected swain in this neighbourhood who has
broken loose with all the desperation that sometimes char-
acterizes very shy people when they do turn the corner !—
and as I am staying with his aunt (an old engagement not
to be got out of) I am the prey of brotherly attentions—' in
vain—in vain ! '   I am really very sorry, though as he is 27
I hope he will soon recover, and if she could have taken to
him you will understand how I should have loved to see her
in a comfortable home of her own.   But I always do feel
one could do anything for a home *but* marry !   All I can do
is to listen to his Cantata !   He (prematurely) composed one,
words and music, which he advised himself to call ' The Consummation of Bliss.'   The night before last I heard this all
through !   Since the fatal ' No ' he is composing one on
Ariadne.   If he sings as Bacchus I don't quite know how I
shall bear it ! !   Don't think me a brute, and he is so good
—and so scientific (the greatest possible attraction for her)
that I wish . . . well, I wish he were someone else ! . . .

(8)

All Hallows Evening, 1881.

. . . I am staying here with a sister of poor Major Poole
—the one who fell at Laings Neck.   His people seem to have
been very much devoted to him and it has been a terrible
sorrow.   His mother is very old and partly paralysed and
has lost her memory.   He was her favorite son, and yet
after she heard of it she forgot it.   But she was troubled by

[1] B.A., a family expression meaning Blighted Attachment.
[2] Her sister.

seeing the tears of the daughters who are at home (one of whom was Major Poole's favourite sister to whom he has left all his sketches) and she remembered enough to know that it was for one fallen in battle, and pulled herself together enough to say, ' I am very sorry for the parents of that poor young man ! ' . . . It seemed to me the most tragic and pathetic thing I have heard for long.   Old Cetewayo refused to eat for 24 hours after his death, which was touching enough. . . .

If the General does me the honor to read ' Daddy Darwin's Dovecot ' I hope he will recognise one turn in the workhouse boy's letter ! . . .

(9)

Sheffield : November 20, 1881.

Dearest Mrs. Smyth,—Your two letters were very welcome and very very kind, but I grudge the use of your poor wrist—and I must thank you off hand for your kindness in putting your approval of ' Daddy Darwin's Dovecot ' into words—such full encouraging words. . . .

Of course the problem for the three past years has been with me whether I should ever redeem from physical collapse my brain vigour, such as it was.   My old doctor up here you know at first believed that I never should, and then it was on the strength of his conviction that I should, after all, that he refused to let me risk Malta last time.   I had to work ' D.D.D.' (looks bad !) very carefully ; very short continuous work muddled me and brought on headache, but I did feel as if I had got the grip of my faculties again, though rather like a spring that has lost elasticity and can't be pressed with a heavy hand.

It is a great pleasure to feel able to follow my *métier* again, from so many points of view.   At times it feels as if this homeless phase of my life would never come to an end . . . and being able to work again is a great help over the time.   Also I am quite convinced it is the only way—if at all —in which I can ever be of any real use to my fellow creatures . . . and it is a great pleasure !

I am so glad you like my new attempt and are so kind as

to tell me so. Word-painting is such a pleasure, like playing a game of skill—to me—and I take such minute pains, and cut and polish, that no praise is so pleasant as the flattery that the word-painting has fallen artistically on the reader's ears! Caldecott complained that I left nothing to an artist and ought never to be illustrated, but he has followed me with such sympathy that he has got the local colour of this neighbourhood in a marvellous fashion. The bare fact of the theft of the House Doves and their recovery at the call of the little lad who loved them is true.

I am busy now trying to do a tale to compete for a Yankee prize of £100—rash, isn't it? I fear there's no chance for me—too good writers against me! But please wish me well. . . .

Violet's letters were delightful. I deeply enjoy such home touches, as even their scrambling conclusions ' Postbag here and the General says it *must* be closed ! ' . . . I can shut my eyes and be in Frimhurst at once ! . . . I do enjoy Frimhurst news—knowing so well, and caring so much for it all. I have a sort of 11th Commandment that keeps me honour-bound from much talking of the possibilities of the future of young people I care for, but other people's love affairs *are* amazingly interesting ! There is for ever the great problem of the two truths : (1) that most pain in the relation of men and women comes from misunderstanding or misknowledge of each other—a misknowledge which is sometimes irreparable—and that therefore the more free and full the intercourse before Gordian knots are tied, the better the chance of either perfect happiness or the avoidance of misery; and that (2) intellectual friendship is a far more binding and deep-seated tie than a mere commonplace admiration and acquaintance—and if one person gets the blade and the other only the handle of that edge-tool it is a sad business. I think I have at last made up my mind as to the only thing to aim at—but I shall reserve this theory for a letter to Violet ! Meanwhile if I *should* hear that those 2 dear children are going to march with the R.E.'s, an Aunt's best benedictions will not be wanting ! . . .

(10)

[*Note.—I add this letter, though of a later date; it was the last in the packet.*]

Taunton : October 19, 1883.

. . . I hasten to warn you that I sent the General a copy of Caldecott's ' Jackanapes ' the other day, and that I have ordered my six André Verse Books to go to you with my best love—a little offering in memory of all that dear Frimhurst and your never-changing kindness did towards the slow process of giving me back the power to work. I never forget it, even when we have not exchanged letters for a while; I never shall forget it dear Mrs. Smyth unless my brain gives way altogether ! . . . When I say I warn you of the books it was because I remembered that when I sent you ' Brothers of Pity,' in your haste to be honest you paid Smith for it ! . . .

I have a favour to ask. I am the happy possessor of a small garden—when I came to it it was a potato patch. My friends have been so good to me and it is now very full (and things *do* grow here !) but my soul is set upon polyanthus and my jobbing gardener says : ' sim as if they be quite out of fashion 'bout here. There *was* a gen'l'm as used to grow 'un but a died some years back.' Now I do so well remember your polyanthus in the long walk, the best I ever saw and your own raising from seed. If they still flourish, knowing how polyanthus increase at the root I think perhaps you could spare me one or two offsets from the different kinds down the walk. . . . *Not if you are saving them for any special purpose,* but if you can spare a few in a mustard tin—or wrapped in a little moss or hay in brown paper—this red earth and reeking climate will soon develop them to my delight and *in memoriam* of the Frimhurst walk. . . .

———

(d)

FROM EDWARD GRIEG

(Translation)

Kopenhagen : April 17, 1879.

Honoured Miss Smyth,—This time there are many kindnesses to thank you for; firstly for being so charming as to
keep your promise; secondly for being so charming as to
write about it; thirdly for being so charming as to send the
charming Variations.   The one thing that is not charming
is . . . the legions upon legions of mistakes in the MS. !
There are moments when I feel as if I were playing the riot-
scene in the ' Meister-Singer ' !   Your permission to correct
these mistakes ' according to taste ' is all very fine,
but . . . !

Well, I am looking forward to the E minor piece, and as
punishment for the mistakes I must insist on hearing the
story behind it.   Such stories have great value for me; I
nearly always have them myself, and when not, the background of the picture seems to me to be lacking.   Our Herzogenbergs will say this is nonsense—and with reason; but
where should we all be without nonsense !   Where music
would be without Wagner? . . . No ! in a far, far worse
case !

I send no messages to the Herzogenbergs because I hope
to find time to write to them to-day.   Goodbye, and, once
more, warmest thanks for what you sent me and friendliest
greetings.

From your
EDWARD GRIEG.

CHAPTER XXVIII

Autumn 1881 to Autumn 1882

I went back to Leipzig late that year and have but few recollections of the winter '81-'82; moreover at this moment the home letters, in which a word sometimes fires a train of memory, give out altogether. But I well remember that for some time past I had suffered under a sense that I was not as much to Lisl as formerly, or at all events, to use a current phrase, not giving satisfaction. From the point of view of work there was no fault to be found, indeed the piles of dated MSS. in my loft bear witness to a period of extreme diligence; the trouble sprang from what was unfortunately a salient characteristic, my knack of constantly forming new ties. Not that she was jealous in the ordinary sense of the word; she knew very well that, come who might, no one could oust her from her place; it was rather that she was distressed and bewildered by what seemed to her indications of a spendthrift moral nature (' ein Vergeuden schöner Kraft,' as she put it).

Until we had met, all in laughing at the exclusive Stockhausen tradition, Lisl had been really carrying it on—less perhaps on principle than because they were a self-sufficing couple; and it is certain that but for the two factors I spoke of, my music, and her childlessness, I should never have been admitted into the bond. As far back as 1880 she had once told me in a moment of irritation that Heinrich sometimes found the *ménage à trois* a trial—as well he might with such an extortionate third—and in face of this all-round insatiability I daresay she asked herself whether I fully appreciated the exception made in my favour.   Much as they both vene- rated Conrad Fiedler the rapid friendship with his wife had not enchanted her, and now there was an English newcomer to reckon with, evidently a remarkable and arresting per- sonality . . . What next?   In one of her letters there is a fine defence of her own instincts in these matters, and she never could understand how I, all in admiring them, could not change my own.

Very differently did my mother, a really jealous being by nature, treat the subject.   Though her contemporary corre- spondence with me has vanished, the most precious bit of her handwriting I possess is dated December 1881, or rather that is the postmark, for she never dated a letter in her life.   A great friend of mine, Captain Hubert Foster in the Royal Engineers, who came to Leipzig that autumn, wrote my news to my mother, and after her death he sent me her beautiful reply.   It is too personal to give here, but the sentence I quoted a few pages back is taken from it; my needs, my happiness were the weapons with which she fought down jealousy ! . . . This letter was sent me with a covering note in which the following words occur : ' Re-reading its con- tents, I am deeply touched to see how constantly your mother thought of you.   I had kept it all these years, I suppose because it shows such tender regard for you, and everything about my friends interests me ; but now I think it may be a pleasure for you to have it.'   Shortly after his visit, a wind- fall having put me in possession of a few extra pounds, I flew over to England at Christmas for a week on a surprise visit, and although I spent two or three days of it with the Garretts that was one of my most flawless re-unions with mother—enough time to enjoy being together, and not enough to rub each other up the wrong way !

As a rule I spent Christmas, which means a good deal to Germans, in the Humboldstrasse, and it saddened Lisl that I chose that moment to disappear.   But on quite other than sentimental grounds was another project combated not only by her but by Aloysius ; namely my intention, announced to them in the spring, of passing my next winter in Italy.

This decision was taken rather suddenly. Desire for contact with other forms of beauty than music, for the South in short, had grown and grown till there was no resisting it, and I felt too that having worked like a galley slave for four years at theory I should be all the better for putting some of it into practice without supervision. That Aloysius fought so hard to dissuade me is a touching proof that the artistic well-being of his pupil preoccupied him more than the inconveniences of her everlasting presence in his house. What a pity, he argued, to get out of harness just when one is beginning to move freely in it ! And he further reminded me that Brahms had re-studied counterpoint from beginning to end when he was over forty. The obvious rejoinder was that I would gladly do the same when I reached that age, or even sooner, and I stuck to my guns. As for Lisl, being herself devoid of world-curiosity, as the Germans call it, she could not fathom my state of mind at all. Her motto might have been a quotation from Carlyle I came across the other day : ' Happy men live in the present for its bounty suffices ; and wise men too, for they know its value.' When a chance of a new experience came along she took it, but in the meantime was quite happy on her own line of rails ; hence these Italian longings were looked upon as one more manifestation of an immoderate hunger for life—the ' Lebensteufel ' she so often bewailed in me. So I went back to England slightly, very slightly, in disgrace with my best friends, and it was settled that if dates fitted in, we were to meet at Venice in the late autumn on my way to Florence *viâ* Switzerland, where I was to be initiated into mountaineering by Wach.

I did a good deal of music, real music, that summer with the von Glehns at Sydenham, and in the course of a projected performance in public of something of mine—a quartett I think—found out for the first time, and wrote to Lisl, that English musicians are refractory to dotted semi-quavers—a

striking symptom of the go-as-you-please theory of life.   I
remember too that the charming singer von zer Mühlen,
whom I often met at the von Glehns, told me that recently,
on his mentioning Lisl and me, Brahms had remarked : ' My
God, children, but those are two musical women tucked away
in the horrible Leipzig ! '   This also was passed on to Lisl,
but in semi-sarcastic vein, for though I was pleased that
others should know the great man thought so highly of us,
his good opinion in no wise added to my stature or flattered
me personally.   And I vicariously felt the same for Lisl ; but
to my amazement that incorrigibly humble person was quite
delighted and thought this tribute a great feather in our
caps.

Towards the end of my stay in England the Garretts came
to Frimhurst.   In spite of their art-y clothes, the effect of
which on Papa's mind I had rather dreaded, they captivated
even him ; and what is more, mother's jealousy was instantly
swamped in her extraordinary appreciation of Rhoda, whom
I think she liked better than all the rest of my friends put
together.   A great point in their favour with Papa was that
they ' braided their hair,' as he put it, so as to leave the forehead uncovered, instead of wearing fringes like his daughters and their friends, which he always maintained reduced
human beings to the level of apes.   There was an amusing
scene at which unfortunately I did not assist.   My mother
had been complaining of the cold in the famous bow window
and the reasonable Agnes suggested a shawl ; but mother,
who though not in her first youth was by no means un-
shapely, replied with some hesitation that she didn't like
shawls ' because they hide the figure so. '   Whereupon Agnes
exclaimed :   ' Isn't that rather kind of them ? '   Awestruck
I asked how this very characteristic remark had been received, and was relieved to hear mother had only laughed.

.   .   .   .   .   .

I sometimes wonder if one's vision of a past incident or a
lost friend is intensified or weakened by the absence of all
written record?   Knowing my habits, Rhoda, who was extremely reserved, had made me promise to destroy her letters

as soon as read, and I did so. In the light of what happened this is a promise I never gave again. All I possess of her now is a bit of heather, plucked after I had left England on Charlotte Brontë's grave, and a little crooked battered stone she once picked up on the beach remarking that by the time I was forty my heart would look like that! . . . It was decided that they were to join me at Florence the following Easter, and in August I left for Switzerland *viâ* Newhaven, Rhoda hurling a forgotten box of 100 cigarettes after me as the boat moved away from the quay.

I stopped at Rouen and like many other people was disappointed with everything except St. Ouen, till towards evening I climbed up the great chalk cliff 350 feet above the town. It had rained all day; the sun was setting, the Seine —all red and yellow and blue—lay at my feet, the new town shrouded in cloud and smoke on one side of me, and on the other the old town with its five grand churches, settled down in an armchair of green and white hills. I wonder if anyone will ever see it like that again? but let no one who has a chance omit to climb that cliff and try. I left Rouen doubting if anything more intense in the way of joy for the eyes could be found in Switzerland.

The Wach chalet in the commune of Wilderswyl was about 1,000 feet above Interlaken, and though its owners were a thing apart, in no way differed from all châlets. There I got to know Wach in quite a new aspect and the one I loved best—a big boy in knickerbockers, madder than any adolescent about mountaineering. So impatient was he to initiate his guest that he would have arranged our first climb for the day after my arrival, but for the gentle icy opposition of Lili, who guessed the fatigues of a long journey third class and insisted on twenty-four hours of rest.

And now let me ask anyone who from youth upwards has greatly loved two things, scenery and adventure, if memory holds anything to compare with such a first experience? The Schildhorn is of course a beginner's mountain but it gives one a taste of the whole thing—an unequalled view of ' the

three Bernese giants,' as it is almost impossible to help calling them, and above all the sonority of perpetual avalanches
—one of the most beautiful noises under heaven. The boys
were then about twelve and fourteen, and there was a
moment when it seemed the younger was about to receive a
thrashing from his father for collapsing in the snow and
declaring, while tears ran down his blue little nose, that he
could go no farther; but who could stand up, or rather lie
down, against Wach? On the top of that mountain I
noticed what was so often to strike me afterwards, that in
the joy of difficulties vanquished the mind of Fainthearts is
miraculously cleansed from all memory of these passing
weaknesses.

Another thing; for my part I have seldom undertaken a
big climb without saying to myself at some particular stage :
' Never again ! '; yet once more safe at home, only one
thought possesses you—how soon funds will allow of another
expedition. I explain this passion, far the most violent in
the way of sport I have ever felt, by two things; firstly, as
Barrès says somewhere, a landscape won by your own
intense effort has a peculiar grip on you—almost a physical
as well as an aesthetic grip ; and secondly there is the danger
not only to yourself but to companions, who may pay for a
false step of yours with their lives. And if that is not an
intoxicating element in pleasure I don't know what is ! Of
danger I had of course no experience on that baby mountain,
yet a premonition—for Wach slipped on a glacier and shot
down a good way before he could stop himself with his axe.
Nothing much would have happened in any case, but it gave
one an idea of the thing.

I began my career as mountain climber with a bit of bad
luck. At a dance in England, saving a fall of the usual kind
in what Lady Ponsonby called our *ton de garnison* neighbourhood where spurs were for ever catching in gowns, I
had strained one of my knees slightly, but felt it for only a
day or two. Needless to say it was this very knee that was
struck bullet-fashion by a bounding bit of rock on the up
journey, about 4,000 ft. from the top. In all I walked eleven

hours with that damaged knee, including leaping down the
mountain with the leg held stiff which of course jarred the
hip, and the result was for the time an end to mountaineering.   The disappointment only ceased to rankle when for the
first time I saw the Gotthard and was well on the way to
Venice, little knowing what awaited me there.

. . . . . .

To my amazement I was met on the platform by Heinrich
only, and horror-stricken I learned that Lisl was once more
in family fetters.   Not only had her mother suddenly turned
up, but also the one being who in their youth had slipped
through the meshes of Frau von Stockhausen's anti-friend
net, and been tolerated as high-born distant cousin—a young
lady of a certain age, called ' Mathilde,' hitherto on mere
cousinly terms with Lisl, but who now at once made common
cause with my enemy in cold-shouldering the foreign
intruder.

Never had anyone a more disastrous first sight of Venice.
I had cut short my stay at home on purpose to see everything with the Herzogenbergs; what happened was the
most humiliating and unsuccessful game of hide-and-seek
ever played, it being understood that the sight of me drove
Frau von Stockhausen into convulsions.   Four days were
spent lurking in corridors, slinking into side chapels, jam-
ming down my parasol over my face in gondolas and so
forth; till at last, given Lisl's dislike of conflicts and utter
helplessness as regards the whole situation, I departed prematurely—in sorrow but still more in anger—for Florence.
I had thought my mother difficult to deal with, but she was
sweet reasonableness itself compared to that beautiful old
termagant.

CHAPTER XXIX

The arrival at Florence was rather dismal, for Venetian wrath was yet undigested and I had no friends there to welcome me, though plenty in store. Julia, Lisl's sister, lived there, also the Hildebrands (intimates of all my group) and the Fiedlers talked of coming later. Meanwhile two things had to be done, (1) choose a dwelling-place, (2) pick up an English girl I had promised to look after—that is, she was to live wherever I did but without our interfering with each other's way of life. My plan of action about finding an apartment was always the same; having taken a ' cabman's room ' in some modest hotel I selected a street or block of buildings the outlook from the back of which—open with plenty of trees—seemed promising. I then searched on doorposts for possible notices of ' rooms to let ' and walked up and down the staircases of such houses till I found what I wanted. Having luck almost at once in the quarter I preferred, Via dei Serragli, I went off to fetch my charge, Amey, the guardianship of whom had come to me as Lisl said—using a wonderful German expression—' as the box on the ear comes to the child.'

Amey was by way of studying painting. I never caught her at it, but before we had walked many yards her true career was revealed, in that she flew at a policeman and began urging him in wonderful French to come with her at

61

once to the market, and arrest several old women whom she had seen pouring shot down the gullets of geese to increase their weight—a usual Italian practice in those days. The idea of beginning Florentine life in a police court did not appeal to me and Amey was infuriated at my apparent indifference to these horrors; so our alliance was ushered in by a brawl in the street followed by her walking off in a rage, to return reluctantly inasmuch as I alone knew where our house was. Poor Amey spent most of her time that winter alternately trying to represent in her sole person a non-existent S.P.C.A., and fulminating at me for merely looking the other way. Otherwise she was a good soul though queer natured. Of course, as we all know, the cruelty to animals one is perpetually witnessing is the one flaw in the otherwise perfect bliss of living in Italy; and the wondering reply you get to protests : ' ma non sono cristiani ! ' (' but they are not Christians ! ') looks as if the old Vatican government were the fountain-head of the mischief, as it certainly is of the beggar plague. But what can a passing stranger do? . . .

My room, a fine airy one with a beautiful view across gardens, roofs, and ' loggie,' cost 17 francs a month! Our landlady was a jovial person who began by telling us she hoped we would receive our gentlemen friends whenever we liked, the significance of which remark did not strike me till years afterwards, though I remember a shade of disappointment passed across her face when I said we had none. We bought our own food and cooked it ourselves in a little kitchen fitted with the usual duplicate arrangements for charcoal fires; and when we were not on speaking terms, which sometimes happened, the silent preparation of our respective cutlets might have been part of some primæval religious rite, the two holes for charcoal being let into a sort of brick altar, and not three feet apart. The worst part of the house was of course the sanitary arrangements, and the road to the best effort of that kind on the part of the architect—the best on our floor at least—lay through my room. This road was of course impassable in war time, a factor which made for peace as far as Amey was concerned.

Not being Pater or the terrible Ruskin, I will not launch forth into ravings about Florence; besides which, my leg being evidently in a bad way, enterprise was checked for the moment. Lest the dreaded fate of immobility should overtake me, which it soon did, I determined to lay in a stock of human companionship, and at once went to call on the Hildebrands. They lived outside the Porta Romana in a convent at S. Francesco di Paola, the immense ground floor of which had been turned into studios. From the floor above, decorated with frescoes by Hildebrand and his friends, and full of beautiful things, you got what is perhaps the most famous view of Florence, and behind the house was a neglected garden. The family consisted of several children, mostly girls —all of them budding sculptors, painters, or poetesses—and Frau Hildebrand, once a celebrated man-enslaver and still gracious and desirable though no longer in her first youth. One almost regretted that so much receptivity to the touch of life had been finally tamed to domestic uses, for nowadays she was rather by way of being fattish and motherly on principle. Yet I remember one evening of reminiscent youthful grace, when after some little domestic festival they all accompanied their guests as far as the Porta Romana; then suddenly she danced a step or two down hill among the fireflies, and I saw a graceful Bacchante hanging aslant between me and the moon. She was a great dear, radiating warmth, kindness, and hospitality, but I got on best with him.

Hildebrand is, I am certain, one of the great artists of all time. Lisl was rather shocked at my saying he impressed me more even than Brahms, but I think the remark was sound, for there are many great composers of modern times, but how many sculptors of Hildebrand's stature, I wonder? He was of a serene gay temperament, absolutely natural, and I think ' a-moral ' is the term to express his complete detachment, in theory at least, from morality and current views on the conduct of his life. Children, for instance, should not be brought up but left to grow like wild flowers; and the results of this principle in his own young family did not appeal to my English notions. Lisl once remarked that if he were not upright and kindly by nature—in fact a good man—he would be a very bad one, and this he allowed was true.

There was a queer mixture of simplicity and shrewdness about him—a lawyer's shrewdness I mean, not the peasant cunning of a Rodin, aware of the market and for all his genius never forgetting it. The public only existed for Hildebrand as a corrective. He used to ask what one thought of his statues, and once when I said a certain arm looked to me too long, he explained that though as a matter of fact it was too short, the remark put him on the track of the real error, which was elsewhere ; a thing I have often felt myself about the judgment of the man in the street—the only criticism of real value, as a rule, to the artist. He was a tremendous arguer and theoriser, and would discourse till all hours of the night on a subject like ' Raumvorstellung ' for instance (' concept of cubic content ' is the nearest English I can find) and its connection with plastic art. His talk was so free from pedantry, so luminous, that any artist, or indeed any cultivated being, could listen to it with pleasure, and watch his clear laughing eyes become like pin-points, as, with raised forefinger, he drove his argument home.

Frau Hildebrand whose brain was not theoretical had lived all her life among artists, knew the jargon and didn't want to be out of it. But alas ! like all creative minds Hildebrand's moved on, and she complained that when after having mastered the latest theory she was carefully expounding it to admiring newcomers, he would suddenly whirl round and cry out impatiently from the other side of the room : ' Ach ! das ist es ja *gar* nicht ! ' (That's not it *at all !* '). She used to laugh at herself for these cultural yearnings and ambitions, but to laugh at one's weaknesses and to give them up are two different matters.

Like many ' picturing artists ' as Germans call them, Hildebrand was deeply musical, played the violin and viola, and could transpose at sight, much to my admiration, whether from the alto, bass, or violin clef, with the greatest ease ; but it was impossible to get him beyond Haydn and

Beethoven. In the same way all he knew or wanted to know of English literature was Shakespeare and ' Tom Jones,' which he thought the finest novel in the world—no great compliment, for the only other novel he had read was ' Elective Affinities.' And this book he actually had the effrontery to defend, as will many a German who knows better. Asked if he considered the perpetual reference to that terrible gardening bore of a lover, the Captain, as ' *der gute Mann* ' (the excellent man) is stimulating to the imagination, he would innocently reply : ' Why not? ' In short the author of ' Wahlverwandschaften ' is Goethe. As for new books, he flatly refused to open one in any language.

Why I speak of him in the past tense I cannot think, for just before the war he was alive and I hope is so still. I went to see them when passing through Munich in 1914 ; he had been very ill and the bounding vitality and loquaciousness of former years were gone, but he talked enthrallingly about modern work and said, with Hildebrand simplicity : ' Compared to these *artists* I feel like a mere workman '— nor I fancy did he wish to feel otherwise. I repeated to him a remark of Rodin's, whom he greatly admired—with reservations—about its being the office of a sculptor to transcend, in the interests of suggestiveness and mystery, the limitations of his models ; and the old pin-point look came back into his eyes as he said : ' It seems to me nothing can exceed the mystery and suggestiveness of Nature.'

Some people complain that his portrait busts slavishly copy Renaissance work, and on the other hand, his treatment of the nude has been found classically cold. My own feeling is that everything he does is so intensely Hildebrand no matter who his progenitors may be, so absolutely free from concession to anything but his own artistic vision, that his work must surely be on the very first line. For many years taboo in Berlin, because when invited by the All-Highest to collaborate in the Sieges-Allee he freely spoke his mind on that terrible subject, he is as good as unknown in England ; indeed I think the only originals of his in the United Kingdom are the bust of Baroness von Stockhausen I referred to, and

a portrait in high relief of Mr. Gerald Balfour which I am
told is at Whittinghame.

Of the other couple of prospective friends, the Brewsters, I
had of course learned a great deal from Lisl, her deep admiration for her extraordinary sister being the main theme of
many letters.[1] It appeared that these relations of hers were
super-humans and that they lived in an Ivory Tower, knowing not a soul in Florence except the Hildebrands.   This
solitary frequentation was born of the fact that once, in pre-
S.Francesco days, Hildebrand found the mysterious lady
who lived on the floor below them sitting patiently on the
stairs with a sprained ankle, whereupon he carried her into
her apartment.   Nothing short of that would have done it.
I knew that Julia Brewster was eleven years older than her
husband (who at that time was thirty-one) and had heard
about their extraordinary views on marriage which did not
commend themselves to Lisl, though, as she often insisted,
they lived in a world of their own and could not be judged by
ordinary standards.   It appeared that they had only gone
through the marriage ceremony in church in order to avoid
wounding the feelings of Julia's family and had found it very
' comic ' at the time—especially some incident about has-
socks which I have forgotten—but it was not looked upon as
a binding engagement.   If either of the couple should weary
of married life or care for someone else, it was understood
that the bond was dissoluble, and there was a firm belief on
both sides that no such event could possibly destroy, or even
essentially interrupt, their ' friendship ' as they called it,
founded as it was on more stable elements than mere marriage ties.   ' Do not be afraid,' they said, ' of anything life
may bring ; face it, assimilate it, and the gods will see you
through.'   (I may add that such was H.B.'s gospel to the
end, though as the years passed he came to realise there is a
thing called human nature, and didn't quarrel with it for
sometimes playing havoc with theories.)

[1] Appendix III., p. 22, No. 4 ; p. 23, No. 5 ; p. 26, No. 11.

This much I had gleaned from hearsay concerning Lisl's relations; face to face with them I soon found out that the real hermit was Julia, her husband being rather an embryonic lover of humanity, hitherto accustomed, owing to circumstances, to pay exclusive attention to abstractions. As I learned many years afterwards Julia was just then beginning to notice in him a new and strange impulse to extend a furtive hand to his fellow creatures and thought it wisest to offer no opposition. Thus it came to pass that instead of being politely warned off the premises as I had half expected, I was warmly welcomed in Via de' Bardi.

My acquaintance with the man destined to become my greatest friend began, it is amusing to reflect, with ' a little aversion ' on my part, although his personality was delightful. Having for years had no real intercourse with anyone save his wife, he was very shy—a shyness like that of a well-brought-up child, and which took the form of extreme simplicity, as though he were falling back on first principles to see him through. In one who was obviously what is called an *âme d'élite* this trait was of charming effect and in spite of it he managed to be witty, amusing, and when he felt one liked him, companionable. He seemed to have read all books, to have thought all thoughts; and last but not least was extremely good-looking, clean shaven but for a moustache, a perfect nose and brow, brown eyes set curiously far apart, and fair fluffy hair. It was the face of a dreamer and yet of an acute observer, and his manner was the gentlest, kindest, most courteous manner imaginable. But alas ! . . . as thinker I found him detestable ! Half American, half English, brought up in France, he was a passionate Latin, and the presence of an Anglo-maniac, loud in praise of the sportsman type of male, and what was worse, in love with Germany, goaded him into paradoxes and *boutades* it was impossible to listen to with equanimity : such as that Shakespeare was an agglomerate of bombast and bad writing; that Goethe's gush about Nature was positively indecent; that a work written without ' de l'affectation ' is coarse; that spontaneity is the death of inspiration, and so on.

His inveterate dislike to everything German was shared, oddly enough, by his wife, in whose appearance and character I now recognise distinct traces of Scandinavia. Julia was the strangest human being, if human she was, that I or anyone else ever came across, fascinating, enigmatic, unapproachable, with a Schiller-like profile and pale yellow hair; and though completely under the spell, I knew far less of her at the end of my two Italian winters than at the beginning. The home medium of this extraordinary couple was French—a fact that deeply impressed Lisl and me; they addressed each other in the second person plural, and though evidently the greatest of friends never uttered a word in presence of others that could suggest anything as *bourgeois* as affection. Given their turn of mind it may be imagined that the matrimonial angle of the Herzogenbergs seemed to them comic, parochial, and slightly redolent of Sauerkraut; moreover Julia spoke of Lisl as one might of some charming, very musical woman one had met somewhere and would be quite pleased to meet again if not pressed to fix the date. I was jealous for my friend, thinking of her uncritical worship of this gently critical sister, but the Brewsters were more amused at my enthusiasm than convinced that anyone who patted her husband's hand in public could be a really civilised human being. In fact the domestic aspect of life was deemed negligible, and my first impression of that household was two dear little fair-haired children, beautifully dressed, to whom, as they slunk out of the drawing-room, no one said good-night. I believe this attitude was modified later; certainly when after many years, during which we never met, their father and I came together again, he had become to his children what he was, I think, to everyone who knew him intimately—the one person who counted.

To sum up, the Brewsters came under no known category; both of them were stimulating, original talkers and quite ready to discuss their ethical scheme, including its application to domestic life, but of course only as a general thesis. On the other hand their friend Frau Hildebrand, human and natural to a fault, and who claimed for herself the wisdom of

Sancho Panza, would privately maintain that all these fine theories must inevitably crumble at the first touch of the realities against which they so carefully fenced themselves in —a proposition I vehemently disputed, being quite carried off my feet by the impersonal magnificence and daring of their outlook. This readiness to cope with any and every turn of the wheel on your own terms went well with my views as to how life should be lived—but I had never dreamed of courage and love of adventure on such a scale as this.

A few weeks after my arrival, and not to my great regret (for as usual it was the woman who at first absorbed all my attention), H. B. suddenly decided to go off lion-hunting in Algeria—a project which his recent mastering of Arabic had perhaps something to do with. But of the wiles of Arabs he knew less, and as we learned later was well exploited, achieving nothing more than once hearing a lion roar in the distance.

.   .   .   .   .   .

One day in November, by which time I was coming to the conclusion that a cripple's lot was evidently to be mine, a telegram was put into my hand. Rhoda had not written for a week and Agnes had let me know she was rather ill . . . this message told me she was dead. . . . Italy slipped away from me and for many weeks I only saw Rustington. . . .

There are few spots on earth, I imagine, of which anyone can say : ' There, at least, I was perfectly happy,' but whenever the beach at Rustington suddenly stands before my mind's eye, that thought swims up with the vision. . . . I am glad to think of her lying within shadow of the old church, close to the stretch of sea we both loved better than any other. . . .

For some reason I never fathomed, Rhoda's death swept away the clouds between me and Lisl. Perhaps she was sorry for me, perhaps she realised that now more than ever I clung to her—the one blessed, and as I believed unchangeable, thing in a cruel changeful world. And I often wonder,

too, whether it was a cry of grief about Rhoda's letters—
' Keep, keep,' I wrote to her, ' the letters of people you
love '—that made her resume the habit, dropped since nearly
two years, of keeping mine.   Anyhow our relation became
from that time onwards what it had been in early days; and
so it remained till it ended.

CHAPTER XXX

On Christmas Day, in my holly-decked apartment, Amey and
I entertained young Heinrich Brockhaus who was passing
through Florence on his way to Rome. Amey had a home
receipt for plum-pudding and I another, given me by Julia's
Irish governess Miss Gardener. Fortunately, as was only
decent, peace and goodwill reigned in our establishment at
that moment, and we stirred our respective messes on the
brick altar in friendly rivalry. I had inspired distrust by
enquiring if it made any real difference whether you mix in
the yolk and the white of an egg separately, or together, but
my plum-pudding won in a canter—as it was bound to do,
according to Miss Gardener, the receipt being Irish.

The bill of fare of the first dinner a cook dishes up remains
for ever engraven on the tablets of memory. We had *prin-
tanière* soup, a roast fowl with tongue and mashed potatoes,
the twin plum-puddings, cheese cakes, and dessert, including
specially chosen bonbons that among other things Lisl and
Lili Wach had sent me. As the former wrote : ' With such
poor little means thy living try to console thee for thy dead.'
Christmas Eve, the real German festival day, I had spent at
S. Francesco, where the children provoked me by foolish
gloating over their presents, while Hildebrand, who loathed
these occasions, sat apart, bored and friendly.

Meanwhile I was almost crippled . . . and Rhoda was

dead. This was the Italy I had looked forward to with such longing !—a place that a first great sorrow made all the more intolerable because of the beauty I saw with my eyes but could not feel. At that time I hated and feared life, passionately envying a nature like Hildebrand's that accommodated itself to the senselessness of it all, and just because it was senseless and inevitable didn't care. Almost nightly I dreamed of my dead friend, dreams such as this. She was declared to be dying, but I knelt beside the bed and said : ' Listen ; I shall go away to-morrow, and if I tell you I shall be coming back again in a month you know you *cannot* die till I do ! ' and she answered with the old amused gleam in her eye : ' Of course I can't; that's rather a good idea—go by all means.' And then I would awake, as tens of thousands awake nightly while the earth is turning smoothly round the sun, asking myself, ' How can I bear this? ' The only key that opens a way out of the torture-house, acceptance, seemed lost for ever. ' Will talking of Rhoda,' I asked Lisl, ' ever be like talking of last year's toothache? ' That question I can answer now ; speaking for myself, certain tragedies in one's life can be put away, not thought of hardly for years if you choose it shall be so ; but the moment you let your mind dwell on them the old ache comes back— to be mastered by weapons Time has put into your hands. One gets over everything . . . and nothing.

I spent two months of that spring of 1883 either in bed or on the sofa. For three weeks the kind Hildebrands insisted on having me at S. Francesco, and being mercifully seized . . . at last . . . by a mania that seizes all sooner or later, I read 42 volumes on Napoleon, fervently blessing Vieusseux, the best lending library in the world. Also I painted a good deal from nature and did caricatures, in which pursuits, strange to say, Hildebrand took great interest. Once I elaborated a theory which he disputed of the laws that govern the perspective of cloisters, drawing many diagrams to prove it; and one of my most cherished possessions is a diagram under which I made him write over his signature : ' Ethel hat *doch* Recht gehabt ! ' (Ethel *was* right after all.)

Knowing how he wriggled out of or forgot things afterwards I thought well to take precautions.

The progress of my acquaintance with Julia was slow and not even sure, one step forward generally meaning two steps back. Visits were strictly rationed on the scale of one per fortnight. She rationed everything. For instance, having learned that Rossetti was her favourite poet and constant solace, I was surprised to find on examining the two volumes of his poems which she had had a year to my certain know-ledge, that the second was intact and of the first only six pages cut; but she explained that she liked her pleasures in small doses. And when I remarked that at that rate it would take her seven years to get through ' The House of Life ' only, she replied : ' So much the better ! ' Such was her tempo, and it may be imagined how it suited mine. I also noticed that the simplest reactions of human nature seemed incomprehensible to her till she had stated them to herself in terms of metaphysics . . . after that all was clear —now she held the clue !

Yet I remember one little scene that made one ask oneself whether this aloofness from things human was not part of a deliberate scheme, whether there were not other possibilities, severely held in check. Physically, as mentally, the last word of distinction, she was more striking looking in a strange way of her own than pretty; but one evening she presented such a ravishing appearance in a new gown, that Hildebrand, though not of an inflammable disposition and severely disciplined by a morbidly jealous wife, was quite in love with her for the moment. And behold the dignified Julia blushing and embarrassed like a schoolgirl ! Finally, when I played a Scotch reel, Hildebrand began dancing about before her—the primitive form of love-making I believe —and oh, wonder ! suddenly she rose and began dancing too ! . . . Pallas Athena cutting capers with a Satyr ! When I afterwards described the scene to Lisl she listened in awe-struck silence without a smile.

By the time spring was really on us I became able to hobble about a little with a stick, and was borne up steps of churches by a herculean Frimhurst friend, Arthur Somerset, then Amateur Champion Heavy Weight Boxer of England. He refused to strip for Hildebrand's benefit, but had no objection to prancing about the studio in a long mustard-coloured ulster, delivering knock-out blows to imaginary opponents. Hildebrand, who delighted in the English, was in ecstasies, laughing undisguisedly while the boxer gravely finished his round, and afterwards he used often to say : ' Where outside England could you produce a fellow like the Champion Boxer ? ' At that time Arthur, fresh from the Colonies, fell in love with every woman he saw, and it would have been unkind to leave me out.   There was also a Swiss painter whose physical development and amorous suscep-tibility almost equalled Arthur's; he also rushed up and down church steps with me in his arms—more in muscular than sentimental rivalry I fancy, but with the same tender results. In fact, thanks to that sprain and consequent helplessness, I was for the first time in my life a pronounced success with the other sex.

Other things I recall in connection with that first winter in Florence, during which time my work forged ahead as never before, are being met on the Piazza Sa. Maria Novella by a man with about twenty crocodiles which he addressed as ' bimbi ' (children), and who, when asked : ' Si domano questi animali?' replied : ' Nossignora, non sono punto ani-mali domestici ' (' Can these animals be tamed ? ' ' No, madame, they are not at all domestic animals ').   Also that dear Reuss turned up, and Hildebrand instantly noticed that whereas in restaurants, where he paid for himself, he gener-ally ordered cold ham and a glass of beer, at S. Francesco his appetite was such as to amaze even the children, who, thinking perhaps of ogres, asked their mother if all Princes ate like that?   Often and often had the Herzogenbergs and I been amused at this very ' durchlauchtige ' trait.

How we made music that spring ! . . . playing every chamber work we could cope with, on Busch's immortal principle

> ' Es ist zur wahren Haus Musik
> Der Muth mehr nöthig als Geschick.'[1]

With Brahms I had of course no success, both Hildebrand and Julia being stubbornly refractory—as was also H. B., who came back a few weeks before I left Florence and with many qualms became our 'cellist. He actually began taking lessons again of his old master, Sbolci, the great local star, and one day when he did extra well, and I kept on exclaiming from the piano : ' Sbolci ! ! ' he thought I was saying ' *Spoiled G* ! '—a mistake which was not cleared up till many years later, for at the time he was too upset to refer to the incident.

And now my dislike of his mentality began to yield to interest, as he proceeded to open up a mind hitherto hermetically sealed to the Latin race. In spite of my mother's leanings the only countries that counted for me were England and Germany, and no John Bull ever held more foolish notions as to French superficiality and moral instability . . . a confession it costs me something to make even thirty years after conversion. It was H. B. who first persuaded me to study Flaubert, Baudelaire, and Verlaine seriously, introduced me to Anatole France, and kindled a flame of enthusiasm for French literature generally that was an endless subject of dispute between me and Lisl—both by letter[2] and otherwise. On that rock, however, I beat in vain ; there is no bridging the gulf between Latin and Teutonic civilisation, and her aversion to French poetry is common to all Germans, though few of them express it as frankly and forcibly as did she . . . (and Johanna Röntgen !).

Just before I left Florence news came that the Brewsters'

[1] ' For music-making in the home, courage is more requisite than skill.'
[2] Appendix IV., p. 125, No. 11 ; p. 126, No. 12.

château near Grenoble, a grand old pile made habitable by them at great expense, had been burned to the ground. Julia, the superwoman, was overwhelmed, and remained invisible for 2 or 3 days, but the bearing of H. B. was a revelation to me; he took it as one might take the loss of an old cigarette-holder. It was understood, my Italy having been a failure owing to my lameness, that I was to come back in the autumn, and early in July I left for Berchtesgaden, where the Herzogenbergs were building a little house, and which lay on the road to my real destination—a Bavarian village called Aibling, where there was a primitive but well-spoken-of mud-bath cure.

·   ·   ·   ·   ·   ·

At Berchtesgaden I had a Wiedersehen with my friends that effaced all memories of the Venice fiasco, he being delighted with my musical output, and she, whose letters had given me a foretaste of the old tender comradeship, apparently bent on bringing its enduringness home to me.

In connection with my adoring reverence for Julia an amusing little psychological study awaited me ; now for the first time a slight tinge of criticism crept into Lisl's appreciation of her wonderful sister. On one point we saw eye to eye. The home life at Frimhurst had always been warm and human, and though, as the demon Brandt child at Leipzig had remarked,[1] I was not fond of small children, I did not like to see them excluded from the general scheme as they were in Via de' Bardi. As for other aspects of life in the Ivory Tower, I discovered that Lisl had but vague notions as to the exact tenets of her strange relations, and above all seemed wholly unacquainted with the Julia I knew, my account of whose opinions and points of view seemed to produce a bewildering effect on her mind. This was not surprising. The Brewsters were not apostles of their own

[1] Appendix, i. p. 245, Vol. I.

creed, least of all among the Gentiles, and apart from her dislike of conflicts Lisl would shrink from discussions that might chill the warm temperature she longed for in that quarter. But in face of my admiring trumpeting forth of their gospel it was difficult to shirk comment, particularly on the burning subject of the marriage bond. She realised, and slightly resented, their gentle ridicule of her own simple, instinctive views, would stoutly defend them, and like Frau Hildebrand maintained that when it comes to the point, everybody, no matter what their theories may be, feels exactly like the concierge and his wife. Still there was no denying the fact that neither of her relations could be called instinctive and simple, and she had nothing to oppose to my amused and rather scornful refrain : ' But . . . you don't *know* them ! ' In short our conversations on the Brewster mentality, as regards this particular point at least, led to nothing, and as they evidently rather distressed her were not persisted in. After all, as she said, there was little likelihood of these fantastic theories of theirs ever being put to the test, so we left it at that.

Meanwhile I pottered about, my leg being still leaden, and incidentally got through a good deal of sketching ; but the great event of that sojourn in Berchtesgaden was that now for the first time I made real friends with Madame Schumann.

It all began over a conversation about her old friend Livia Frege, to whom, though she saw her faults, she was deeply attached. I always thought neither of the Herzogenbergs appreciated Frau Livia properly, and at that moment she was quite in Lisl's black books because of an absurd incident that had happened in Leipzig that spring. All three of them were dining at the Wachs' when it came out that this was the fiftieth anniversary of Livia's first appearance as concert singer, and presently Herzogenberg rose to bring the usual toast. He was a delightful speaker, graceful, witty, and human, but at times absent-minded, and alas ! when the critical moment arrived, the name honoured ones there present were begged to celebrate was not Frau Frege but . . .

Frau Wach! Of course everyone laughed, but Livia's was *le rire jaune*. Though a great artist, and now a great lady, she took speeches with the seriousness of the *bourgeoise* she was by birth and early associations, and all the evening sarcastic allusions to his little slip—uttered of course in a laughing way—rained on poor Herzogenberg. This Lisl thought both stupid and ungracious, which of course it was; and when Frau Schumann pleaded her old friend was like that, Lisl maintained it was a great pity to be like that, in short the discussion became heated. And as I entirely agreed with Frau Schumann's remarks about spots on the sun, and not only admired but really loved Frau Livia, a strong wave of sympathy set in from that hour.

With all her sixty odd years Frau Schumann was more a child than any of us, and up to that time, as she afterwards confessed, the new element in the life of her beloved Lisl had rather upset her. But once Frau Schumann accepted you it was generously done. I had written a little 'Prelude and Fugue for Thin People,' thus styled because the hands crossed rapidly and continually, deeply invading each other's territory. This piece she was determined to study, and when I gently demurred, from modesty of course, she flared up in her own peculiar fashion with: 'Aber *so* stark bin ich doch nicht!' ('I'm not as fat as all that!')—a phrase that gave play to that endearing little lisp of hers. Her daughters reported her as completely engrossed in this athletic problem, murmuring to herself amidst her struggles: 'Gehen *muss* es aber!' ('It *must* be managed!') and in the end it was dedicated to her, title and all, by special request. She had visited England regularly for nearly half a century, but all the English she knew was 'Alright!' spoken as one word and thrown into her German haphazard, as often as not inappropriately. One day, fancying I had offended her, I sent over an apologetic note to her lodging, and presently, back came a card with 'ALRIGHT!' written on it, for once applied as intended. Another time I found her examining a sketch I had made of the fine old cloisters at Berchtesgaden, the colour effect of which I was rather pleased with; after a painful silence she remarked : ' But surely those cloisters are not all blue and yellow like an Austrian bank note? ' She then hastily added : ' But what do I know about painting? nothing at all ! ' and I had to assure and reassure her that I was not at all hurt.

There is one charming Frau Schumann story of this period —a conversation Herzogenberg overheard while I was at Berchtesgaden—which I hope has never found its way into print; anyhow an English version must be prefaced by the remark that, in Germany, crotchets, quavers, and semi-quavers are called fourths, eighths and sixteenths. In the Schumann household the eldest daughter, Marie, did the accounts, and one day she suddenly asked (I must give the German first) : ' Mama, wieviel gabst du mir soeben?—ein und ein fünftel Mark, nicht wahr? ' The astonished reply was : ' Aber Kind, besinn' dich doch ! Fünftel giebt's ja nicht, blos viertel, achtel, and sechzehntel !' (' Mama, what did you give me just now? one mark and a fifth, wasn't it? ' —' But, child, reflect ! . . . there are no such things as fifths, only fourths, eighths, and sixteenths.') This anec-dote, together with the one about Joachim and the metro-nome, looks as if music and arithmetic don't go together.

I always think with amusement of one of Frau Schu-mann's unexpected little rages, because one so often suffers under the cause oneself. Two or three of her humble satel-lites had followed her to Berchtesgaden, much encouraged thereto by her daughters, who found their mother's holiday passion for cards excessive; and one day, just as they had started a game of Skat, one of the satellites observed that if they had thought of it they might have played dummy-whist instead. ' There ! ' cried Frau Schumann, ' if there is one thing I abominate it is people who as soon as you have settled down to one game suggest another, or when you are going to play one piece ask for some other piece. . . . Ach ! diese ungeregelten Geister ' (these undisciplined spirits !), and so on, till her wrath died down in Lisl's peals of laugh-ter. It wasn't everyone however who had Lisl's courage and could carry it off ; in other company the air was often thunderous for quite a long time after one of these outbursts, till suddenly the thunderer herself came forth with her indescribably beautiful smile from behind the clouds, and all was well.   These are the faults that endear people to you almost more than their virtues.

CHAPTER XXXI

SUMMER 1883 TO DECEMBER 1883

I ONLY stayed a short time at Berchtesgaden, the pressing matter being to get my leg cured, and departed for Aibling with a half-promise from the Herzogenbergs to join me there later. And it was further arranged that on my way back to Italy in the late autumn I should stay with the Schumanns at Frankfort. . . . O glory!

Aibling, like all places where you have finally got rid of a haunting terror—for Johnny's fate had been much in my mind, as in my mother's—is a loved recollection. But for a diminutive Kur Haus it was an enchanting, absolutely primitive village, cut in two by a couple of clear brown streams running parallel to each other, and spanned every hundred yards or so by wooden bridges—and at the back of beyond was a most rugged threatening-looking section of the Alps. I gathered from the stationmaster that accommodation was scarce and humble, and went off to the only place he could suggest, the one hotel being of course beyond my means. Finding no one in the passage I knocked at the door of what seemed to be the 'gute Stube,' and receiving no answer opened it with a polite : 'May I come in?', to find myself in presence of three cows. Presently a young female farm hand advanced out of the gloom and showed me the room they were in the habit, so she said, of letting. The chest of drawers, I was told, belonged to 'der Mutter' and were filled with her 'Kram' (old stays, bodices, and hobbles for the cows)—in fact the only drawer that could be put at my disposal was in the base of the sofa-bed, a thing without head or tail-board, higher in the centre too than at the ends, so that one's pillows were generally on the floor. There was one cup in the house but no saucer, one knife, one fork, and some glasses, all of which were produced as a great favour from the mother's cupboards. I lived in that house three whole days. The peasant (that is ' die Mutter ') waited on me with a baby on one arm, while a soprano of the third-rate Italian kind sang wildly in the Kur Haus opposite, practising for a concert. And to crown all, a place which shall be nameless was in the cows' drawing-room. When I moved on elsewhere I stuck to the peasant as *masseuse* because of her powerful ' technik,' which she accounted for by saying : ' Ich bin ja recht viel mit dem lieben Viech umgegangen ' (' I have had much truck with the dear beasts ').

My next visit was to the doctor, who turned out to be a born healer though not of the Harley Street type. He lived in an old ancient little house all gables and corners, with a beautiful sundial and motto painted on it ; and as once more nobody responded to my knockings I walked straight into an old-fashioned room, full of worm-eaten carved furniture, good taste, and dirt. Seated at a S. Jerome-like table, in the midst of the litter characteristic of that saint, was a man with filthy hands, muddy riding boots, rusty spurs, and a blue-eyed intelligent face, who had lost his voice and spoke, in hoarse whisper, a dialect that puzzled even his German patients. I at once saw he knew all about my case, and went off with the loan of an electric battery, evidently home-made and coated with oil and peat mud. To cut a long story short, he and the baths cured me completely in three weeks, but for a shrunk muscle which had yet to be expanded by exercise.

I spent an exquisite August there, learning quantities of Rossetti by heart while under treatment ; and one evening, following one of the little rivers up a rocky valley, laughing young voices rang out, and round the corner I came upon some twenty naked youths, bathing, skylarking, and chasing each other among the trees. Here at last was a bit of old Greece . . . and it was my miserable duty to walk on hurriedly looking the other way ! . . . By and by friends turned up, a certain Lord and Lady P. They had just been with my mother and Mary at Aix, where he had vainly wooed my lovely sister with costly gifts, including a beautiful fan—declined scornfully by her but gladly accepted by me. As I said before, my old Whig friend's advice never to refuse a good offer had been followed ever since.

After the P.'s left, by a wonderful bit of luck I came in for one of the village ceremonies that still survive in Catholic Alpine districts, the consecration of the ' Aibling Veteran Society's ' new banner. No fewer than fifty-seven societies attended this festival with thirteen bands. At their head marched a magnificent peasant girl dressed like a *vivandière* (I wish I had asked why) followed by twenty Aibling virgins in white muslin and blue ribbons, whose twenty self-conscious, stuck-up-looking countenances shone blowsily beneath flowery wreaths. All the women and most of the men wore gorgeous old peasant costumes, and as the procession wound among the little bridges, crossing and re-crossing the rivulets to the sound of Volkslieder beautifully played, I could have wept that, knowing nothing of the festival, I had not urged the Herzogenbergs to come one day sooner. When they did arrive they fell head over ears in love with the place, as I had promised them they would, and a week later I started for England, happier than I had been for months.

. . . . . .

I went home *via* Rothenburg an der Tauber, then little known, but a place most people interested in mediæval towns have visited since. Conrad Fiedler who had never been there wrote a scoffing letter about my enthusiasm ; how, he asked, can anyone who has seen Italian architecture rave about German gothic ? a point of view I never could understand. Meanwhile I envied Bavaria a form of government that enabled her King to forbid the modernisation of Rothen-

burg, and thought with a pang of certain factories on the
outskirts of Hildesheim—not to speak of Chester.

. . . . .

How the sadness of that return to England came back to
me the other day, when, passing through Frimhurst, which
is to let, I sought, and found traces of the big ' R.G.' Rhoda
had carved in the beech-tree opposite the schoolroom window! Of course my first visit was to Rustington, my first
walk to the churchyard. Nothing wrings the heart more
sharply than remembering the jokes of a recently lost friend;
as I laid on the grave a wreath I had made of the heather
and many-tinted ferns she had admired round Frimhurst just
a year ago, it flashed across me that she had once said I
handled flowers as if I were buckling up the straps of a harness! . . . In the hall her coat was still hanging, her stick
still standing in its old place, and her favourite dog had
learned, as dogs will, not to miss her. . . . On her writing-
table was a caricature I had drawn of myself going away in
a rage from the Parrys', because he wouldn't play me Beethoven's Opus 111 when I wanted him to, and under it written in her strange strong handwriting : ' Ethel, the versatile
wax statue, going away from Knight's Croft.' . . . And the
beach without her . . . and the hopeless bewilderment of a
first great sorrow re-lived on the spot where you had been so
happy! . . . Of Agnes, who carried on Rhoda's work and
responsibilities, and is alive now to see their fruition, I will
only say that grief such as hers makes me half ashamed to
have spoken so much of my own.

. . . . .

The Frimhurst situation I came home to this time was,
if anything, more fantastic than ever. I lit upon a tragi-
comic letter to Lisl describing it in full; the unutterable
jollity of the young ones; the chatter at the breakfast table
which always fascinated me afresh; the ever-recurring financial crises; Papa's announcement that in *two or three
years* (!) we must let Frimhurst; mother's tears at this pro-

spect; her countless new and gorgeous gowns; my estimate of their cost; and finally the abstention of us younger ones from butter and sugar—an attempt at bringing moral weight to bear on our parents which entirely missed fire. We children thought they must love our home less than we did, otherwise surely they would take action, but of course it was the common shrinking of minds no longer young and elastic from drastic resolutions. As I explained to Lisl, who enquired why the mother I so much admired let things slide in this way, the force of her character exhausted itself in moments, and she was not good at sustained effort; but I am glad to say I added : ' Yet oh ! what a " ganzer Kerl " (a real good sort) she is, and how thoroughly I approve of her ! ' Well I might.

That summer I recall a little incident that illustrates how quick and kind she could be. Some exceedingly high and mighty people of the ' nice ' set had come to tea, and suddenly there entered, much to our horror, a gawky adolescent, son of neighbours such as everyone who lives in the country has to cope with—gentlefolk in their own estimation and engaged in a severe struggle to establish the fact. My mother was always wonderfully kind to the parents of this youth, who on this occasion remarked, as he advanced towards her wiping his hands on an unpleasant looking handkerchief : ' Excuse me, but I suffer from warm hands.' The high and mighty ones looked unutterable things, but my mother, cordially shaking the sticky paw, said at once : ' I know you suffer from a very warm *heart* ! ' . . . How rude she was sometimes—for instance when she considered her daughters' admirers treated her ' like a cypher '—but how dear and delightful she could be when she chose !

There was an unusually dramatic carriage adventure soon after my return. The ' quiet ' horse, Dandy, reared as some soldiers were marching by, fell backwards alongside the cart, and lay there plunging. One of the officers, who turned out to be our old friend Lord William Seymour, was off his horse and on Dandy's head in a second, but the animal was so entangled in traces and straps that it took a company of

Guardsmen half an hour to set him free.   After which Papa,
the reins wound as usual round his weak, gouty wrists,
drove quietly home as if nothing had happened.   That made,
so the others said, four accidents in five weeks; and I may
add that when my mother was involved she was not in the
least alarmed, only provoked, thinking such scenes ridiculous
and rather unseemly.   What with our stable adventures, and
the fact that we were still exceeding our income by about
£200 a year, yet going on as usual, no wonder Uncle Charles
maintained with more emphasis than ever that ' the Irish
strain predominated.'   On the other hand some of our sporting visitors found our ways quite to their taste, and once an
old friend of ours, Henry Allfrey of the 60th Rifles, remarked
to a brother officer : ' I always spend Sunday afternoon at
Frimhurst—they're ready to ride the pig or shoot the cow or
anything.'

.   .   .   .   .   .

In the autumn I met for the first time the Empress
Eugénie, who after the death of the Prince Imperial had
settled at Farnborough, and since 1883 has been the most
wonderful friend to me and mine.   I remember saying to the
Duchesse de Mouchy that it was hard to believe that she
could ever have been more beautiful than now, and the reply
was : ' I think in some ways she is more beautiful now than
when she was young, because years and sorrow have done
away with the accidents of beauty—youth itself for instance,
and colouring—and revealed the exquisiteness of design.'
And as first impression another incident may be recorded—
a very characteristic one.   A fat middle-aged Jewess of vast
possessions, whose elaborate red-gold wig indicated what the
colour of her hair may have been in her youth, and who possibly had resembled the Empress in other respects some
twenty-five or thirty years ago (which she proclaimed to the
world was the case), informed her hostess over the tea-table
at Farnborough Hill that she was constantly being taken for
her in London.   A thrill of secret horror and amusement ran
through the assembled company, but the Empress's rejoin-

der, innocent of the faintest tinge of secret irony, was:
' Mais c'est très flatteur pour moi, Madame, puisque je suis
bien plus âgée que vous '—the first of innumerable lessons
in good manners one was to learn in that school.

.   .   .   .   .   .

October and November of that year I spent in the North
with Alice and Mary. At Muirhouse, the old Davidsons'
adorable place on the Firth of Forth where Alice and Harry
lived in the summer, many of the happiest days of my life
have been passed; there too, especially after she and my
brother-in-law settled there permanently, I really got to
know Alice, of whom I had seen far less in my youth than of
my special pal and contemporary, Mary. Though the Firth
is not quite the sea it is the next best thing, and a beautiful
wood ran down the cliff right to the beach. Mrs. Davidson
remains for me the perfect type of a Scotch gentlewoman,
and for some strange reason, since no one would have expected it, this gentle, tall, stately lady was fond of me—
perhaps because I was so devoted to her. Her husband on
the contrary was tiny, vivacious, witty, and versatile, and
but for his essential Scotchness might almost have been a
Latin; in contact with these two I first became aware that
theirs is the branch of the Anglo-Saxon race I most admire.
They all loved music and beauty generally, and would listen
for hours to soft Brahms and Schubert songs, but when I
tried them with Bach's Organ Toccata in D major, Mr.
Davidson ran away, saying that sort of music sounded best
in the next room.

He was an inimitable teller of Scotch stories, and one of
these, though perhaps it is well known, I must do my best
to preserve, because I so often use it against foreigners who
declare there is only one vowel in the English language.
The dialogue takes place between a salesman of woollen
goods (B), and a customer who is testing them between his
finger and thumb (A). With many apologies to Scotland I
shall endeavour to spell phonetically and give a translation.

Original	Translation
A. Ooh?	Wool?
B. Eye, ooh.	Yes, wool.
A. Ah ooh?	All wool?
B. Eye, ah ooh.	Yes, all wool.
A. Ah eh ooh?	All one wool?
B. Eye, ah eh ooh.	Yes, all one wool.

After this, the foreign interlocutor is generally too flustered to object that these are Scotch, not English, vowels.

Though the two dear brothers-in-law, Harry Davidson and Charlie Hunter, are dead, their wives are alive, so I will only say about them that it always makes me happy to know I was a favourite sister-in-law of Harry's, and that to Charlie, a great man to hounds, I owe my chief joy that year and in many years to come, for he mounted me whenever the hunting season found me in England. That November a String Quintett of mine, that was to be produced in Leipzig early in the New Year, was in course of rehearsal there, and Lisl wrote, only half in fun : ' I believe you think more of how that wonderful horse jumps than how I like the new third movement ! '—a charge that our correspondence, in which every bar of that Quintett is discussed again and again, amply disproves ; but the irritation at my passion for sport continued long after she had ceased to fear it might crowd out a nobler passion.

It was in connection with this Quintett that I began if not to dislike, yet rather to distrust, Joachim. Longing that my mother should hear something of mine, and considering that what was good enough for Leipzig was good enough for London, I begged Lisl to suggest his playing it at St. James's Hall; all the more since when it had suited his book, if I may use the expression, he often produced works far less ripe than mine. But Joachim beat about the bush, said he preferred a Quartett which he knew I didn't think much of, and which as a matter of fact I had torn up, and the end of it was . . . nothing at all. I had no ambition whatever as regards England then, but I did want my mother to have a great pleasure—something to show for all the bother I had caused them. She was wildly excited about this Quintett being produced, and would persist in talking about my ' success,' as she called it, to all sorts of kind bores who then of course talked about it to me, and I longed to brain them all. All my life I have hated no word as I hate that vulgar, meritricious word ' success.' I tried my hardest not to snub dear mother, and she herself was more than satisfied with me that summer, writing to me afterwards with characteristic generosity, that I had been ' an angel '! But knowing how otherwise angelic one could be with people far less dearly loved but who never rubbed you up the wrong way, as usual I felt helplessly guilty towards her in my heart when the time came for crossing the Channel again.

CHAPTER XXXII

December 1883 to Spring 1884

This time my route to Italy lay over Frankfort where the Schumanns had lived for some years. Every detail of that visit—from the colour of the music-room curtains to the subdued creaking of the front door, which, according to my hostess, defeated every joiner in the town—lives in my memory; nevertheless, having come across two letters of mine to Lisl fresh from the mint, one written under the sacred roof, the other in the train for Munich, I shall let these speak for me.

(1)

At Frau Schumann's ! ! ! December 1883.

' My Darling,—It really has come true ! I am under Frau Schumann's roof at last and in spite of the awfulness of it am wildly happy. I really meant to stay only two days but then dear kind Frau S. proposed doing the Quintett to-morrow and my staying till Monday. As that fell through I proposed going to-morrow (Sunday). This she wouldn't have, so I stay till Monday after all. As ill-luck would have it I was out both yesterday and to-day at her practising time, but this evening she is sure to play.

' The first day she and I went off to hear " Lakmé " by Delibes, and when we got there found it was to be

" Martha." I had never heard the Opera, and she not for a long time, and we *were* so amused. How young and *unblasirt*[1] she is! Yesterday we two went to the Museum concert, an awful programme; a Saint Saëns symphony, another novelty of an awful description, Arie out of the Meistersinger and Euryanthe, sung by the " exquisite " Götz, and . . . thank God for all His mercies . . . the G moll of Mozart. Sitting next us was Frau Viardot, such a bright clever-looking woman, with a personal and professional friendship for Saint Saëns, on which account Frau Schumann who of course hated the symphony endeavoured to control her feelings. Do you know that symphony? It begins with a passage for solo flute or clarinet, something like this, or worse ' (*here follows a musical quotation*) ' and seeing Frau Schumann's face—horror, resignation, politeness, renewed horror, chasing each other across it—I began to laugh so dreadfully that I didn't know how to hide it. You can imagine how comic it all was, but I was full of admiration for her patience and consideration of Frau Viardot's feel-ings . . . I get on very well with Marie and Eugenie[2] and find the latter as attractive on further acquaintance as I did at first, but I think both their minds want poking up; they give out so very little of what is in them. At home they are charming with her, or it is their humour to be so now. I like to hear Eugenie chaff her, as yesterday when Frau S. said she always read the papers and Eugenie said : " Ja Mama, doch nur die Mordgeschichten " (*Yes, Mama, but only the murder cases*). And oh! the funny, half-vexed, half-amused face with which she protested : " Nein, Kind, warum denn gar die Mordgeschichten? Wie kannst du denn so was sagen? " (*Nay, child, why then the murder cases? How canst thou say such a thing?*) Do you know I have actually stopped being frightened of her . . . They are calling to me to go out with them! . . . Heavens! I am late! More to-morrow. . . .'

---

[1] The reverse of *blasée*.
[2] Frau Schumann's daughters.

(2)

In the train to Munich.

'. . . I am dreadfully sorry to leave Frankfurt but so happy to have had the privilege of being there. I wish I could make Frau Schumann see that. She would go on about " wir haben Ihnen doch so wenig anbieten können " (*we have been able to do so little to amuse you*) and it is so difficult for such as me to tell her without its seeming mere phrases what it is to one being in that house. And, do you know, the feeling of unaccustomed awe and reverence—so unlike what I have for anyone else—clogs me; and I feel a difficulty that never bothers me otherwise in expressing what I feel. I am perpetually reviewing our respective situations and thinking what a wretched object I am compared with her, and how I'd like to do something desperate for her; and so on in the most fruitless fashion. She played me the A minor fugue this morning. I think I care more for her Bach playing than anyone's in this world—O I forgot Brahms ! I was thinking of Rubinstein, etc.

' With the girls I get on admirably, Marie quite transformed, so lively and jolly. They are very funny together and find me more than comic, so we amuse each other well. Our start for the party that evening was very funny. Eugenie nearly pulled Frau S.'s cap off wrapping her up, and then when the cab came it was so small we could hardly get into it, and Marie was in a fury and saying : " Nein, da bleib' ich doch zehnmal lieber zu Haus " (*No ! if it comes to that, I'd ten times rather stay at home*) as if she had been doing anything but grumble all day at having to go. And then she and Frau S. abused the cab-driver in a tragic tone I cannot describe, but which you, knowing the people, can well imagine, for having so small a cab, and he privately informed me it was not his fault if four such unusually stout people (me stout ! !) got in at once. I laughed so at the whole thing, as did Eugenie, that they ended by laughing too and we had a jolly evening; and Frau Schumann played the E major Paganini study and " Warum " and some other little pieces so divinely and looked so beautiful that if I tried to hold forth about it I should assuredly fall into " excess." Y. Z. sang weakly and charmingly, and he and I and Eugenie sat at a " Katzen Tisch "[1] and were very jolly, and sending Frau Schumann and Marie home stayed on ourselves and played idiotic games and the fool generally. I was so sorry F. left before I came; I do like her much, with her clown's pathos and nice eyes and shyness of Frau Schumann. . . . Well you see, I am just as unreasonable about Frau S. as ever, and did she do wrong and you catechise me about it should vex you as much as ever, for I feel her faults without even wishing she had not got them—I am perfectly indifferent to them and cannot bother even to think of them. As nature she is the most wonderful, delightful experience I know and I simply bask in it and try to make it more and more my own. I will write from Munich, my darling, and tell you about the Fiedlers. O how I long to be settled and at work again !

'Your E.'

This longing was not to be satisfied immediately, for while staying with the Fiedlers at Munich I developed a mysterious illness which probably was rheumatic fever. Anyhow I at once became delirious and broke the ' German Record for Fever survived by the Patient '—a speciality as many subsequent illnesses proved, and it is pleasant to excel in any line. Dreading something infectious I entreated to be taken to the hospital, but this they would not hear of, and again I said to myself what wonderful friends were mine, though the one nearest to me in many ways by temperament, the one who understood everything instinctively and without cavilling, was dead. For ten days my head was enveloped in ice and could not be touched, and as I had gone to bed with my hair, which was long and thick, in a loose pigtail, there seemed nothing for it but to cut it off—a distressing necessity. But Fate intervened in the person of Mary's

---

[1] A little side table that Germans call the Cat's Table.

mother, who with the aid of oil, a mackintosh cover, and infinite patience, accomplished the miracle of disentanglement after exactly three days of almost ceaseless toil. In the second week of the New Year I started for Florence, quite well though skin and bone, my Quintett having meanwhile been performed in Leipzig, as may be read in an admirable letter from Lisl on criticism.[1]

On the journey I fell in with an old English friend—a widow, deeply religious on ultra-Protestant lines, whose husband used to beat her. She had often told me her greatest grief was knowing for certain that he was now in Hell, so it was astonishing to learn she intended doing a round of Italian churches, praying in each to be re-united with him as soon as possible. When I related this incident to Hildebrand he remarked as usual : ' Where, I ask you, could one find a widow like that except in England ? ' I again took up my abode in Via dei Serragli, where nothing was changed except that Amey was now studying Art elsewhere. My landlady, finally despairing of tips from furtive male visitors, stole my best boots first thing. After this exploit, with an idea perhaps of making me forget a rash offer to pay for them herself, she took to sticking bunches of violets in rickety wine-glasses on my over-crowded writing-table ; also to screaming ' chi è? ' in the passage, as proof of vigilance, whenever the door bell rang. Implored to abandon this ear-splitting practice, she remarked it would be the Signorina's own fault if more things were stolen, and shrugged her shoulders with a wry smile when I meaningly said I would take the risk. She was an old rip, as my father would have put it, but I think of her with sympathy—if only because one day, when I dropped three things in rapid succession, she remarked while picking them up : ' Bella cosa che la terra ferma tutto ! ' (It's lucky that the ground stops everything).

That spring in Italy more than made up for the previous year's failure. I worked as never before and contrived

[1] Appendix IV., p. 124, No. 8.

between whiles, alone and happy, to see most of the principal Umbrian towns; also Rome, where, the lodging of my desires being owned by a hairdresser who declared he never let rooms, inspiration prompted me to let down my hair, whereupon he gave in at once. In Hildebrand vein I ask, where except in Italy could you find a landlord like that?

An exquisite trait in the Italians, the only race I am uncritically in love with, is this easy response to a human touch, a certain closeness to nature which welds all ranks together at the base.   Their heads may be in different social strata but the feet of all are on that rock.   In spite of imperious authority on the one side and unbounded reverence on the other, my old friend of later years, that greatest of great ladies Donna Laura Minghetti, treated her butler and was treated by him as an equal at bottom, and it is the same throughout Italian society.   That very spring I am writing about, thanks to my own aristocratic friend, the Dowager Duchess of Sermoneta (*née* Ellis), who took me to all sorts of otherwise invisible villas, I was privileged to see a certain fat Marchesa, bearer of an historic name, rating her gardener so furiously that apoplexy seemed imminent, when the old man gently put his hand on her arm and said : ' But, *figlia mia,* peas won't grow in the open in February.'   My very first essay in shopping the year before had given me a taste of the quality I mean, to which I owe as many twinges of delight, walking the country, as to the scenery itself. They had told me that people who have a soul above haggling are looked upon by Italian shopkeepers as dull and unsportsmanlike, in fact that to buy anything without bargaining is equivalent to shooting a sitting pheasant.   I bargained therefore over a certain teapot as keenly as my knowledge of the language allowed; suddenly it was put into my hands at my own price, with the remark : ' Do me at least the pleasure to break it soon ! ' . . . And then the politeness of them, the serene disregard of red tape in Post Offices and other solemn places !   At that time attempts were being made to bring home to the people the dangers of spitting. and noticing that this national custom was nevertheless in full swing, I once asked casually in an up-to-date hospital whether spitting was forbidden in corridors? The answer was ' Sissignora : ma faccia pure il Suo commodo ' (Yes, Madam, but don't let that inconvenience you). How I loved, how I love the Italians ! . . .

I used to walk by night miles and miles along the Arno and once had a nightmare of an experience. On the narrow river path, hemmed in on the other side by impenetrable vineyard fences, I met a rough-looking man who stared and passed on. I am not nervous about tramps as a rule but this fellow was alarming—big, brutal looking, with a slight suggestion of insanity. The moon was perpetually dodging in and out among rushing clouds, and looking back presently I saw the man had turned and was following me. I quickened my pace and found he was doing the same. I began to run, so did he. I must have run for about a quarter of a mile and was in extreme physical distress, when a transient beam shewed a break in the fence; I shot in and my pursuer overran the scent. Then I flew down a rough path and soon hit a road within sight of habitations. After that I always walked at night with a revolver, knowing that if I produced it tramps would think I was mad and leave me alone. (Whatever you do in Italy the explanation is : ' è pazza !') These walks terrified Frau Hildebrand, but there was a vein of adventurousness in Julia (who, by the by, under the humanising influence of H.B.'s presence was more approachable this year) which responded to unconventionality. She liked action in others as long as she herself was in no way involved.

In March Lisl had a very severe illness. Remembering Rhoda I was terror-stricken and begged to be allowed to start for Leipzig, but Herzogenberg wouldn't hear of it— said she was to be kept quiet and asked comically whether I really considered myself the right person? Bottom was their favourite character and I promised ' to roar an it were a nightingale,' but all in vain, and to make it worse Julia remarked : ' One must be *very well* to enjoy you.' Sadly I wished, as often since, that one could combine the advantages of one's own temperament with those of someone else's.

That year there was a further crop of the Shakespeare battles which abounded during the eighteen years of my friendship with H. B. (for I count from 1890 when we met again in England.) I had been swept away by Salvini's ' Othello,' but unfortunately went to see him as ' Lear,' which, like all his rôles except Othello, was mere ranting. Still more unfortunately I found myself sitting next H. B. Many of Shakespeare's plays got on his nerves and at that time he considered ' King Lear ' the work of a savage—an opinion held, privately, by many cultivated Frenchmen, as I have found out since. Later in life, weaned from exclusively Latin tastes in literature, I think he came to feel Shakespeare differently; anyhow I know he considered ' Hamlet ' the finest play in existence. But if two great friends have a perennial quarrel on a given subject, neither ever gathers exactly what the other's opinion is, particularly if one of them gets exasperated, as I invariably did on that theme. In later years we made it a rule never to discuss Shakespeare. . . .

The Fiedlers came to Florence in April, but the blend with the Brewsters was not quite a success, Mary not appealing to Julia, partly because of a quality of hers I delighted in—a touch of the peasant (' roughness ' is a poor equivalent of the word that exactly expresses it, ' Derbheit '). I have a recollection of being with the Fiedlers by chance in some place where burghers were dancing, where we were bored and silent, and where she who, like me, cared for the good things of life, suddenly exclaimed in broad Bavarian : (it may have been a quotation but I never forgot it) ' Tanzen können mer nit, reden und amüsant sein können mer auch nit, aber Champagner trinken können mer schon, damit die Leit was zu schaun haben und sich ärgern ' (We can't dance, we can't talk and be amusing, but we *can* drink champagne, so that people may stare and feel cross). Whereupon she ordered two bottles. I owe to Fiedler a notable experience of German solemnity and lack of sense of humour—notable because connected with one of their demi-gods—for it was he who introduced me at Florence to the celebrated Roman historian Gregorovius. When I caught his name, I innocently said : ' Why, I thought Gregorovius was an *Ancient* Roman,' upon which the great man turned on his heel and cut me ever after. Nowadays I might keep such a remark to myself, but surely it was very harmless?

Hildebrand was wild that year on portrait busts—his finest I think are of that period—and had talked of doing one of me, but the idea of sitting is always unwelcome to active people, and eventually he decided to take a cast of my face to start with. At the best of times this is a horrible experience ; your hair is tied back with bandages, you are laid out on two chairs and swathed in sheets, your face is smeared with cold cream, your eyes sealed with clay, and quills are put up your nostrils and into your mouth. Then comes the plaster-pouring, and your whole face is gradually buried under a wet weight of several pounds. I felt I was stifling and my heart bursting but thought it was only nerves, for everyone present spoke in agitated whispers as at an operation. Then I lost consciousness, and came to, to find the plaster had been hastily torn off by Hildebrand, his wife having noticed that my hands had turned green and that there was a bubble of blood at the end of one quill, the others having fallen out altogether. In fact I was suffocating. In spite of her and Fiedler we started again, and the result was an appalling thing, wholly useless to work by, which ever after was called ' Ethel's death mask.' I was just off on a long-planned expedition, and for reasons which will be explained later the bust was never executed.

CHAPTER XXXIII

Spring 1884

Among many kindred experiences none floats more magically poetic on the horizon of my memory than the one I am about to relate. My scheme was to walk through the Casentino and across the Apennines into the Romagna, planning so as not to be more than two days' journey from the railway towards the end, in case funds should give out. In Italy you really can count on the weather, and my only luggage was a camel's hair Salzburg cape, a comb and toothbrush, a tiny bit of soap, an iron-shod stick, an Ordnance map, and a revolver. The bulk of my money, a piteous little sum of course, was stowed away in various hems. I had got up the country thoroughly beforehand, knew where I should strike monasteries, art treasures off the ordinary beat, and the best point for what I had set my heart on—a simultaneous view of the Adriatic and the Mediterranean. For a fortnight I walked and scrambled in that noble landscape, passing from the delicate Casentino to rocky solitudes of a quite other order of sternness to anything I had seen in Switzerland. Sometimes you came upon a tiny group of human habitations huddled together in the unexpected greenness of a gorge; otherwise not a soul was to be seen.

I generally timed myself to arrive about nightfall at some Monastery, sleeping in the outhouse provided by monks for Woman the Leper, or sometimes I hit off the Albergo (neither an inn nor yet a pothouse) of a mountain village. Twice or thrice I slept in the open, under a jutting rock or behind a heap of sweet-smelling herb-shot hay, my cape rolled into a pillow, for the nights were almost as warm as the days and the only spell of chilliness was at sunset. But the chief jewels in that little circle of precious memories are two incidents, one spiritual, the other temporal, that fell in the last two days of my wanderings.

I had spent a couple of nights in a certain monastery that clung like a limpet to a precipitous wall of rock, what the Order was I forget, but the monks' habit was white. The Prior was a short peasant, the expression on his round face a blend of shrewdness, childishness, and spirituality. Some first remark of his seemed to call for the explanation that I was a Protestant, whereupon he said gently : ' The best Christian I have ever known was a Protestant—he helped me once in my youth when I had just joined the Order '; then he was silent, and I saw he was peacefully contemplating a past tragedy. One of those saints who without effort, and seemingly without intention, draw souls forth from their shells as the first warm day draws bodies out of their houses, that monk knew more about me in two days than many a confessor might learn about his regular penitents in a lifetime. I told him about my music, about the absorbing passion for sport and games, about Rhoda's death and the impossibility of bearing moral pain, about the pull of life and the constant longing for calm, the fascination of difficulties and barriers, the need of human contact and affection, the love of one's own ways, in short all there was to tell of the ' Lebensteufel ' that so often bewildered and distressed Lisl. . . .

One can fancy what his commentary was—the old, old receipt for the peace that the world cannot give, the necessity of turning away from life, and, when trouble comes, of acceptation. (We met again that evening, I and that most difficult of words !) And once or twice he murmured, more to himself than to me : ' It will take many years . . . yes, many, many for certain . . . but some day please God you will learn the lesson.' On the second evening, the few francs I had tried to give him having been refused in accordance with the rules of the Order, I asked him in desperation how to repay them for their hospitality? A gleam of mischief came into his eye : ' Well, if you like to give me fifty centesimi,' he said, ' that much I can accept with a good conscience if I say a few Masses for you . . . and I don't suppose you have any objection though you are not a Catholic. Then he added : ' I should have mentioned you many times at the Sacrifice anyhow for nothing.' . . . The last sight I had of him was at five o'clock next morning, standing at the top of the rugged path that led to the valley three thousand feet below and once more crying, with uplifted hand, ' Figlia mia, figlia mia ! turn your back on life !—it is the only way.'

Towards sunset I arrived at a little village from which a two hours' walk next morning would take me to the station in time to catch the train for Florence. My money was all gone and I was rather sad, for at the critical moment clouds had come up on the eastern horizon, and though I caught a shimmer of sea on the west, the Adriatic had remained invisible. Thus the chief object of the expedition had not been achieved, and certainly the Prior would not expect one to learn resignation in twelve hours. While I was waiting for supper, as indeed at the moment of my arrival, everyone was discussing what could have happened to the Signor Barone, so of course I asked who the Signor Barone might be? They pointed to one of those fantastic fortress-like villages, hamlet and castle combined, that cluster among Italian mountains— *that* was where the Signor Barone lived. It appeared he was a Florentine noble, who like the Prior had turned his back on the world—not from saintliness, but in order to live, year in, year out, the life of a hunter; a man who knew not fatigue, whose rifle brought down everything it was pointed at, who sometimes on his way from the chase honoured that establishment by passing the night there, and might now be expected any moment. Presently much rumbling of wheels, cracking of whips, and shouting sent everyone flying out into the yard, and in came five dogs, followed by a tall, bronzed, well set-up man between forty-five and fifty—good-looking but for rather a red nose, and evidently a gentleman though a little run to seed. We saluted each other politely and I went on smoking cigarettes and devouring newspapers after the manner of people fresh from the wilds. Meanwhile the Barone sat down to a simple meal and ate as ravenously as I was reading, drinking his own wine, I noticed, which some-one fetched out of a rough hunting cart.

Presently he lit a perfect cigar of the brand H. B. patron-ised and we began to talk, passing through the divine weather to whatever may have been the European situation at the moment, and thence to personal topics. I told him I was an English girl wintering in Italy, explained how I came to be in that village, how unfortunately I had missed the great view and had now concluded what was probably the most perfect experience life had to offer. He was greatly interested, specially in the Ordnance map and my red-inked route, which, as one who knew every inch of the country, its art treasures and beauties of every kind, he found well plan-ned; indeed it was pleasant to hear him abounding generally, in the Hildebrand sense, as to the merits of the Anglo-Saxon race. ' But you *must* see the two seas,' he cried, ' it is one of the most curious sights in the world. Do try again; this wind is bringing up just the right weather.' Whereupon I explained that I had come to the end of my cash and had no alternative but to go back whence I came. The Barone, who I saw had an idea in his head, had got as far as saying: ' Well, will you do this? ' when he suddenly rushed to the window and thundered out ' Stop! ' in a fashion that brought the departing hunting-cart up short. He then pro-duced his card, which had a Florentine address on it, in-formed me that he lived up yonder in the mountains, which I already knew, and had many horses and carriages at his disposal. What he proposed was that his men should bring them down with provisions and that he should escort me next day to another spot I had not yet seen, whence a still finer view of the two seas was to be obtained, the road to which ran through century-old chestnut woods all the way; and for that day he much hoped I would do him the honour to be his guest. ' Can you cook, by the by? ' he asked; I

replied I could, after a fashion.   ' Enough no doubt,' he
said, ' to broil a couple of beefsteaks at a forge half way up
the pass, and my man shall bring the meat with him. . . .
Now I earnestly entreat you not to deny me this great
pleasure.' . . .

I looked at the Barone, who, with his sombrero, velvet
coat, high boots, and distinguished though slightly dilapi-
dated air, might have stood for the portrait of Don Juan
approaching the fifties—Don Juan disgusted perhaps for the
moment with town life and building up in the pure mountain
air for further adventures.   All this was noted, but also that
he was a gentleman, and I thought the risk could be taken ;
so after very slight hesitation I gratefully fell in with the
plan, left him to make the arrangements, and went up to
bed.

The start was fixed for seven A.M. and our cavalcade consisted of three carriages, four horses, and four mules, three
of the latter being hitched on somehow in harum-scarum tan-
dem style.   They never pulled an ounce and not infrequently
careered along beside the horses.   We went off at full gallop,
dogs and all, across the valley, and struggled up the mountain road, reaching a sort of primitive forge at about ten
o'clock.   Frying-pans and all things needful were produced
from one of the carriages, and the Barone was kind enough
to say I handled the beefsteaks in a manner that inspired
confidence.   We conversed in French, much to my relief,
and he revealed himself as a cultivated man with great knowledge of literature, not to speak of the perfect manners which
of course had struck me the night before.   I mentioned the
Prior ; the Barone knew him and said the mountains were
full of saintly men of that type.   ' I don't find the mountains
make a saint of me,' he added, ' but then I don't want to be
one, nor, though you are impressed by him for the moment,
do you, I fancy.'   Let no one think this was said sugges-
tively, unpleasantly ; it was just a quiet reflection—and a true
one.   The last stage was a three-quarters of an hour's stiff
climb on foot.   Path there was none, and it was well that I
had declined the offer of a mule, for I cannot think less than

four could have conveyed our paraphernalia up that place. Our bourne was a sort of grassy bridge, shaded by chestnuts, which connected two forest-clad mountains; on either side, peering at each other above the tree tops, were twin peaks, wrought in the glowing, dark red rock that makes that part of the Apennines look at sunset like the upper reaches of Hell. From the bridge you gazed right and left for miles and miles till your eye met the two seas. And now the Barone began to lament and rave, for àlas! once more the Adriatic had stubbornly shrouded herself in haze. I never saw a man more distressed, and what touched me was his evident fear lest I should think I had been lured thither under false pretences; he actually appealed to the driver-in-chief to confirm his statement that nothing could be more favourable than the weather conditions. This may have been a bit of the Italian wiliness I find so delightful, for of course the servant backed up the master, and went on after the manner of his countrymen to inveigh against the undependableness of what Mr. Wells calls 'that ancient mother of surprises, the sea.' The Mediterranean, he added in a spirit of justice, seldom failed to oblige, it was always the other; 'In somma è un birbone quel Mar Adriatico,' he said in conclusion.[1]

Meanwhile the other servants were spreading out the feast on a table-cloth of exquisite old linen, embroidered and becoronetted, and the silver and glass though not in a high state of polish were beautiful in quality and design. No rough hunter's meal this, but a Decameronian banquet; chickens and tongues that put my beefsteaks into the shade, game pies, *foie gras,* and above all wonderful salads unlike anything I had ever tasted, which years afterwards I used to madden that old epicure Donna Laura by raving about, for of course I had forgotten details. I knew there was Chianti in the world such as that now before me, though like the salads I had never met it; but the Cordon Rouge was a cherished old friend. While we smoked over our coffee and

---

[1] In short that Adriatic is a rascal.

liqueurs the servants had their turn, and caroused behind some distant bushes on a jutting-out bastion of rock. I don't remember that we laughed much; it was pleasant, rather thoughtful talk, and we had silences too, like old comrades of travel. After one of these the Barone suddenly said : ' This sort of thing would be unthinkable with any but an English girl. You are cold young people after all—full of vitality . . . but cold.' I said that depended; if you were out on an excursion in quest of beauty, well . . . that was what you were out for, and quite enough too (or sapient words to that effect), and the moment passed. Perhaps he was giving me an opening on the off-chance of its being taken, but I don't think so : anyhow that was our one and only approach to the danger zone.

The wild drive down again was such as to suggest that the whole arsenal of *fiaschi* had been emptied behind those bushes, and as often happens when you are leaving a scene, never, I said to myself, can the superb landscape have looked so alluring. In vain one's eye sought the twin peaks from the valley below; my companion told me there was scarce a spot from which they could be seen. They might have been H. B. and Julia. . . .

The Barone had let me know delicately that he considered me his guest during the whole extra twenty-four hours I had stayed on at his request, and having only just money enough left for breakfast and railway ticket I had accepted the position without demur. He now told me that after dinner a little surprise awaited me, but first let me say that, apparently determined I should have a thorough change from the fare of the last two weeks, his own cook prepared the repast, and the champagne was of some brand he had spoken of at lunch as far better than Cordon Rouge ' I like a *crescendo,*' he remarked as he filled my glass, ' what says Mademoiselle the Musician ? ' And *crescendo* it was. In all he did that day to please me, there was a splendid gesture as unlike a parvenu's display as he himself was unlike Sir Gorgius Midas; one guessed he lived sparely enough out hunting, but, as an American friend of mine once put it, found the pleasures of the table ' compensating ' when youth is past, and cultivated them at home.

Then came the crown of those fairy-tale hours he fashioned for me. After dinner I was taken into a barn-like annex with raftered ceiling, illumined not with petroleum lamps but wax candles . . . (he had thought of everything!). And there, making profound obeisances, stood a little band of wandering musicians, beaten up from Heaven knows where and at what trouble—a violin or two, a 'cello, a couple of zithers, a guitar, some strangely shaped wood instrument, not of the hautbois but of the clarinet family (which surprised me) and a discreet mingling of tambourine and other percussion. The Barone told them I was a young musician from afar—a very distinguished one he of course added—and bade them see to it that their national music should please me; after which he led me to a big sofa covered with skins where we sat in state like a King and Queen. They played deliciously, with the intense rhythm of South Latin races—a rhythm we Anglo-Saxons not only have lost ourselves but seem incapable of appreciating in others. The culminating point was when the leader rose, and with grace none but Italians can hope to attain, handed me his violin and begged for the honour of my collaboration. Most of their performance was by heart, but for certain numbers they had dirty little bits of MS. music (like London brass bands) and it was in one or two of these that I took part.

Thus the day came to a close; I said goodbye to the Barone, who was going off very early next morning by train in the other direction (something to do with a rifle), promised to visit him in his mountain abode when next I should come to Italy, and . . . never saw him again! . . .

As Epilogue I will add that walking home from the station at Florence, to my horror I met Lady Ribbesdale, a handsome, stately Scotchwoman of the attractive barrier type, one of my youthful ' passions,' who looked rather startled, as well she might. My straw hat might have been borrowed off a scarecrow, my boots had not been blacked for a fortnight, and my blouse had only once been washed—and that by me in a mountain stream. I hastily shifted the cape on to my left arm and never knew if she caught sight of the revolver with its knotted strap (the buckle had been torn off long since). But I do know that she remarked to the Duchess of Sermoneta that Mrs. Smyth would be much distressed if she were to learn that her daughter was rambling about alone in such an extraordinary get up; wherein she did my mother injustice.

The Duchess told me all about the Barone. He was of bluest blood, had run through two fortunes in his youth on the usual lines, fell in love with and married a penniless girl, got tired of her, settled what was left of a rapidly dwindling third fortune on his family, and being a great sportsman retired to one of his remote castles . . . not without feminine solace. There were meteor-like appearances in Florence, where he saw his wife and daughters and was considered an original rather than an outcast. Soon after I mislaid his card, and by the time I revisited Italy many years afterwards I had forgotten his name and lost sight of the Duchess, who no longer lived in Florence. Like the Prior he crossed my path—then the bush closed behind him for ever. Perhaps this is no misfortune. Even I, an incorrigible sequel hunter, hold that certain very perfect experiences should have no sequel.

CHAPTER XXXIV

Spring 1884 to Spring 1885

Both before and after this trip of mine, Julia having now ceased to ration my visits, I saw the Brewsters constantly, and found them more and more delightful. One of the great advantages of the amiable habit some friends have of keeping one's letters is, that a memoir writer can check present-day recollections by contemporary evidence. For that reason I was glad to come across a letter of mine, dated April 1884, addressed to a friend who knew the Brewsters slightly and had asked for my impressions.

' . . . Her great idea is that he is to be a sort of Prophet, for which reason she encourages him in a bad habit of stooping from the neck, declaring it makes him look scholarly and unsmart! On the same lines she, the diplomat's daughter, is fond of assuring him that he hasn't the knack of associating with his fellow creatures, but this I think is partly because she herself loathes the world and wants his company in a dual solitude. Last year I once said to her that I thought his manners, though not traditional, were absolute perfection, and felt certain that if he chose he would have a great success in the world; and I saw at once how she shied away from the idea. . . . No one ever fascinated me more utterly than Julia does, though perhaps a good deal of it is the charm of things mysterious and unfathomable; one can't help hoping she may turn out to be human after all. . . . ! They are the deepest of friends and I imagine were once passionately devoted to each other; but even if that part died down, as I suppose it always does, it wouldn't matter, for he is the sort of man it is impossible, besides all the rest, not to be fond of in a most comfortable way. Speaking for myself, what with comparing notes about mankind, morals, art, literature, anything and everything, what with the laughter and fighting and utter good comradeship, I have never had such a delightful relation with any man in my life . . . .'

.   .   .   .   .

I have forgotten to say that Frau von Stockhausen had taken up her residence in Florence early in the spring, and, to my great admiration, was learning Swedish . . . at her age! Under the eye of her son-in-law, the one person of whom she stood in awe, she now developed an elaborate friendliness towards me, which though gratifying was rather alarming; and though they did not say so I don't think her daughters (for of course I wrote the glad news to Lisl) were taken in for a moment. It is never soothing to one's vanity to be disliked by striking, and, when they choose, fascinating personalities, and by degrees, being optimistic in such matters, my alarm subsided, leaving the field to unmixed self-congratulation. The high-water mark of my favour was reached during another violent illness, rather on the lines of the previous one, which suddenly overtook me shortly after my return from the mountains. Fruit, flowers, and *billets-doux* were showered upon me, and once or twice my former enemy actually hovered about my bedside! All this because, as I learned later, a foolish young doctor whom the Hilde-brands considered a genius announced I was in a galloping consumption and could not live more than three weeks!

This news must have intoxicated Frau von Stockhausen, and if an incubus is about to be removed you sometimes almost love it. Or possibly, being an inveterate old come-dian, the part of noble, generous, forgiving mother, which went so well with the beautiful powdered hair and delicate head-draperies, appealed to her. Or again, remembering Venice and Leipzig, she may have thought it wise to construct at the eleventh hour a screen between herself and possible reproaches after my death from Lisl. The one thing certain is that her previous sentiments towards me were fervent affection compared to what she felt at that moment.

I think that Florence group of friends must have been quite mad; this time I had no rheumatic pains, only a cough, a racking head, and fantastically high fever; and three days after being condemned to the grave I was sitting up in bed playing the violin and eating with appetite—symptoms the doctor considered conclusive. Julia had already telegraphed to my mother to come at once, and had also written, but in a characteristic fit of other-worldliness had put ' Warnborough, Hampshire,' instead of ' Farnborough, Hampshire,' and as no country had been mentioned, the enterprising Florentine postal authorities, who no doubt heard of New Hampshire, U.S.A., sent all the documents to America. (Long after I was back at Frimhurst and in blooming health they came trickling in, much to the astonishment of my mother, for I had made one of my lightning recoveries and she had hardly grasped that I had ever been ill at all.)

Meanwhile the sudden collapse confidently predicted by the doctor failed to set in, and after a week or so he remarked for the first time that certain natures had the power to throw off the germs of tuberculosis in an astonishing manner. My friends were much relieved to hear this and congratulated me on my splendid constitution . . . but the joy of one venerable friend seemed to me a little overdone. Three weeks later H. B. went off to Grenoble, where a new château was being reared on the site of the old one, and Julia and I left together for Berchtesgaden to join the Herzogenbergs. As Frau von Stockhausen was due there in a week it was unanimously agreed that my stay should last exactly six days, after which I left for England.

.   .   .   .   .

The last time I had been at Frimhurst, being now considered a financial expert, mother and I had gone thoroughly into the ways and means, and there is no doubt whatever that the problem of saving £200 or more on our yearly expenditure was soluble. A scheme had been drawn up between us which Papa, all in resenting it, could but admit was sound, and certain economies had been started at once. Others were to follow, and I had gone away full of hope. Alas! on returning this summer I learned from the others, who as I said were heart and soul in the matter (though Nina's bills did not look like it), that things had drifted back almost at once into the old channel and that the letting of Frimhurst was now imminent. It appeared that mother, who was then at Homburg with Violet, was far more reconciled to the idea than my father—partly perhaps because, though she would have died rather than admit it, the prospect of a change was not wholly unwelcome, especially if it meant living abroad for a while; but mainly, I think, because women are more thorough in these matters than men, less content with tinkering at a situation. Certainly when she came back from Homburg such initiative as there was came from her.

We now had a very decent little organ at Frimley Church and I became bitten with organ playing, which, as a sort of athletic exercise, appealed to me far more than the violin, not to speak of the prospect of tackling Bach on his own instrument. I determined to have lessons by and by in Leipzig (which I did) and meanwhile accepted with enthusiasm the invitation of our one really musical neighbour, Sir William Cope, to spend a week-end with them and meet his old friend Sir Frederick Ouseley, the well-known organist and composer.

Strange to say a new musical experience awaited me at Bramshill, Sir Frederick, who had studied music at Leipzig under Mendelssohn himself, being one of the very last of the old race of improvisers. He would ask you to give him a theme for a fugue; you invented, of course, as crackjaw a one as possible, and off he started. A good deal of it was learned padding, but immensely musical and effective, and I who had heard nothing like it at Leipzig or elsewhere, was much impressed. Several members of the Westminster Abbey Choir had also been asked to meet him and sang part songs exquisitely in that superb old hall. But the most exciting thing was that at meals a slip of music was placed beside each of us, according to our voice, and the pitch being given with a tuning-fork, we sang grace at sight on Gregorian tunes unearthed by Sir William, who was a thorough musical antiquarian. At each repast new tunes appeared, and the effect was so indescribably solemn that it was difficult to settle down to one's soup. This is the only incident of any kind I can recall during that summer.

.   .   .   .   .   .

I had known for some time that Salomonstrasse 19 was among the many monuments of dead and gone burgher ideals doomed to demolishment; that summer the blow fell, so that when I went back to Leipzig in October, new quarters, with the indispensable outlook over green, had to be found. The loss of the dear attic suite would have been heartbreaking but for the fact that my days in Leipzig were numbered; for it was now an open secret that Herzogenberg had accepted the post offered him by Joachim (Professor of Composition at the Hochschule) and of course I was to follow them to Berlin. Having to say goodbye to certain friends in Leipzig would be very sad, but on the other hand I looked forward to studying the Prussians—after all the hub of the German Empire—at close quarters.

I remember vividly two incidents in that winter season. When I think of one of them my blood boils even now; the other is among the most delightful memories of my life.

The first was connected with the Egyptian Campaign of 1884-5, throughout the course of which I had been lectured right and left by the Germans even more severely than during the South African War. The culminating point was the death of Gordon, a hideous tragedy that made me ashamed to look anyone in the face and was the beginning of a lifelong horror of the Liberal Party. A day or two after the news came I was sitting in the Limburger's box at a Gewandhaus concert, and so was the Commandant of the Leipzig garrison, a well-known 1870 General of the thin, snappy type. Suddenly, during the interval, he turned on me, and in loud rasping tones expressed his opinion of a nation that left its best servants in the lurch. The offensiveness of his manner was indescribable, but being only too conscious of deep national humiliation, I let the waves meet over my head. At last Frau Limburger, in spite of the absurd awe in which these military bigwigs are held, took up the cudgels and asked why they should arraign poor me for the sins of the English Government? To this the Commandant solemnly replied that on the contrary it was the duty of right-thinking people to seize every opportunity of bringing home ' our German feeling in this matter ' to all and any members of the offending race. I am quoting verbatim from a contemporary record the words of a distinguished General Officer to a young stranger dwelling in their midst! . . . This time, and no mistake, I realised that as regards our country Germany was a huge cistern full to the brim of hatred—military hatred anyhow—and that I was sitting under the escape pipe.

It is a relief to turn to the other incident, the realisation of a long cherished hope—namely my mother's visit to Leipzig, which fell in April. She was very well just then, and as, whether I approved or not, her cupboards were full of gorgeous garments, I begged her to bring a few with her—a weakness for which no one will blame me. Naturally I wanted her to be a success in every way, and as it turned out her triumphal progress among my friends flattered my fondest desires. I never saw her more entirely at her best, more radiant. Of the effect of the music on her I have already spoken, and knowing how it would increase her pleasure I used to play beforehand the themes and chief beauties of everything she was going to hear. My dear kind friends competed with each other for her presence in their ' Logen,' lent her their carriages, and generally showered hospitality upon her. But what made me happiest was her adoration of Lisl, who was so perfect with her that even now, thinking of it, my eyes fill with tears. They saw each other daily and mother's room was always stocked with flowers sent by her; ' I have always loved you for loving them,' she said. After Lisl, I think Frau Limburger was nearest to her heart; she

saw at once how the jolly home life, more reminiscent of
Frimhurst than anything I found elsewhere in Leipzig, must
appeal to me, and knew how generously I had been allowed
to share it. Of course too she at once detected the breeding
hidden beneath eccentricities of manner that endeared that
old friend to one rather than otherwise—in a word saw eye
to eye with me in everything.

Her German, at first a little wild and intermixed with
French, daily came back to her more and more, and as ever
she took the bull by the horns. There was one extraordinary
conversational effort with Herr Frege, an absent-minded old
gentleman not quick at the uptake under any circumstances,
who knew not a word of any language but his own, and who
had remarked to her, as politeness required, that she must
be very proud of her Fräulein Tochter. ' O ja ! ' said my
mother, ' aber . . .'—well, I will not try to quote her reply,
which was an endeavour to convey that she sometimes felt
like a hen that has hatched a duckling, but unfortunately she
could not recall at the moment the German for hen, hatched,
or duckling. It happened at luncheon and I was far away,
but saw her appeal once or twice to neighbours, point to an
egg, make a gesture of swimming, and my attention being
by this time thoroughly aroused, heard the bewildered Herr
Frege slowly saying : ' So, so,—Ihr Fräulein Tochter geht
also gern auf's Wasser? ' (' Ah, indeed, your daughter is
fond of boating? ') This my mother understood and went
off into fits of laughter as did everyone else, but I am certain
old Frege never had the faintest idea what it was all about.

The finale was a grand dinner-party given by her to many
whose kindness to me had been unwearying for the last seven
years. She looked amazingly handsome, wearing all her
diamonds, and insisted on Herzogenberg taking her in to
dinner—a touch everyone appreciated—Lisl being on the
other side of her left-hand neighbour. Dr. Philipp Fiedler
wrote a really charming poem in her honour, full of course
of kindly references to her daughter. Limburger's speech,
for there were several, was brilliant, funny, and in English,
and she took Wach's, the polished diction of which was a

little beyond her, for granted, asking me afterwards if his German wasn't rather *difficult*. The next day she went back to England, and I am certain was not exaggerating when she said many and many a time afterwards that she had never been happier in her life than during that fortnight.

.   .   .   .   .

Soon afterwards the Herzogenbergs left Leipzig, and I, who was going next day to Crostewitz (where I usually spent ten days or so before returning to Frimhurst), went to the station to see the last of them, as the phrase runs, . . . to see the last of them, as one says hundreds of times in a lifetime with an unforeboding heart. I remember few dates, but that date, May 7, will be remembered to my dying day. As the train moved off and slowly rounded the curve, I saw Lisl waving at the window . . . never to see her again in this world, except in dreams.

APPENDIX IV

(a)

FROM ELISABETH VON HERZOGENBERG (LISL)

(1)

[Written to me when I was in Italy]

Leipzig: November 5, 1882.

(*In German.*) . . . You ascribe to Hildebrand qualities he certainly has *not*, and you know how much I like and am attracted by him. But he is a man who is only a good fellow just as long as his feeling lies that way, never from sense of duty: in principle he hates everything that binds— duty, conscience, law (except the law of Beauty) and morality. Quietly, and without his realising it, life has sometimes taught him better, but at bottom he is still the same. . . . On the other hand all you say about Julia delights me, and I subscribe to every word. I hope you will get closer

116

and closer to each other, and that you may more and more feel the blessing her presence brings with it. . . . I do like your saying that you feel ' like a great rough egoistic young colt ' beside her ! . . . it is so true, yet how fond I am of you, my old one, in spite of all your vices ! . . .

I thought of you specially yesterday when Rubinstein was here. He played Schumann's F ♯ major and some glorious Chopins and was so dear and amiable—and not at all in the love-making mood, thank Heaven. Though he was dead tired after rehearsing ' The Maccabees ' for four hours, he himself suggested playing, and but for one or two coarse touches in the Schumann played divinely. In a fit of good-nature I had asked little A. to come, and she flirted beyond what is permissible with Nikisch. (*In English.*) He kissed her hand every time she poured him out wine ; he's a regular Jack the Maiden Killer and I think it's quite a shame. She is, I think, quite naïve, but rather silly. They have such terrible trouble at home, poor girls, that's why I asked her. . . .

There are fine moments in ' The Maccabees ' but that's all (*in German*) and on the whole I have the impression of a creative action that is a necessity to the creator but not to the world. Feebleness is oddly mingled with plenty of temperament, much perfume, and very much colour ; but . . . the fruit is dead. And this man maintains in his blind madness that German ' inwardness ' (*Innerlichkeit*) means nothing, or rather is another word for impotence, whereby of course he is thinking of Brahms ! He said some nice things about the ugly Joachim affair, and thinks he started the whole business in order to marry an English Lady Somebody ! ' If that is so,' he added grimly, ' then I have no use for his Beethoven Concerto and his *inwardness* and all the rest of it ! ' Though this is nonsense from the point of view of art, humanly speaking it was warm and sympathetic, and I was glad to hear the frivolous R. talking in that style.

I have not told you, I think, that Frau Joachim has been here and that I visited her in her hotel. I considered it my duty, though it wasn't easy, for I dreaded what the impression might be. But it was good beyond all expectation ; she threw her arms round my neck, sobbing, and was so simple —merely the mother, the lioness robbed of her cubs—that I was deeply touched. Still I cannot get rid of the feeling that she has let herself drift in the direction of cheap, trivial, sentimental yearnings, and gazed forth right and left with immoderate lust of conquest; not with any evil intention, but after the fashion of people whose souls are poorly furnished. Things are different now; I think sorrow has ripened and ennobled her and that took hold of me. Her despair when she speaks about the children (they have taken the daughters to England) is so touching. Imagine! not a soul, except Frau O. and myself went to see her, and in Berlin everyone cuts her—so cowardly and evil is the world! And the worst of all are the virtuous women, who make me perfectly furious.[1]

It is amusing to think of your giving Hildebrand lessons in counterpoint! Of course you are the one who will learn most, and that is the important part of it. I am glad you like Julia's children so much. I said you would. You'll get to understand Harry better by and by; he is not an easy subject! . . .

(2)

Leipzig: January 2, 1883.

(*In German.*) . . . Heinrich's Variations gave me immense pleasure. The thing came to him in a good hour; the theme is beautiful, finely articulated, prolific, and the variations are, as they should be, independent growths that nevertheless depend on the theme. I can't put it properly but you will know what I mean. A true theme for variations has a *paterfamilias* character that one recognises at once, and the children should show heredity and yet each have its own individual physiognomy and value. . . .

We heard ' Paradise and the Peri ' once more the other day and I loved it more than ever—also ethically, though the poem moralises in such an infuriating fashion and is really impossible to enjoy.[2] But even in the poem there are certain moments that transcend the temporal, and the repen-

---

[1] Later, when Herzogenberg accepted a post offered him by Joachim at the Hochschule, Lisl did not call on Frau Joachim who was still living in Berlin.

[2] Ungeniessbar.

tant sinner is a figure that always makes me shed uncritical
tears.   Who can resist the words ' There was a time when,'
etc.? . . . The music is admirable almost throughout, and
yesterday the scoring revealed to me a wealth of beauty I
never noticed before, so much so that I asked myself : ' Is it
I who have learned to listen, or has it learned to sound? '
We go but seldom to concerts, perhaps once in three weeks
to the Gewandhaus, and for that reason I enjoy as never before, and am sometimes utterly overwhelmed with the sort
of gratitude you know of—as expressed in the ' Trilogy of
Gratitude.'   But the longer I live the more do I stand in
stupid amazement before figures such as Beethoven and
Mozart, increasingly beset with vain questionings.   It is
only because we are accustomed to them that we don't go off
our heads, and though I sometimes long to read biographies,
and now mean to start on Theyer, I see how childish it is to
try and find the key to such miracles in records of lives and
activities.   Each night when such a one is born is a kind of
Christmas Day, and the only thing that should sound in their
honour is the Song of the Angels.   I can't quarrel therefore
with Spitta's tone of panegyric in his Life of Bach, but the
word one longs to hear, which might bring one nearer to the
secret of such creative power, is never said !   The German
Mystics might have managed it, but I think silence is best.
Well, there is no end to learning in Art, and for that reason
one might almost wish to reach extreme old age.

Frau Schumann dined with us at the Wachs, after playing
the Mendelssohn Concerto divinely.   Lili was charming, but
as regards her Frau Schumann is in bonds.   To thaw her
requires a certain amount of initiative; if I hadn't taken my
courage in both hands with her from the first she would
never have shown me all her sweetness (*Holdheit*). . . .

(3)

Hosterwitz : September 2, 1883.

(*In English.*)   My oldest best darling,—I am going to
write you a letter in my flowingest English, all of it.   Don't
laugh.   How dear and kind that little moist red electric letter of yours was, and how it caressed my soul and how

gladly I poked it into my pocket after having read the descriptive parts of it to Henry and my father, who asked me (an hour after) if I liked red ink? ' No,' I said, ' by no means, don't say so, nor does Ethel, but of course she can't have had ink in her hotel so the electric machine must do its best ! ' Old little one, how pleased I am you were pleased with that quaint old Rothenburg. My brother loves it above everything and I am truly sorry we couldn't be there together. We were so happy and peaceful at Munich and I did enjoy you so, my Ethel, and felt over and over again how much it is to have you, and how happy I am about you, in spite of my unhappy moments. I think I couldn't be happier if you were always as you are sometimes (indeed often) and if that can console you for future times, write that behind your ears, old one!

How glad she'll be now, at home once more and in new clean dresses and stockings, the poor lost child, wrapped up again in all the comfort and warmth and cosiness of home ! I even feel what it must be like here in our poor halved home, without mother or sister, but there is something in sitting at the old table one had one's feet under as a child, and seeing again all the good old pictures, and green chairs, and forks and knives, that is not to be compared with anything else. And how much more so for you, whom a longed-for sweet atmosphere of home embraces—not only such little details—and sisters, and little Bob and nice old butlers (that steal, but with attachment) and your beloved English land, your heath and your moor, your big trees and your village green ! . . . O I envy you, my darling, the fulness of your joy and the strength of your impressions. I well know there's a shade on all that, and that its name is Rhoda, but I know too one is able to enjoy and suffer alternately, and at the same time nearly, in an incomprehensible and not less true way. I do hope your joy will have sunny strength enough not to let you feel the chill of the cloud.

My darling, when will she go to Rustington and will she write immediately? And how's my leg and shoulder that I rubbed and pinched, and does she always think of me as her best friend and worrier?—for I worry you often, I know; but it being a part of me you must bear it, as I bear yours, my old darling, and love you not less for all that, my child.

Poor Lily ! Her Kadi, as we call him you know, was

really ill with gastric fever; and scarcely re-established, still quite weak and slender and sentimental, away he marched, tempted again by his old tempter, ' the Guide-Fox,'[1] on a great and long excursion, leaving poor Lily in terror and dismay, but incapable of protest, as she always is when those she loves show a strong will. . . . Good-bye, my best child; I'll write better next time; it's my last dreadful pen. Write soon again and love your faithful

LISL.

(4)

Leipzig : October 8, 1883.

(*In German.*) . . . My reward for that tiresome time at Dresden was 10 days with Julia. How I enjoyed her! how proud I am of her both as human being and sister, and how happy I count myself to stand with her as I do! We talked a great deal—mostly in passages and on staircases as usual, when there was neither time nor opportunity. As questioner and listener she is always just what one wants, and has, among other wonderful qualities, that of pushing back everything in one that is weak and drawing out the best. . . .

(5)

October 10, 1883. (*In German.*) . . . Julia's children are charming; they give me joy mingled with a little pain. At times I delighted in them, freed from all thoughts of self, but there were weaker moments in which my own needs came between us and clouded my vision. When others are happy with their children, each laying a protecting hand on some little head, it hurts me that no one seems to think of me, and sometimes it is hard to fight down one's tears. One word would be enough to banish the mood, but no one says it. . . . Whether all this never occurs to Julia, or whether she merely cannot find the word, I don't know; but this dead silence in the one region in which one needs help, and longs for one of those sympathetic touches that atone for so much

---

[1] A mountain guide.

and work such miracles, is amazing on the part of a being
so richly endowed, and in many ways so generous; who,
moreover, often refers to this or that incident obviously with
the idea of pleasing and making one communicative. At
times I am forced to conclude she has no notion how it is
with me, how I have longed, how I still long, and what it
has cost me to appear so calm. The terrible phrase we have
so often laughed at : ' knowing through pity ' (*durch Mitleid
wissend*) often recurred to me, and exactly expresses what I
was asking for . . . and didn't get. Once more you see
how near you are to me in that I tell you this, certain that
you know me well enough not to see any reproach in it;
merely the confession that I am human, and cannot associate
with the gods without feeling that something is lacking. . .

(6)

October 19, 1883. (*In German.*) . . . Julia thought our
Venice attempt last year a great mistake and that it was
foolish of me to bring two such elemental people as you and
my mother together. She knows how to put herself in the
place of both of you, and that is why it hurts me that such
a many-sided being should evince no comprehension for *my*
state of mind. That leaves you more indifferent, you incorrigible little wretch—as usual chiefly interested in the great
' I,' and wanting to know what Julia said of you, and how
she looked while saying it ! . . . At Aibling you would have
entered more fully into my little troubles . . . I remember
one special evening, and am not ungrateful, my child, but
you know how slow I am at dropping one part and taking up
another. And though I know—*I know*—the pedal-point is
indestructible, in the meantime, what with your sorrow for a
dead friend and your interest in a new living one I come off
rather badly. . . . You say I made no allusion to your sad,
sad letter from Rustington, but that was because I felt that
you alone could help yourself there . . . that *I* could not
help you . . . in fact I sometimes feel that I am of no real
use to you at all—merely the dumping-ground you need.
Rhoda and the past, Julia and the future, are your real pre-
occupations, and if I listen well that is all you ask.

. . . I have grown fonder of Harry than ever before, and though his views are not mine I respect the iron consistency with which he carries them out and accepts the consequences.[1] I have met no one who is such a perfect, harmonious result of culture in the best sense of the word. Compared to him we are all peasants . . . but once in an unguarded moment Julia confessed to me that it was a strain (*anstrengend*) being his wife . . . this in spite of the deep love and intimacy between them ! . . .

. . . I don't think that phrase of hers about you which I quoted was meant ironically . . . but who shall interpret Julia? Yet how clear and limpid is the general impression ! (*Gesammterscheinung*).   She said a nice thing about you— that you have the rare and healthy quality of understanding that feelings of friendship fluctuate, are sometimes on the surface and at other times in the depths. I think I too can lay claim to this virtue and have successfully survived many of your phrases. But I do wish one could synchronise better and that people wouldn't dive just at the moment you want them most . . .

Ah ! my Ethel, my child, let me tease you a little now and then—for I am so fond of you !

(7)

January 11, 1884.   (*In English.*) . . . Darling, of course I don't, how could I? find fault with you for thinking as you do of Julia, though I don't understand these things when they ' monologise '—is that the word?—and in spite of Julia's kindnesses and consideration this is the case.   Nor can I quite help feeling with a kind of bitterness how very easily a miser like she seems to do marvellous things when she sends a chicken and a bottle of wine in your illness.   Of course where one economises one's effects the power is doubled, specially if one has to do with you, you old magnifying-glass—but I think of myself and Lili who love you from the deepest depths of our hearts . . . and it makes me sad !

---

[1] A sentiment which, put to the test later, was to fail her.

(8)

[The reference in this letter is to a String Quintett of mine that had just been produced at Leipzig.]

January 27, 1884. (*In German.*) . . . Yesterday was a great day, but until we saw how the public would like it the motherly hearts of Lili and myself beat horribly. One doesn't really enjoy the work of someone dear to you at a public performance (as I always feel when Heinrich's things are being done) and my real pleasure was at the rehearsal on Saturday, when my old heart beat with joy only. At the concert I was oppressed by a feeling almost of shame for the work of art thus laying bare its soul—specially in the C♯ minor movement, when I felt as if you were undressing before the horrid Leipzig public ! But luckily they know nothing about what that piece might tell them ! In other respects, too, I listened differently as one of the public, in some ways more sharply; both I and Heinrich noticed for the first time that there are too many stopping places in the first movement, and afterwards made the remark to each other in the same breath. . . . Strange how clearly a wretched thing like a public makes one see; one is then feeling with the man in the street, more naïvely, more amateurishly—at the same moment more stupidly and more intelligently . . . Thürmer (*the viola*) played wonderfully in the C♯ movement, especially the E♯ at the end,—a point I drove into him well at the very first rehearsal. . . .

[The full significance of the following letters, written after our meeting in the summer of 1884, will become apparent when the first chapter of Part III has been read.]

(9)

July 30, 1884.

(*In English.*) . . . Good-bye, my child, love me, and put up with me—for I take pains to think myself into your soul. . . . The world is much too complicated for me, and I thank Heaven that there are some things deep and simple at the same time ! . . .

(10)

August 11, 1884.

(*In German.*) . . . Believe in me, as I do in you, beloved child. Whatever you ask of me would seem as nothing—it is good to be united thus! I hold you to my heart; tell me you feel how I love you. . . . L.

(11)

September 22, 1884.

(*In German.*) . . . I will gladly read the articles on Flaubert and Baudelaire, but I believe more and more in the limitations of taste set by nationality. I am too German by instinct and education ever to feel more than respect for an ' artist ' like Flaubert. For me, the manure heap on which his flowers bloom never loses its stench—(*Gestank*)—a feeling every Frenchman would jeer at. The French indifference to subject-matter, whether in literature or painting, is too foreign to our nature and notions; to us it is important what an artist uses his powers on, not only how he uses them—such is the tradition we have inherited from Schiller and Goethe—and a puddle in which the sun reflects itself remains a puddle. But these gentlemen fancy that everything their magical pen touches is thereby lifted into the region of Art, and demand of their readers an indifference on this point that none but such as possess French culture can achieve. The consequence of that principle is that a dying frog may inspire as fine a work of art as the Virgin Mary— a statement I myself was once obliged to sit and listen to ! . . .

My darling, tell me often that you love me—it strengthens me in the faith of being able to be something to you now ! . . .

YOUR OLD MOTHER.

(12)

October 5, 1884.

(*In German.*) . . . So the Röntgens have played you the new Brahms Symphony !—another of my few musical joys taken from me! It always happens that when I have been specially counting on something of the sort as regards you, Fate snatches it away from me. I am ever too late! Not that I reproach the R's for having played it to you, that would be too ridiculous, but . . . I wish it had been I! Still I am delighted that you are so impressed and that the two movements you like best are my favourites.

The Andante touches me as do few things in music, so restrained, and in spite of its tenderness, so virile—an exquisite product of matured power. When first I heard it I thought involuntarily of a giant holding his breath for fear of waking a child. How adorable and beautifully articulated the first theme is—and the divine G major bit!

The man who can write that is not on the down-grade as Levi declares him to be ; but Levi has become blind in that direction. . . .

Last night I read the articles on Flaubert and Baudelaire. Bourget's characterisation of this literature as the Art of a Decadence—of a subtle but dying culture—is so exactly my own feeling, that I ask nothing more in justification of my own antipathy. If a Frenchman, an admirer too of this Art, pronounces that sort of funeral oration on it, we who lack sympathy for it may well feel exonerated! . . .

Julia is in Berchtesgaden, Harry in the Sologne, where he has shot, so he writes to my father, $1\frac{1}{2}$ hares in 6 weeks! .

(*In English.*) We meet again then on Thursday! Good-bye, old friend of mine, we'll have a good time this winter, and you shall feel again the old, old story, that no one can love you truer than

YOUR MOTHER LISL.

(b)

From My Mother

(1)

[After Rhoda's death]

November 1882. My own, own darling,—I can think of
nothing but you! I know so well how miserable you are—
such a dear noble, charming woman and who loved you so!
My darling how I wish I were near just to hold your hand
and listen to you talk of her. Would you like to come home
for a bit? we will pay your journey; *do,* dear, if you have the
least thought of liking to do so; it must be so hard to bear
this great sorrow without anyone to share it that you care
for. Papa sends his dear love.

YOUR DEVOTED MOTHER.

(2)

[After her visit to Leipzig]

April 1885. My own darling,—Here I am, safe and sound,
and pronounced to be looking much better—' more lively '
for my delightful fortnight. How I enjoyed it no words can
say, but *you know,* and it will always be such a source of
retrospective happiness. We had a beastly enough passage
this time but I did not give in! My own pet, don't forget
to let me know my share of the coffee, tips, etc.—at least
two £s—and tell me how Frau von Herzogenberg is and
give her my love. I don't think she has an idea how I really
do love her and would do anything in the world for her! I
have been talking to the family till I am half dead, to say
nothing of travelling without stopping from 12 yesterday till
12 to-day. I found a dear little note of welcome from Nina,
who is at Bonningtons and returns to-morrow. The dear

girls V. and N. and Bob are quite well. I send you this photo of him to comfort you! do tell me how you like it.

Ever, my own, dear kind, thoughtful, loving girl,

Your happy and devoted
MOTHER.

(c)

FROM FRAU LIVIA FREGE

[Translation]

Leipzig: February 10, 1884.

My Ethel,—I wonder if by any chance your thoughts are with me? For three weeks I have been laid up with a bad cough and may not leave my room. Every evening I lie for many hours thinking and thinking—as often as not of you—and I write you long imaginary letters that are nothing but Psalms of Thanksgiving for your affection. I have been saying to myself that in all my life no one has ever cared for me in the way you do. Many have been kind to me, many, too, were fond of me, but all these got something in return; it may have been assistance, amusement, pleasure in my singing, what you will—there was something to offer in exchange for love. But you, who only knew me as a cross-grained old woman! . . . Real affection is always a gift. I have often said to my self that you are the embodiment of a spirit that once upon a time, perhaps, lived in and rang out of my singing. When, in days gone by, I sang with passionate enthusiasm the Spring, the flowers, the birds, the human heart, I think the atoms transmogrified themselves into one who came to meet me in the form of love personified . . . you!

Again a night lies between these lines. How often I conjure up the thought of your inner self; are you busy composing, or is the dull mood still on you?—No! I feel certain that you are in good spirits again! I myself am weighed down by many things just now; how much there is in one's life that no words can convey! For me, at such times, the Aria in the Passion ' Have mercy, Lord, on me ' expresses it best; what unearthly things the violin says . . . how it laments with one! Only those who have suffered deeply can understand that Aria.

To turn to a very different subject, there is a Masked Ball here to-morrow; the young people are busy trying on costumes and inventing new dances, and all Leipzig, that is to say that particular group, perambulates the streets in a state of mental intoxication. You ought to be here to invent something really funny; no one seems to have a notion how that sort of thing ought to be done.

Forgive my bad writing; half my being is nervous aches and pains, but with my whole heart I embrace thee, beloved child.

Always thy
LIVIA.

PART III

IN THE DESERT

pared to do an indefinite number of times to the very end.
But apart from other considerations the case in question
seems to me unusual, puzzling, indeed almost inexplicable as
psychological study.   I spoke of a way of looking at moral
problems, as with eyes devoid of eyelashes, which even in
the days of youthful enthusiasm struck me as characteris-
tically German ; it may be that in this experience with my
friend I struck a primal strain of nationality.   Be that as it
may, after all these years I think I can undertake to tell the
story fairly and without bitterness ; almost as impersonally,
too, as if it had happened—which sometimes seems to be the
case—to someone else.   But first I must go back a little.

It may be remembered that the Brewsters held unusual
views concerning the bond between man and wife, views
which up to the time of my arrival on the scene had not been
put to the proof by the touch of reality.   My second visit to
Florence was fated to supply the test.   Harry Brewster and
I, two natures to all appearance diametrically opposed, had
gradually come to realise that our roots were in the same soil
—and this I think is the real meaning of the phrase to complete one another—that there was between us one of those
links that are part of the Eternity which lies behind and
before Time.   A chance wind having fanned and revealed at
the last moment, as so often happens, what had long been
smouldering in either heart, unsuspected by the other, the
situation had been frankly faced and discussed by all three of
us ; and I then learned, to my astonishment, that his feeling
for me was of long standing, and that the present eventuality
had not only been foreseen by Julia from the first, but fre-
quently discussed between them.   To sum up the position as
baldly as possible, Julia, who believed the whole thing to be
imaginary on both sides, maintained it was incumbent on us
to establish, in the course of further intercourse, whether
realities or illusions were in question.   After that—and
surely there was no hurry—the next step could be decided
on.   This view H. B. allowed was reasonable.   My position,
however, was, that there could be no next step, inasmuch as

it was my obvious duty to break off intercourse with him at once and for ever. And when I left Italy that chapter was closed as far as I was concerned.

I then went, as has been related, to Berchtesgaden, and there, accustomed as I was to lay bare my life before her, Lisl had learned all there was to know. Blame neither attached to me nor was laid at my door; we saw eye to eye in all points, and parted, as may be imagined, more closely if more tragically knit than ever.

But before I had been many weeks in England it became manifest that the chapter was not closed after all, and a correspondence began between my two Florentine friends and myself which continued throughout the following winter—the winter which culminated in my mother's visit to Leipzig. The point under discussion was whether my policy of cutting the cable was appropriate to this particular case, whether it would not be to the advantage of all three of us (which was H. B.'s contention) that he and I should continue friends —not necessarily meeting, but at least corresponding.

If the people concerned in a drama such as this are respectively cruel, treacherous, faithless, or hypocritical, any and every development is conceivable; but in this case, insane as we may all seem, neither were H. B. and I bent on pursuing a selfish end regardless of giving pain, nor was Julia consciously playing a part. The story of those months —a fantastic chapter in psychology—will never be told by me, if only for the reason that it is not my story alone; what has been said must suffice—and I think it will suffice—more or less to explain Lisl's subsequent action. And if asked how I came to swerve from my decision not even to discuss the ' friendship ' theory, I can only say that the case was not as simple as it seems, and that a very genuine doubt existed in my mind as to how I ought to act—a doubt shared at times, though I think against her better judgment, by Lisl herself.

.   .   .   .   .   .

That winter was not a happy time for either her or me. Every turn in the situation, every action, every thought of

. . . Not till I was back in England did the longed-
for letter, dated June 15, arrive, and if in comparison with
others I was to receive later it is still almost loving, there
was a new tone in it—the work of disintegration had begun.
Its gist was that our common life could not continue for the
present, and that if it gave me as much pain to read these
words as her to write them, she thought I would nevertheless see, on reflection, that it was inevitable. Of breach not
a word; on the contrary entreaties for ' good ' letters that
should show her I understood and accepted the situation.
This was not all however; reproaches were levelled against
others, demands made, past incidents raked up, and my replies were as may be imagined; in fact it was a correspondence between two worn-out people, disputing as to which
particular wave had cast the vessel on the rocks, and whether
shipbuilder, chartmaker, or captain was to blame.

Suddenly her letters ceased altogether. As I afterwards
learned a new figure had now come on the scene, a woman
whose chronic jealousy was a legend, and who during my
long spell of delightful intercourse with her and her husband
had had cause, in early days—perhaps during a week—for
jealousy. It had happened long ago, the whole thing was
utterly harmless, born of high spirits and vanity, indeed
more jocular on both sides than anything else; still it was the
only time in my life I had done anything distantly approaching to what Lady Ponsonby called ' prigging hairpins ' and
no doubt I deserved the drubbing administered by Lisl after
confession. Since this peccadillo jealousy had died down—
as well it might—and all three of us had been the best of
friends and comrades ever afterwards.

It is only fair to say that this lady was much attached to
Julia Brewster, and rather late in the day had developed into
a strong upholder of the domestic hearth—as beseems a con-
vert, a jealous woman, and a mother; all the same I sometimes wonder whether in that summer of 1885 some real
cause of complaint against her husband accounted for the
zeal with which they both joined in the hue and cry led by
my old enemy. Men and women are mean on different lines,

and there is a particular sort of male meanness inherent in the relations of the sexes which permits erring husbands to go great lengths in the way of propitiation; otherwise I cannot account for this belated double-barrelled zeal against me. But its effect was deadly, for it appears to have been a necessity of Lisl's nature to harden her heart against me before she could summon up courage to break our bond; and just because these two were by way of being my friends, their influence told where ancient animosity such as that of her relations would probably have achieved nothing.

I meanwhile was at Frimhurst, asking myself in anguish what could be the meaning of this second, still more terrifying silence. Clotilde Limburger was staying with us, as arranged between our respective mothers in April. I know that my sisters, who were of her own age, delighted in her, and I believe she enjoyed herself, but the rest is a mist. Only one thing stood out clearly in connection with her coming, that given provincial conditions it was wonderful of Frau Limburger to let her come at all; for Leipzig was already gossiping about Lisl and me, and it would have been easy to find some pretext for postponing the visit. But none was put forward, and though there may have been a suspicion at home that something was wrong, no one said anything, and life went on as usual.

At length in August came a letter in which only the exquisite handwriting—she used German characters and made them strong, flowing, and decorative—reminded me of Lisl. As I said before there were no fresh accusations to bring, but everything I was and ever had been was drawn by the hand of a stranger—almost of an enemy. It appeared I was a Juggernaut car driven by a 'Lebensteufel,' or rather a wild horsewomen blinded by self-love, galloping rough-shod over all I met. It was conceded that I was innocent of desire to wreck any fellow mortal's happiness, least of all that of a woman I dearly loved, but of what avail, asks the writer, are innocence and excellent intentions if none the less devastation marks your path? . . . And harshly as she judged me, the rest of the situation she gauged correctly; reading what she had to relate, as one divorced from theories and at last in contact with the realities of a situation, it became evident to me that human nature had indeed prevailed over super-humanity. The scales fell from my eyes and I suddenly saw myself, not as coadjutor in a noble reading of Destiny, but simply as thief of my friend's goods. . . .

Lisl had spoken of devastation; but if, for a passing moment, negotiations between the Brewsters had come to a deadlock, it was mainly owing to the evil genius of that group, my old enemy.   Where tact, wisdom, moderation, fairness were needed, bitter, reckless violence held the field—but that too I only learned long afterwards; meanwhile what more obvious than that I, and I alone, was responsible for everything? . . . To return to the letter, I was upbraided for venturing to reproach the writer for her long silence, for mentioning my own pain at all in this connection seeing what others were suffering, for speaking as if I had any claim on her as compared to the claims of others.   Then came bitter self-reproaches for having played her part so ill during the past winter, and I guessed she felt that from the first her line should have been : ' Break with him, now, or our friendship must come to an end.'   Would it have changed anything? possibly, for the time being. . . for life was inconceivable to me without Lisl; but no such ultimatum had been pre-sented—an omission for which she was never to forgive her-self.   And now, she wrote, having thus failed her sister, her expiation must be to give me up; the only reparation I could make was to accept the fact . . . and disappear.   Hardly believing my eyes I read that, given my faculty of getting all there was to be got out of life, I should no doubt find con-solation; and last of all, what cut me to the heart most, came the words : ' the foundering of our little boat is but an episode in the general shipwreck.' . . .

Re-living this shock, as I did the other day thirty-three years afterwards, it seems to me strange that I did not go mad. For seven years my life had been as inextricably mixed up with the Herzogenberg's lives, whether musically or

humanly, as if I really had been their own child; so much
so that when owing to her parents' jealousy I had to keep
away from the house even for a day or two, it seemed to us
a small tragedy. And such was my bottomless faith in Lis!,
that though her letters abound in protestations of undying
fidelity—a thing that strikes me curiously now—in none of
mine is to be found the slightest word to call them forth.
As soon would I have asked a promise from the sun to rise
daily. If therefore the idea of even a temporary separation
seemed to me, at first, monstrous, the core of the anguish
was suddenly finding myself confronted with a total stranger.
Had she written words such as these: ' However long our
parting may last, if for ever and ever, believe in my faith
and love as I do in yours; keep my picture bright and untar-
nished before your eyes, as I will yours before mine,' then I
think—or so it seems to me now—that I could have achieved
resignation. Of course her ' distress ' is spoken of, but
every word which could suggest that our past was a living,
aching memory in her heart seemed to have been carefully
eliminated.

I wrote to her, bewildered, appealingly, in despair, and
received one or two more letters in reply, each colder than
the last; finally, on September 3, in the very words I should
use to-day, I bade her farewell till better days should dawn,
and silence fell between us—a silence to be broken by her,
for one brief moment only, two years later.

As epilogue to this part of my story let me say that I am
now old enough to realise how great a rôle our own hopes
and desires play, without our knowing it, in the shaping of
our course. This conceded, I can only say my mistaken
reading of Julia's soul was honest, and that if that time were
to be lived through again, I believe, given the lights I then
possessed, that I should act as I did then; to do otherwise
would have been to use a measure unfit for the standard of
that case as I saw it. This I know; into that mistake of
mine I put better stuff than into many a blameless enterprise
of later years. And after all, if, as I said, the word ' suc-

cess ' does not mean for me all it implies, still less does the word ' failure '; how will our wisdom and our foolishness look to us in another world? Nevertheless I had been faithless to my own instincts—and for that the penalty had to be paid. The strands of what was to become the fundamental relation of my life were severed, not to be re-joined for many years. I burned my boats and went into the Desert.

.   .   .   .   .   .

And now the question was, how my future life should be shaped. Lili Wach, who had suspected nothing, was now told all—as far as such things can be told in letters. She never admitted for a moment that the breach could be anything but a passing necessity, and urged that for more reasons than one it was my obvious course to vanish for a while from the German scene. If I effaced myself in every way the waters would surely subside, whereas my presence among people who knew us both could only increase the gossip, turmoil and bitterness. Eventually I came to be ot this opinion, and the fact that Herzogenberg was to enter on his duties in Berlin, not in 1886 but that very autumn, simplified matters. So I took the hardest resolution of my life— to remain quietly in England instead of going back to face the situation, which was my passionate desire. It was never easy to work at home—but I then believed I should never again work anywhere.

My mother, now fully informed, was perfect; the Leipzig visit had shown her my normal life abroad, and having learned to love Lisl she knew exactly what the breach signified in every sense. Being at bottom a very reasonable woman, she maintained that for the time being Lisl had probably no choice but to break off relations; but she too felt certain that inasmuch as no one accused me of anything but blindness and lack of judgment, all would come right in the end.

Meanwhile Lili Wach hoped much, and so did I, from a meeting between her and Lisl (hitherto successfully evaded by the latter) which was to come off in the early winter. But this last and best card was played in vain. It was impossible, wrote Lili, to elicit any satisfactory explanation of her attitude towards me. She had begun by saying it was forced upon her by others, then retracted and passionately declared it was herself who willed it so. The separation . . . yes, Lili Wach had answered—that I too accepted now as inevitable; but how should I or anyone who had watched our relation all these years understand the accompanying circumstances? how came Lisl, for instance, to forward to her the letter of a third person who knew me but superficially, and who held that at bottom I was of a light nature, one incapable of deep feeling, who played with human material as a sculptor plays with clay? I can imagine the gentle, mordant irony with which Lili would ask how the judgment of an outsider could possibly affect that of people who had known me for years and years? . . . and perhaps poor Lisl regretted that piteous attempt at self-justification. Then Lili had tried by every means in her power to hold up before unwilling eyes the picture of their common friend, feeling the while that she was achieving nothing. At last, after repeated entreaties not to pursue the subject, it had been dropped as hopeless, and therewith a painful interview had come to an end.

There is a wonderful poem by Goethe [1] about the way the gods lead you into mischief, and pass on, leaving you to bear the consequences as best you may. Often and often I thought of that poem in connection with the activities of the couple I spoke of; for this letter, the stone that brought down the avalanche, was from the husband! Surely there was something fantastic and impersonal about such a Nemesis for a harmless little flirtation . . . ? For that reason I bore these blind instruments of Fate no grudge and met them with pleasure in after years.

I will not dwell upon other incidents of those nightmare months, on the campaign of defamation embarked on by my old enemy, at Florence and elsewhere, reports of which reached my mother and must have caused her anguish. At

---

[1] Harfenspieler. Nr. 2. ' Wer nie sein Brod mit Thränen ass.'

last Conrad Fiedler wrote to Lisl urging her to break her
damning silence—a silence the world could but interpret in
one way, namely, that I had committed some heinous crime,
and that my best friend, having now found me out, had repu-
diated me. Her reply was that those whose feelings it was
her first duty to consult asked but one thing of her, to discuss the matter with no one, and that she was bound to respect that wish ! . . . Finally, I made up my mind to return
to Leipzig in about a year's time, come what may—a decision
approved by the Fiedlers who insisted that I should begin by
staying at Crostewitz. Thus the world would see that they,
who possessed all the facts, knew I had done nothing disgraceful.

Before passing on, one word. . . . The other day, re-
reading that indictment of Lisl's, I felt, and remembered
feeling at the time, that much of it was true ; indeed I have
seldom received a similar letter, unless from the obviously
stupid and malignant, without realising that herein lies the
sting. The whole difference between real friends and people
who, without being active enemies, are not well disposed towards you, is, that the former see your faults but love you
because of certain other qualities, whereas the latter see the
faults only and not unnaturally dislike you. And even in the
case of active hatred and malice how comes it that just such
and such a monstrous charge is brought ? You know it is
untrue ; the left arm happens to be too long ; but what makes
it appear too short to the eye of ignorance or malevolence ?
Where is the error, and can it be corrected without imperil-
ling something essential ?

This has always seemed to me a great problem not only in
character but in art, and that is why I mention it here.

CHAPTER XXXVI

Summer 1885 to Autumn 1886

In the course of that summer of 1885 Violet became engaged to Dick Hippisley, an admirer specially backed by Aunt Judy, and of course a member of the Corps she favoured. It was evidently someone's duty to set the ball rolling, for one day the station-master at Farnborough had remarked to Harry Davidson : ' Your good lady and Miss Mary were snapped up pretty quick, but this lot don't seem to go off somehow.' The event greatly excited the many mothers of marriageable daughters who abound in neighbourhoods such as ours. One of these, my dear Mrs. Napier, who was still in command at Sandhurst, met my mother on the platform shortly after the engagement became known : ' O my *dear* Mrs. Smyth,' she cried before all the porters, ' I *do* congratulate you ! . . . that *nice* Mr. Hippisley ! . . . Do tell him he could have had *any two* of my girls for the asking and welcome ! ' This engagement, and the fact that Dick Hippisley celebrated the occasion by at once christening us ' the Smyth Family Robinson,' are the only incidents, together with Clotilde Limburger's visit, that I can recall during that summer. But an event was soon to happen which profoundly affected my whole outlook.

That autumn staying up at Muirhouse I met Harry's sister-in-law, wife of the present Archbishop of Canterbury, then Dean of Windsor. Following my principle of not speaking of the living I will only say that thanks to her friendship, the kindness of the Dean, and that house of refuge the Deanery, life became possible to me during the next

ballooning secret, something to do with a valve, had been betrayed to the Italian military authorities, and his senior, a certain Major X., had been heard saying that in his opinion Templer was the traitor. The two men notoriously hated each other, and at that moment our friend was more amused than angry. But next day a strange thing happened; he found a blackbird with its beak cut off nailed to his door, and being versed in the symbolism of the country folk, with whom he was on excellent terms, knew this was a friendly warning that the ' beaks ' were after him and that if guilty he had better ' fly ' the country. Two days later the Hippisleys got a note from him saying he was under arrest at Chatham and would they come at once? It appeared that everything depended on his being able to account satisfactorily for his whereabouts on three given days in the month before last—a serious undertaking for a man who forgot today where he had been yesterday—but since he and the Hippisleys were constantly meeting he thought that perhaps they could help him.

Now Violet is blessed with a fabulous memory, so much so that when she was a tiny child Johnny used to amuse himself by teaching her the names of all the Derby winners for decades upon decades. Casual visitors were put on to ask her suddenly: ' What horse won the Derby in such and such a year?' and never was she caught tripping. On this occasion, therefore, she applied herself hopefully to the task of reconstructing Major Templer's past, working from dates it was possible to fix, such as a golden wedding, a meet of the hounds, the painting of the Warren animals' portraits, and so on. One more interview with the prisoner and the task was accomplished, nor could a Q.C. sent down to cross-examine her find a flaw. She was *subpœnaed*, the trial began, and she drove into Chatham four days running, but was never called as the case for the prosecution collapsed. The Government withdrew the charge, and Major Templer ' left the court without a stain on his character.'

It was a monstrous business, and our friend St. John Brodrick, who was then at the War Office, subsequently asked Violet why she had not written to him at once instead of letting them make such fools of themselves? Her reply was that no one could suppose the authorities would start a case like that on such flimsy evidence; after which it is unnecessary to remark that Violet was then a very young woman.

.   .   .   .   .   .

I have always had a passion for walking tours, and in the summer of 1886 the Hippisleys, their retriever ' Hurry,' and I embarked on a tour in Cornwall, which began with an absurd incident set in the atmosphere of a recently married man's tender susceptibilities. Arrived at Falmouth whence we were to proceed on foot, Violet suddenly remembered that a former admirer, a Mr. S., had a beautiful house on the bay and also a sailing yacht, so a letter was dispatched announcing our arrival. It soon became evident that her friend, who instantly presented himself, was not clear in his mind as to which of us was Mrs. Hippisley, and as it seemed advisable in order to get the maximum of favours out of him to leave the matter in doubt, I persuaded her to take off her wedding-ring. Alas! the plan succeeded only too well, and ere long, at Dick's earnest entreaties, the ring was restored to its place; and to his honour be it said our host bore the shock like a man, his kindness suffering no diminution. Among other places he took us to was a long spit of rocky land, half buried in monster geraniums, fuchsias, and roses. At its extreme end was a beautiful old church, the eighty-years-old parson of which had spent three-quarters of his life lying flat on a scaffolding under the roof, patiently covering beam after beam with fantastic carving. The light was too bad to judge of the result, but this vision of an old man who knew how to live needed no special illumination.

On the other hand, for quite other reasons I shall never forget a very hot morning in Falmouth waters—a dead calm, and that dreadful little yacht rocking in a slight swell, while each of us drearily trailed a mackerel line and hated Mr. S. for continually telling us we had caught a fish and should

haul it in.   At length one of us crudely suggested the boat
and we were rowed to shore in the nick of time, having the
presence of mind to take with us the luncheon we had hitherto been unable even to look at.   Once safe on the beach it
seemed incredible that we could ever have loathed the very
idea of dressed crab.   .

Our general plan was to begin by walking along the coast-
guard path to Land's End, and as Violet's head was not
good, Hurry's collar was buckled round her waist and Dick
led her by the chain like a monkey.   Once when he and I
scrambled down to a cove to bathe, a huge boulder of serpentine decorously dividing us, she was chained up aloft lest she
should slip or become affected with the madness of the
Gadarene swine.   Economy being our principle we afterwards held a laundry festival in the cove, to assist at which
Violet was carefully piloted down, and then for the first time
we noticed, having to carry them ourselves, that things
washed in the sea never dry.   This was one of the many occasions when Violet, asked to take a short cut across a wide,
dull peninsula, refused to play the walking-tour game and
sent Dick off to ' raise anything on wheels.'   Soon we were
driving six miles to the nearest town in an ancient wagon-
ette, from every anatomical projection of which intimate garments hung flapping in what is called in those parts a gentle
breeze.

Altogether I wasted much breath on that tour trying to
check Violet's backslidings from austerity.   There were
arrivals—not on foot—at hotels, where what I thought over-
sumptuous repasts were ordered for themselves and Hurry
by the other two, Dick, though a frugal eater, being in the
early acquiescent stage of married life and loth to leave his
wife alone with her soaring appetite.   As it was my great
ambition to keep somewhere near our estimate of daily expenditure, at last I proposed ordering two dinners and one
plate of scraps for the dog, the result to be divided among
us.   The plan was adopted, no one went hungry, and we
' put threes ' into the bills.   But when it came to Dick ordering a pint of champagne for the exhausted Violet, and

suggesting that threes should be put into that bill too, this essay in finance was rejected by me, and what is more Dick never heard the last of it.

It is difficult not to launch into a paragraph beginning : ' The beauties of this most romantic county exceeded all expectation '; taking that as written I will go on to say that Gladstone's first Home Rule Bill had just foundered the Liberal Party, and throughout our wanderings two things struck us : firstly the beautiful diction of the country folk, which reminded one of Highlander's talk, and secondly the sensibleness of the questions constantly addressed to us as visitors from the Far East. Again and again we would hear the remark : ' Mr. Gladstone is a very clever man, but so are Lord Hartington and John Bright—and good men too, both of them. Now why are *they* against the Bill? ' and in spite of Papa's and my opinion of radicals I conceived great hopes for the future since character still seemed a factor in politics. At Helston we chanced on a political meeting at which Mr. Courtney, afterwards Lord Courtney, was to speak, and for the first time in my life I entered the political arena with a volley of questions. I knew my facts, and was inordinately flattered when the Chairman remarked with some irritation that ' notice ought to have been given of this very severe cross-examination.' What with our excitement at finding a meeting on, and pushing in with the crowd, we had forgotten Hurry's existence, and when we emerged he was nowhere to be seen. He was an exceptionally sagacious dog however, and Violet declared that as in his place she would go back to the four cross roads we had passed just before reaching the town, and wait, no doubt we should find him there. And sure enough there he was, sitting motionless and staring with all his eyes down the Helston road.

Many years afterwards Violet met Lord Courtney and asked him if he remembered the Home Rule meeting? He replied ' Most vividly ' and told her he had often wondered who the questioner was. If not too polite he might have added ' in such an extraordinary get up,' for the talent so many women possess of presenting a workmanlike and at the same time pleasing appearance has been denied me. When I rang at the front door of the house my dear Mrs. Benson had lived in when her husband was Bishop of Truro, the footman politely informed me the back door was round there behind the laurel bushes.

As regards climbing and what are called risky adventures, Dick and I were of one mind and body. I particularly remember a visit to one of those tin-mines that run for miles under the sea. Clad in revolting garments that greasy clay had stiffened to the texture of armour, we clambered down a narrow shaft by a perpendicular ladder, the rungs of which were coated with the same deposit. The descent seemed interminable. All the time a huge vertical beam, the mine pump I believe, rose and fell, groaning and throbbing, within nine inches of our shrinking backs; and as we passed gallery after gallery, pinpoints of light fastened themselves on to the beam or were shed in passing, as men kept stepping on and off this agitating moving ladder.

In the meantime, while Dick and I were in the bowels of the earth, Violet was having a nice little experience about which hangs the peculiar odour of dissenting circles. Getting bored with waiting she decided to go home, and an overseer of some sort kindly offered to show her the road; but on the way his attentions became so pressing that the situation needed firmness and presence of mind. As they approached the village, however, this unpleasant individual begged her to fall behind and follow him from a distance, lest to be seen walking with a strange young lady might compromise him !! . . .

But far and away the most vivid of our Cornish impressions, indeed one of the supreme memories of my life, is a celebrated cave in the Scilly Islands called 'The Piper's Hole,' the mouth of which is only just above high water mark; and as the passage you are invited to enter runs down hill in a fairly steep incline, you start in a far from neutral frame of mind. Turning to the right you are in complete darkness, and the first of a bundle of torches is lit and stuck in an iron ring fixed in the cave wall, while the thunder of boulders pushed to and fro by the breakers seems hardly three feet above your head. As you go on the passage winds and narrows, and ever fresh torches are stuck into further rings, till the walls meet in a V point and you think this is the end of all things. Not at all; squeezing through a crevice the last torch is kindled and lo! a second cave, its floor a little blue fresh-water lake full of fishes. The guide waves his torch to and fro, almost touching the surface, but without disturbing the quiet circling movement below; then you realise with a slight shock that these tiny silver fishes are blind. And to complete a vision of the underworld that might belong in the Eleventh Book of the Odyssey, there, on the other side, attached to a massive chain, black and motionless, lies Charon's boat! . . . A cleft in the rugged dome was pointed out to us, and we were told that it led by difficult tortuous ways to the land above and was negotiable with the aid of ladders and ropes; but seeing on our faces a strong desire to try it the guide hastily added : ' So I've heard tell, but I daresay there's no truth in it ! ' And unfortunately we had no time to put the matter to the test.

Other abiding impressions of Cornwall are the incredible colour of the serpentine rock all round the promontory, either dark fiery red, or dark fiery green ; Tintagel, where Dick and I undertook a really perilous climb; the wonderful line of cliffs called Bedruthan Steps, against which gigantic waves for ever dash, no matter what the weather, as they do on the coast of Clare ; and finally the Vale of Lanherne, of which it may be said that one thing alone conveys an idea of such beauty—the name. There is a large Roman Catholic convent there, with a fine picture or two in the Church, and it was pleasant in that ultra nonconformist district to hear the nuns spoken of with so much love and admiration.

We all four enjoyed that Cornish tour from beginning to end, but for me it lies in my memory wrapped in a tissue of gold, for many years afterwards The Piper's Hole suggested the scene of the Third Act in my opera ' The Wreckers.' Indeed on this tour were gathered the legend and most of the impressions which, passed on to H. B.—as

one might hand rough sketches and a palette to a painter—
were wrought by him into the libretto he wrote for me.

As for that last scene, I shall probably not live to see my
dream realised.   These things can only be adequately tackled
in countries where there is a genuine popular demand for
opera, and consequently a subsidy, part of which is devoted
to a thing the public insists on—the production of new
works.   At Munich in 1914 the most astonishing machinist I
ever met brought his genius to bear on the Piper's Hole de-
coration with enthusiasm, inventing a device for bringing the
sea right on to the stage ; and the ideal performance of ' The
Wreckers,' for which I had waited ten years, was to have
taken place on Feb. 20, 1915 !

But in this country the only necessities of life recognised
by our ratepayers are things like drains and water-supply—
and thus it will be in England for ever and ever.

.   .   .   .   .   .

It was towards the end of my exile that a family expression sprang into being to which we still have recourse when
someone cuts in at a crisis with gloomy and unhelpful sug-
gestions.

I have forgotten to mention that on Sunday evenings a
short service was held in the drawing-room at 9 o'clock, in
presence of the assembled household, the chief feature being
a sermon culled from one of the calf-bound ' Suffer-Day '
volumes that possessed the tables during 24 hours of each
week.   On this particular Sunday, Barbara Hamley being
among the edified congregation, the discourse began, according to my father's rendering, with the remarkable words :

' To-day we are more serious than useful ' (*usual*).

CHAPTER XXXVII

AUTUMN 1886 TO AUTUMN 1887

As the time for my return to Leipzig drew near, my mother did what she had often suggested doing and what Lili Wach had urged should be done—she herself wrote to Lisl. What she said I do not know though I can well imagine. The reply was a singularly beautiful letter, written in German. Gentle and implacable, it is mainly an entreaty to my mother to see, and help me to see, that not her own will and action but Fate stood—and must always stand, given the circumstances—between us. And the word I longed for, an assurance that the old faith and affection were still alive, was not to be found in those pages.

.   .   .   .   .   .

I left England in September, going direct to Engelberg where the Fiedlers were staying. More than a year had passed and Lisl had steadily refused to discuss the reasons of our now notorious breach with any of our mutual acquaintances. This being so, Conrad decided to constitute himself my champion in Leipzig, more especially since I now felt free to show him certain letters proving that Lisl had been told everything from the first, and that I was guiltless of deception, treachery, or anything that could alienate anyone's sympathies, let alone merit social ostracism; also that if it was a question of apportioning blame for what had happened, others were at least as culpable as I. He thereupon wrote once more to Lisl, demanding as an act of *bare justice* that she should corroborate certain statements he proposed to make in certain quarters; and this time he gained his point.

Meanwhile I again shouldered my pack and started forth on a solitary tramp across the beautiful Joch Pass to visit the Wachs at the Ried. Lili Wach, who feared that a bitter ordeal awaited me at Leipzig and was incapable herself of grasping nettles successfully, was evidently relieved to learn that Conrad was taking action in my behalf, and with the certainty of our passing the winter together I left for Crostewitz.

.   .   .   .   .

The return to my old haunts taught me one thing, that human nature is kindlier than pessimists would have one believe. The Fiedlers told me that many of my old friends, notably Frau Limburger, had refused from the first to believe ill of me; that others had dimly suspected a situation unsuitable to the convenient black-and-white methods of melodrama; and that even those who had cheerfully believed the worst were not sorry to know they were wrong. Perhaps no one likes being taken in too grossly.

But one bitter disappointment awaited me; I ought to have foreseen it perhaps, but . . . I didn't. Soon after my return the Fiedlers left for Munich *via* Berlin, and Mary was full of the representations she meant to make to Lisl, which, she believed, must surely change the whole situation.

Alas! the result merely showed what, when she chose to put them forth, Lisl's powers of persuasion and fascination could achieve. Up to now the two had been on rather distant terms; there was lack of affinity to start with, moreover when, as was the case with the Fiedlers, a husband interested Lisl more than the wife, she took no pains to conceal the fact—and Mary was accustomed to adulation. But on this occasion, as I read between the lines, she laid herself out to capture the whole position . . . and succeeded. In the pages upon pages I got from Berlin there is not the faintest allusion to the real point at issue, the harshness and brutality with which the breach had been effected, the early attempt to make the Fiedlers drop me, and all the rest of it, nor is my everlasting question ' does she speak kindly of me? ' as much as referred to. On the other hand change upon change is rung on Lisl's tragic and beautiful appearance in mourning (she had recently lost her father), the nobility of her character, the desperate position she was placed in, the inevitableness of our separation, and the sufferings of other persons involved—who as it happened were less than nothing to the writer. Not that my sorrows were forgotten or that I was reproached or blamed in these loving effusions; but the magic of Lisl, acting on an impressionable being for the first time wooed by her and treated as an equal, had caused Mary to forget, or gloss over, everything that was not to her interlocutor's advantage!

Knowing how everyone coveted Conrad's good opinion, far be it from me to blame Lisl for the masterliness with which she conducted what I always called in my mind the ' Berlin Congress,' including the winning round of my own particular friend, Conrad's wife. She was not only a great artist musically speaking; there was a quality about her which would have made this frankest, most sincere of beings a superb actress if the Stage had been her vocation. When deeply moved she had command of extraordinarily beautiful language, to which her letters, in the original at least, bear witness—letters written at lightning speed with scarce a stumble or an erasure. In conversation her voice, not a striking one as a rule, would then acquire a thrilling metallic ring, her expression a fineness, her gestures a rare grace and beauty, for all their violence, that carried everything before her. No wonder the gratified Mary forgot her brief; even Conrad must have been under the spell, for in a beautiful letter [1] he wrote me from Munich, full of wise counsel, the main issues are not mentioned! Feeling that after all I had been left in the lurch in a matter at least as vital to me as my good name, I wrote bitterly, and presently the interchange of letters ceased.

    .   .   .   .   .   .

I settled down in new rooms in the Hauptmannstrasse, the quarter once favoured by the Geistinger. . . . How many of

---

[1] Appendix V., ii. p. 179.

us have stood in a street, wondering, as we gaze up stupidly
at certain windows, what our connection is with someone
young, keen, and happy who used to stand there doing the
same thing ! . . . The Geistinger had left Leipzig long
since, and the first time I passed her house that autumn
three children were laughing and quarrelling in her balcony
. . . but there was another street on the other side of the
town through which I never passed again. . . . Most of my
Saturday and Sunday afternoons were spent at Dölitz, the
Limburgers' country house, riding, and playing tennis or
bowls according to the weather, Ella, my particular friend,
wife of the eldest son Julius, being in Egypt. I remember
that one day I and Clotilde (who had acquired a taste for
dangerous games during her stay in England) shot down
stairs on a shutter and were rather pleased to find none of
her brothers evinced any desire to do likewise. We hoped
herewith to have begun the undermining of a prevalent German notion that women are but poor, timid creatures.

In January I flew home to assist at the marriage of my
youngest and only unmarried sister to Hugh Eastwood of
the K.D.G.'s, on which occasion for the last time in my life
I acted as bridesmaid. A week later the couple started for
India ; Bob, who had been ill, was sent to Egypt in quest of
a few months' sunshine ; and I returned to Leipzig—in premature possession of some beautiful sapphires my mother
had always meant to leave me in her Will.

From February onwards I was no longer alone in my lodgings. Ella Limburger, who had been suffering severely
under the doglessness of the East, met in the streets of
Vienna, fell in love with, purchased, and brought home, a
huge sprawling yellow-and-white puppy of the long-haired
kind generally seen dragging washerwomen's carts. Half
St. Bernard, and the rest what you please, Marco was an
entrancing animal, but as there were already three sporting
dogs of Julius's about the house, Ella yielded to my passionate entreaties and gave him to me.

For twelve years that dog was the joy of my life, and

latterly the terror of my friends. I have had the privilege of rushing to the assistance of Royalty—our most kind and faithful friend the Duke of Connaught—who on endeavouring to leave a note at my cottage had been driven hastily back into the high road by Marco, slamming the wicket just in time. And another old friend, Sir William Butler, declared that nothing would induce him to approach my door unless clad in riding boots. In fact like many other geniuses Marco became nerve-rasped and ferocious in his old age, but in his youth, though always a desperate character, he was wholly amiable, and took to life on the third floor, his head reposing on the pedals of a seldom silent piano, as if washerwomen had never been heard of.

A greater philosopher, a more perfect comrade for a busy woman, can never have existed; if, in the stress of work, I put off his dinner too long, all he did was to shut his eyes and moan very, very softly, like a baby. I gave him a toy, a thing called ' Marco's purse '—really a little netted blue bag with long strings, which eventually became a repulsive object but nevertheless travelled with us everywhere, wrapped in fold upon fold of *Weekly Times*. Sometimes when bored, after many yawns and sighs he would get up and lay his head on my lap; but at the words ' Don't bother, Marco,' he would stand still, reflecting, then suddenly pounce on his purse, roll over on to his back, hold it up between his paws, and making it sway backwards and forwards, alternately catch it in his mouth and let it go again. Having worked off his energy this way, he would get up, lie down very carefully on the exact centre of the purse, and go heavily to sleep —an object-lesson to many human beings.

That February the weather was arctic, a fact linked in my mind with the capricious digestion of young dogs and the frequent necessity of rising from my bed and hastily putting on ulster and slippers, in order to conduct poor Marco down to the street. I almost became a Socialist owing to the chivalrous conduct of the second-floor lodger, no less a person than the great Bebel himself, who, finding me shivering in the *porte cochère* one night, insisted on my going upstairs instantly, and in due course conducted the invalid back to his own quarters. Wherever I went Marco went, and wherever Marco went he made history. I had noticed that sometimes, even without his purse, he would roll over gently on to his back, yawn, and rub his nose with a large white paw; this odd trait was developed into a trick called ' eat your paw,' about which there was something so subtly appealing, that even old Frau Limburger, who disliked and dreaded dogs, was melted at the sight.

I never knew a more hilarious temperament than Marco's —so much so that, invited to attend a rehearsal Brahms was holding of his piano quintett at the flat of Brodsky the violinist, it seemed advisable for once to leave him in the street. I was seated at the piano turning over, when suddenly the door burst open and with a bound Marco was beside me, while the cellist's desk, taken in his stride, went crash. Having spoken disparagingly of the great man's sense of humour, it is only fair to say he rose to this occasion and declared the whole thing took him back to the Harlequinades of his youth. . . . During the two bereft winters I spent in Leipzig, anything more markedly kind, fatherly, and delicate than Brahms's manner to me cannot be imagined; but I had always known that with all his faults he had a heart of gold.

.   .   .   .   .   .

What chiefly remains in my memory concerning that very critical epoch is the wonderful kindness shown me. My great trouble was mentioned by no one except Lili Wach, and I am thankful to think that in after years I was able in some measure to make up for what must have been a painful spell of her life. If three people have been in closest alliance, and two of these are violently separated, each still clinging to the third, the situation of that third is not an enviable one—more especially in the case of a temperament so unwarlike, so delicate and shrinking, that among the many nicknames bestowed by me upon her, the favourite and most appropriate was ' the Sensitive Plant.' Yet behind all, carefully dissimulated in ordinary life, was what the other lacked, passion; that is why her friendship was so satisfying in deep waters. Nevertheless endless discussions that led to nothing wore us out, and eventually, though she never gave up hope of better times coming, we avoided by mutual consent the subject that was in the forefront of both our minds.

Looking back through those months, many and many a sudden grip of a friendly hand do I recall—trifles light as air but which made all the difference. For instance I remember how Julius Limburger, the prodigal son of the family—a young man much criticised in Leipzig but whom I always loved for his kind heart—took me by the arm one day and said in his rough fashion: ' Now look here, you are still young, hang it all, and I won't have you moping like this; you're to come to the next Gewandhaus Ball, mind that!' And I did go to the ball, for the first time since many years, and Julius made it his business to smother me in partners from start to finish.

But I think with most delight of a sudden touch of humour in dear simple Frau Röntgen. Her great worth of character had always impressed and attracted me, but that winter deepened and intensified my feeling, such a friend did she prove herself, so sure and delicate was her instinct how and when to help. Some acquaintance of hers was in trouble and spoke of it, adding: ' but you never liked her, I know.' I said: ' I don't dislike anyone who is unhappy,' whereupon Frau Röntgen remarked cheerfully: ' My dear Ethel, don't tell me you have developed into a " Thränen Lise "' (tearful Lise) ' that's not at all your line, believe me!'—the allusion being to an exceedingly dull old spinster whose speciality it was to weep with the afflicted no matter on how slight an acquaintance. This little joke was like a breath of fresh air in the Catacombs. On another occasion, when I sang her a particularly cheerful little song I had just composed, she clapped me on the shoulder and said: ' So eine Musik lass' ich mir von Ihnen gefallen!' (That's the sort of music I like to hear from you).

There was one case of wobbling which I record, firstly because it ended well, and secondly because it was characteristic and funny, though I did not feel amused at the time. During my year in England Frau Livia had made no sign—which was not surprising, for we did not correspond regularly and she was not one to rush on the horns of a dilemma; but when she learned I was returning to Leipzig she wrote, not exactly unkindly, but urging me to stay away, on the ground that girls of whom certain things had been said—*whether deservedly or not*—did well to remain ' unterm Schutz des elterlichen Daches ' (under the protection of the home roof). And the finishing touch, I thought, was a suggestion that I should compose the Psalm about the waters going over one's head, on which theme she felt certain I should ' produce a masterpiece ' ! !

Like Bonnemaman I kept a draft of my furious reply, the gist of which was that I had done nothing disgraceful and should most certainly come back. As for ' the conflict of duties ' for herself which she mentioned, she could be quite easy in her mind, since wild horses would not drag me across her doorstep. The tone of the letter was true to the deep affection and respect I bore her, but dynamite was not lacking and it must have pulverised her for the moment. Nevertheless in my heart I felt sorry for this German equivalent of an Early Victorian lady, temperamentally as incapable of understanding complicated situations as a child of ten ; and when I really turned up, Conrad's activities having preceded me, I got a dear note begging me to go and see her. Of course I went at once, was met by two outstretched arms, and not only was all well, but I think the incident brought home to us how deeply we were attached to each other in a region that no passing differences can affect—the region of elective affinity.

.   .   .   .   .   .

When I returned to England that summer Marco had a colossal success—except perhaps with my little nieces and nephews, who having learned what his duties would have been had he remained in his own station of life, naturally expected him to drag their go-carts. But this, unfortunately, was the one and only request he refused to comply with, having I suppose seen enough of that sort of thing in days gone by.   Strangers used to ask curiously what breed he was, and when I casually answered : ' Oh, he's a Wiener-Hund ' they looked knowing and were quite satisfied. Mother adored him, even when he lay under a certain wicker-table at tea-time, and, getting up, walked about as under a canopy, bearing plates and teacups.   As at Leipzig, he went everywhere with me, and one night at the Edward Clives, when there was a fight under the dinner table between Marco and the Clive dog, I remember the presence of mind displayed by beautiful Violet Howard, Lilla Clive's sister, who seizing her full glass of champagne, leaped up on to her chair and stood there—a bewitching vision in green and gold.

One feat of Marco's, and it shall be the last, I cannot refrain from recording.   In the schoolroom there was one of those old-fashioned bookcases in two sections, consisting of a cupboard below, about $3\frac{1}{2}$ feet high, and four shelves on the top—between the two parts a six-inch ledge.   You placed a glove on the top shelf and Marco would leap on to the ledge, change feet in a flash, rear up, snap the glove, and descend with his back to the bookcase.   I never saw a heavy domestic dog capable of such a performance, though Charlie Hunter once had a dapple-grey cob that could have done it on the side of a house built to scale.

During these years I have been reviewing, Bob had been through Wellington and afterwards with an Army coach; but being like myself bad at examinations, he failed to pass, and was now doing militia training at Guildford with a view to getting into the Army by the back door.   None of a family devoted to scenery cares about it more than he, so we determined to explore the Wye country in the priceless company of Marco.

The peculiarity of walking-tours is, that for the reason quoted from Barrès, one is as entrancing as another, provided you plan them properly.   True, there was no sea this time, no Piper's Hole, but it was England's beauty in a

' du ' ! . . . I may have wronged her, but I still see no other explanation.

This was the last communication I ever had from her, and with it began the bitterest epoch in my experience; for though, as will be shown, I had re-acquired a certain grip on life and work, it seemed to me I might some day find myself hating Lisl.

There are people who appear to find a relief and a solution in hatred; perhaps because it has a false air of showing character and facing facts. I think I always felt dimly that this apparently strong, healthy growth is in reality the child of stupidity and sterility; yet it took me years to understand that if the implacable not only repel but inspire pity—and a touch of contempt—it is because they are dead and do not know it. . . the charnel house masquerading in the Pageant of Life. And if the generous attract and uplift—even when difficult to live with, like my mother—it is because these are really alive, and the only fit company for the living. I hadn't yet got as far as hatred; it was rather that the Centre of Indifference seemed to have been reached. The old tenderness would still ' tread softly round and gaze at me from far,' but it was becoming easier to drive that gentle ghost away. Thus month by month the sadness within deepened, and this was the mood in which what turned out to be my last winter in dear Leipzig was lived.

CHAPTER XXXVIII

Autumn 1887 to Spring 1888

Almost immediately after our return from the Wye, Bob and I again started forth in each other's company, this time for Germany where it was his laudable intention to learn German, one of the most difficult of languages, in three months ! But anyhow the admission that knowledge of foreign tongues might come in useful in a soldier's career was something to be thankful for; a few years back, good linguists like my friend Captain Hubert Foster had been looked upon almost as decadents, certainly as doubtful chips of the old John Bull block. At my advice Bob put himself under the wing of Johanna Röntgen who had a perfect passion for teaching anybody anything [as also for learning herself] and of course they began their studies with ' Egmont,' the one play of ' our Goethe ' calculated to appeal to a budding soldier.

In Johanna's spare hours she taught drawing, and I think the Bible, at an infant school for 3d. an hour or some such sum, and towards Christmas I remember she showed me with great pride some little cardboard models of Leipzig and District made by her pupils—an excellent way of teaching them to observe. It seemed though that each model had an inordinate number of poles with ' Verboten ' placards, and I pointed this out to Johanna, adding in my folly that it was rather a shame to drag the ' Verboten ' bogie into these wretched infants' games, thereby checking healthy instincts of rebellion without which every child is a bore. But

Johanna replied triumphantly that I evidently knew very little about children—German children anyway—for as it happened those ' Verboten ' poles were to them the supreme ecstasy of the thing. ' The only difficulty,' she added, ' is to stop them putting one at each end of the Grimmasche Strasse '—this being a great highway that cuts the town E. and W., in fact the Oxford Street of Leipzig !

I have often said to myself that nothing illustrates the difference between the Germans and ourselves more perfectly than this little incident, except perhaps another that does not belong in the eighties, but which I must stretch a point to record here as natural sequence to the Johanna method.

Kreisler, who of course is an Austrian, was once travelling with his wife from Rome to Naples when, as so often happens in the Campagna, the train pulled up three or four miles out of Rome for the reason that a herd of bullocks were reposing on the line. At this moment Kreisler noticed that his famous Stradivarius had been left behind at the Hotel ; uttering imprecations he hurled himself out on to the line, made his wife pitch out their hand baggage, including violin No. II, and then received her flying form in his arms, the floor of the carriage being about four and a half feet above the ground. All this time their two fellow travellers, Germans, had been ceaselessly expressing their scandalisation, reminding the young Austrian that to get out between the stations was ' strengstens verboten,' Kreisler in his agitation not even bothering to reply. Suddenly, as the engine gave a piercing and prolonged whistle—less alarming in Italy than elsewhere, for there are many stages yet to come—Frau Kreisler's bag was seen to be missing. ' Hand me down that bag on the middle seat please . . . quick,' said Kreisler. ' I shall do nothing of the sort,' replied one of the Germans and slammed the door. Whereupon Kreisler, swarming up the side of the carriage, wrenched the door open, pushed past the German, and while the train was slowly getting into its stride jumped after the bag to the ground. He told me he should never, never forgive himself for not having punched the head of the man who slammed the door, and being of a passionate temperament got quite white when he spoke of the incident, which had happened at least three years previously.

.   .   .   .   .   .

Early in the music season I at last met the great violinist Sarasate in private life, and was amazed to find this sad, tragic, romantic looking man literally bubbling over with fun. That evening he had stepped for a moment into a ' Carmen ' performance and went into peals of laughter at the idea of any public accepting our admirable but hideous prima-donna, Moran-Olden, as ' Carmen '; although he greatly disliked Germans, it was well worth coming to Germany, he said, to see such a ' trait de mœurs.' Talking to him I realised for the first time that though Spaniards thoroughly endorse Mérimée's story, on which the libretto is based, the treatment of it in the Opera infuriates them, as does also the mitigated French handling of their desperate national rhythms. I knew too little of Spanish music to contest the point and as I love ' Carmen ' hope this is a purity of feeling to which only Spaniards need aspire; but all musically cultivated countrymen of his I have met since are of the same opinion as Sarasate.

As regards another audacious foreigner's work, Gounod's ' Faust,' revived that winter in Leipzig, my life in Germany had been one long battle from the first, the banalisation of their great play being a crime the Germans are unable to forgive, though there as elsewhere the only people who matter, the gallery, love the music in spite of themselves. Connoisseurs like the Herzogenbergs and the Röntgens, while grudgingly allowing the ' relative ' beauty of some of the music, asked how any cultivated person who knew Goethe could sit out the Opera? I wonder what they would have said to an English version of the play produced by Irving in the eighties, in the course of which Faust informs Mephistopheles that he intends to make an honest woman of Margaret, but is persuaded by the other to drop the idea !

Whether this amazing interpolation was a concession to English prudery or a gratuitous piece of hypocrisy I never made out. As managers are wild to get the sympathies of the audience with the hero and heroine at any cost, it may have been put in to prove that Faust had a better nature . . . unfortunately counteracted by Mephistopheles. Anyhow it was one of those occasions on which one murmurs : ' Alas my country ! '

I think it was in November that Fanny Davies and Brodsky played a Violin Sonata of mine in the ' Kammermusik,' and Bob remembers the critics unanimously said it was devoid of feminine charm and therefore unworthy a woman— the good old remark I was so often to hear again. Lucy Tait, Edith Davidson's sister, who was passing through Leipzig at that moment, and whom her brother-in-law the Dean had described as one of those people who never miss a train but always come by the next, arrived in the middle of the first movement (very good time-keeping for her) and was ushered through a back entrance on to the platform itself in full view of the whole audience—a severe punishment for one of a particularly retiring disposition. Our Christmas was spent at the Limburgers—sequel to many delightful Saturday and Sunday afternoons at Dölitz in the late autumn. The way the brother was admitted as a matter of course into the bosom of this and other families at that intimate season, shows how wide and delicate was the German reading of friendship for the sister. He himself became quite sentimental over it, and no wonder.

All this time I was wishing to goodness he would apply himself more assiduously to the task of learning German, and above all regretted his absurd passion for music which resulted in his going night after night to concerts and the Opera instead of following my old plan of attending the Drama. . . . Alas ! there was no youthful Geistinger to keep him up to the mark ! When we both went back to England in the middle of January, I for a fortnight's hunting, he for good and all, I felt that it was in some obscure way my fault that he hadn't learned more ; but he has since assured me that it was not for lack of being worried almost to death on the subject by me.

The great frost of February and March 1888 I shall always remember because of a rather horrible skating adventure I had. The country round about Leipzig, as all students of Napoleon's campaigns know, is intersected by countless little rivers—one dirtier and more sluggish than the other—which however atone for their existence by flowing through beautiful woods. Consequently this year, the ice being in places three feet thick, the skater was in Paradise. One moonlight evening a party of some eight or ten of us started forth down the river, had supper in a woodland restaurant thrown open in this unexpected burst of winter prosperity, and timed our return so as to be back in Leipzig about 11 P.M. On the way home one of my skates got loose, and a nice shy English boy called Mynors, son of a clergyman, having stopped to help me, we two and Marco fell behind the rest. Flying along to catch them up, the thermometer any number of degrees below zero, suddenly I found myself in the river (about four and a half feet deep just there) my skates well embedded in the muddy bottom! It was a gully of warm water flowing out of a factory hidden away in the trees, and skinned over with ice.

I wish I could relate that Marco flew to my assistance, but as a matter of fact he stuck in his toes, slid a yard or two, and hurriedly made for the bank, where, in spite of commands and entreaties, he sat down—actually sat down—and watched the proceedings dispassionately On either side of me the ice was eighteen inches thick but the gully was too wide to lift oneself out, nor could Mr. Mynors get purchase enough to take a pull. Eventually we hit upon a brilliant idea which was that I, exhausted and half frozen to death, should make one final leaping heave upwards, turning as I rose, while Mr. Mynors, aiming the point of his stick at the buckle of my Norfolk jacket, was to give a mighty prod and shove. Painful as it sounds the manœuvre was a success, and presently I was on my back on firm ice, but before the bank was reached my petticoats were stiff and clanking.

It was no time to sit down and fiddle with skates, one of mine being half off already, so we linked arms and jog-trotted the four miles to Leipzig. Now as ill luck would have it my landlady was attending a wedding supper and alas! there was nothing in my room by way of stimulant except half a bottle of Lager beer! . . . I begged Mr. Mynors to fly at top speed to a restaurant for some brandy, got into bed and lay there, dreading a return of one of my violent illnesses, for I was shivering to such an extent that the bed shook under me. At last, after what seemed to me an eternity, came a knock; then a hand appeared, stiffly holding out a bottle! . . . Quite exasperated by this un-timely display of English prudishness, I thundered to the poor boy, who probably had never seen a woman in bed in his life, to come in at once—which he did with a reluctance that even then amused me. And the point of the story, showing what the human body can assimilate under certain conditions, is, that I drank about a pint of most villainous raw spirit at a draught, fell instantly into a drunken sleep, and woke up next day without even a headache.

In the March of that year I sent Joachim the Violin Sonata, hoping that though it had been mercilessly slated by the Press, he might perhaps be of a different opinion and see his way to performing it in London. I recommend his answer [1] to the attention of any young musician assured by a great authority that he has no talent, for this, according to Joachim, was my case; he added a hope that I would not resent his expressing this conviction (which by the by he solemnly retracted twelve years later when I didn't care two straws what he thought) and comforted himself by reflecting that if my musical bent was genuine it would survive his lack of appreciation. I felt this was true, and the day came when I was glad never to have been among his favourites; as a rule pedantry and total absence of the sacred spark were their chief characteristics, and with very, very few excep-

[1] Appendix V., ii. p. 181.

tions they all fizzled out in after life. Still the letter was
not an agreeable one to receive, particularly at that moment,
and one little dig at him I allowed myself. I said that of
course an honest opinion could never be resented, but at the
same time I much wondered if he considered Mr. So and So
a genuine talent—this being a youth never heard of before
or since, whose deadly dull Opus I. he had recently produced
in London, and whose mama was a giver of smart musical
parties, at which the Joachim Quartett performed about once
a fortnight, for fabulous fees, throughout the season.

This letter received no reply.

.   .   .   .   .   .

All this time I had been seeing a great deal of the von
Webers, people I had met off and on in Leipzig society for
many years, but who, though cultivated and musical, were
not in the sacred Herzogenberg set. Weber, a captain in the
Leipzig regiment, was either grandson or nephew of the composer, and his wife a Jewess, niece of old Madame Schwabe's;
but what gave special point to intercourse with this
couple was the constant presence in their house of Weber's
great friend, Count Paul Vizthum, a Saxon officer on the
Head Quarters Staff. But for the fact that I knew he was
deeply in love with a young married woman, a friend of
mine, I think I should have completely succumbed to the
charm of Vizthum, a sort of Bayard nearer forty than thirty,
not exactly handsome but of a magnificent presence and a
grand seigneur. These three got into the habit of coming to
supper with me—a supper of cold ham and beer, though
sometimes one of the party would bring a *pâté de foie gras*
or a particularly admirable sausage, and on one occasion
(somebody's birthday) there was champagne. Now I come
to think of it the spectacle must have been unusual . . .
these immense Saxon officers tramping up three pairs of
stairs to my door, depositing their helmets and swords and
all the rest of it on my piano, and settling down to a frugal
meal with a musical student, just for the sake of a little
pleasant talk.

I never met any of the trio again, though sometimes I seem to remember a passing glimpse of Vizthum at Dresden, but the poor Webers' subsequent history was tragic. Gustav Mahler, who was then one of the conductors at the Leipzig Opera, fell in love with her and his passion was reciprocated—as well it might be, for in spite of his ugliness he had demoniacal charm. A scandal would mean leaving the Army, and Weber shut his eyes as long as was possible, but Mahler, a tyrannical lover, never hesitated to compromise his mistresses. Things were getting critical, when one day, travelling to Dresden in the company of strangers, Weber suddenly burst out laughing, drew a revolver, and began taking William Tell-like shots at the head-rests between the seats. He was overpowered, the train brought to a standstill, and they took him to the police station raving mad—thence to an asylum. Always considered rather queer in the Army, the Mahler business had broken down his brain. I afterwards heard he had lucid intervals, that his wife in an agony of remorse refused to see her lover again . . . and the rest is silence.

Mahler's life was full of incidents of this sort, and knowing him even as slightly as I did I can well believe it, not being able to conceive that any woman who loved and was beloved by him could resist him. I felt this even when I saw him last (it was at Vienna in 1907) worn out, exasperated, prematurely aged, wrestling with the Habsburgs as personified by the Intendant of the Opera House he had made the first in the world. He was far and away the finest conductor I ever knew, with the most all-embracing musical instinct, and it is one of the small tragedies of my life that just when he was considering the question of producing ' The Wreckers ' at Vienna they drove him from office. When he was gone even his enemies regretted their action; but the ideal of art he set, his passionate refusal to abate one jot or tittle of his artistic demands, the magnitude and purity of his vision, these are things that start a tradition and linger after sunset. . . . At the time I am speaking of in Leipzig I saw but little of him, and we didn't get on ; I was too young and raw then to appreciate this grim personality, intercourse with whom was like handling a bomb cased in razor-edges. But later on, when years had endowed me with seeing eyes, I thought with deep sympathy of poor Frau von Weber—whom he probably considered a mere passing fancy!

Throughout the greater part of the winter of 1887-88 the Griegs were in Leipzig and it is then that my real friendship with them began. When Grieg appeared on a platform, whether alone or accompanying his wife's superb rendering of his songs, the audience went mad, but there was a simplicity and purity of spirit about them that success could not tarnish. Out of action, these two tiny people looked like wooden figures from a Noah's Ark, the transfiguration which ensued when they got to work being all the more astonishing. Frau Grieg sang in Norwegian of course and one often had only a vague idea as to the meaning of the words, but her performance was, as Vernon Lee once said about someone else's singing, ' explosive literature,' and one wept, laughed, and thrilled with excitement or horror without knowing why. The song over, she again became Noah's wife. Grieg is one of the very few composers I have met from whose lips you might hear as frank a confession as he once made concerning one of his later works. I had been so enthusiastic, and he was always so keen to get at honest impressions, that I ventured to say the coda of one of the movements seemed not quite up to the level of the rest. ' Ah yes ! ' he said, shrugging his shoulders, ' at that point inspiration gave out and I had to finish without ! '—I remember too on a certain occasion his being invited for a huge sum to conduct not only his own work but the whole programme, and refusing on the ground that he was too bad a conductor. ' But the public won't mind that,' pleaded the manager, ' they'll come to *see* you conduct : besides which, as you conduct your own music you surely can get along with other people's well enough for all purposes? ' At this remark Grieg shook his pale yellow mane angrily : ' My own music? ' he snapped, ' any fool can conduct his own music but that's no reason for murdering other people's '—and the manager had to drop the subject.

But of all the composers I have known the most delightful as personality was Tschaïkowsky, between whom and myself a relation now sprang up that surely would have ripened into close friendship had circumstances favoured us; so large-minded was he, that I think he would have put up unresentingly with all I had to give his work—a very relative admiration. Accustomed to the uncouth, almost brutal manners affected by many German musicians as part of the make-up and one of the symptoms of genius, it was a relief to find in this Russian, who even the rough diamonds allowed was a master on his own lines, a polished cultivated gentleman and man of the world. Even his detestation of Brahms's music failed to check my sympathy—and that I think is strong testimony to his charm! He would argue with me about Brahms by the hour, strum passages on the piano and ask if they were not hideous, declaring I must be under hypnotic influence, since to admire this awkward pedant did not square with what he was kind enough to call the soundness of my instinct on other points. Another thing that puzzled him was my devotion to Marco, of whom he was secretly terrified, but this trait he considered to be a form of English spleen and it puzzled him less than the other madness. For thirty years I have meant to enquire whether dogs play no part in the Russian scheme of life or whether Tschaïkowsky's views were peculiar to himself; anyhow it amused me, reading his Memoirs, to find Marco and Brahms bracketed together as eccentricities of his young English friend.

On one point we were quite of one mind, the neglect in my school, to which I have already alluded, of colour; ' not one of them can instrumentate ' he said, and he earnestly begged me to turn my attention at once to the orchestra and not be prudish about using the medium for all it is worth. ' What happens,' he asked, ' in ordinary conversation? If you have to do with really alive people, listen to the inflections in the voices . . . there's instrumentation for you ! ' And I followed his advice on the spot, went to concerts with the sole object of studying orchestral effects, filled notebook upon notebook with impressions, and ever since have been at least as much interested in sounds as in sense, considering the two things indivisible.

    .   .   .   .   .   .

I must not forget to record one more strange manifestation of the German spirit witnessed during that spring of 1888— an incident of the same order as the scenes with the peppery stationer and the egregious Commandant of the Leipzig garrison, but more astounding, even than these, in that the hero was one of my most intimate friends.

It will be remembered that most of the great German doctors had pronounced the Crown Prince's malady to be cancer, and that Sir Morell Mackenzie, called in by the Crown Princess, was of a different opinion. No one who was not in Germany at that moment can realise the charges to which an inspired Press will go, the least of the charges brought against this noble woman being, that the whole thing was a plot between her and Morell Mackenzie to secure her the pension of a German Empress, inasmuch as an heir stricken with a mortal disease might possibly be excluded from succession !

One day, at the height of this disgraceful business, I was lunching at the Wachs, Lili as it turned out being ill in bed, and naturally I imagined that Wach would share my horror and distress. Not at all ! The discussion began fairly temperately, by his asking me how English doctors would have liked it had the Prince Consort been similarly afflicted and a German doctor called in to reverse their decision ? I replied that though they would in all probability have hated it, such a scandal as this malignant Press campaign was absolutely unthinkable in England. But my remarks were brushed aside angrily, Wach's voice rose and rose, so did mine, and finally when I said : ' but after all she is an English Princess,' he bounded up, rushed round to my side of the table and vociferated—his clenched fist within three inches of my nose : ' How *dare* you say she is an English Princess? she

married our Crown Prince and is a German . . . a GERMAN
. . a GERMAN ! ! do you understand? '

At this point all the children fled from the table, pelted
down the corridor, and as I learned afterwards burst into
their mother's room, half in terror, half in wild delight,
screaming : ' Mama ! Mama ! der Papa schlägt die Ethel ! '
(Papa is hitting Ethel.) . . . Meanwhile I too had jumped
up, and declaring I would not stand being spoken to like that
by anybody, rushed into the corridor, seized hat and coat,
banged the door behind me, and struggling into my garments, rushed down the three flights of stairs into the street.
But hardly was I fifty yards from the house when I heard my
name being called, and there was the Professor, table nap-
kin in hand, tearing after me, his longish stiff dark hair
standing erect in the wind. Being devoted to him of course
I accepted his apologies without difficulty, and was led back
in triumph to the deserted luncheon table ; the children, a
little disappointed that after all murder had not been done,
were collected again and the meal went on in peace. But my
amazement at this extraordinary display survives undimin-
ished to the present hour.

APPENDIX V

(PP. 179 TO 186)

(a)

FROM DR. CONRAD FIEDLER

(*Translation*)

Munich : January 3, 1887.

Dear Miss Ethel,—Why I am writing to you instead of Mary is partly because she is not well and I greatly doubt if you will get the long expected letter before you start for England.   She began it, and fragments of it are lying in her blotter, but she hesitated to finish and despatch it.   It is impossible to portray certain complicated inward conditions with clearness and certainty, and every such attempt is fraught with the danger of doing violence to intricate conflicts of sensations such as these.   In fact it is a hopeless task, and the more conscientious you are, the more you shrink from trying to formulate what can only be felt and guessed.   I only saw parts of the letter Mary wrote you from Berlin, but doubt if she could add anything to it in compliance with your demand for absolute clearness in this matter.

She saw Frau von Herzogenberg oftener than I did, but in our first interview I at once gained a different picture of her attitude and state of mind to that based on impressions gathered from you, and I cannot deny that I was glad it was so; had it been otherwise it would have distressed me greatly. But do not think that for that reason I have lost imagination for your position, or weakened in the sense of justice that has prompted me from the first to defend your attitude and actions against misconstruction, and resent the imputation to you of unworthy motives, or points of view which are not yours. Only I think that in certain points you yourself are unjust; firstly in that you charge Frau von H. with having miserably betrayed and sacrificed you and your character to her own people; then, again, in that you ask her to reduce the intricate tangle of feelings and duties which, without fault of her own, she finds herself involved in, to a question of one or two fixed possibilities; and lastly in that you press for a decision which, matters being as they are, cannot be arrived at.

You say the present state of things cannot continue; but as I see the matter you cannot look to any change from without—only to finding strength in yourself to begin life over again in a certain sense. I realise profoundly the anguish of the inward experience to which you have been, and still are, subjected; it is one of those situations in which existence itself is at stake—an ordeal in which a nature either survives or goes under. But you yourself say you are conscious of a reserve of strength. Meanwhile, in order to aid your powers to new development you ask to be delivered from a state of uncertainty which, alas! is inherent in the nature of the case! . . .

Your inward relations with Frau von Herzogenberg have perforce lost their simplicity, their limpidity, their innocence; that fact cannot be altered. It is neither a question of the old affection surviving, or of its ceasing; what has happened is a clouding-over (*Verdunkelung*) of the whole relation which cannot be got rid of. I see no way out of it but that you find strength to close with the past, and instead of wearing yourself out seeking the solution of an insoluble problem, devote your energies to new aims. Not that I would have you cut out of your existence such an important part of your inner life as your friendship with Frau von H. has been through all these years—that is impossible; but it seems to me you must sink it, like a treasure you possess, in the deepest part of your soul, there to be kept safe till the changes of life, or circumstances themselves, bring it once more to the surface. And then perhaps you will find that this mutual treasure has been faithfully guarded in another breast; but for the moment it is my firm conviction that all attempts to restore a thing that can no longer subsist as it did formerly can only be disastrous. Meanwhile the calm you need in order to find yourself again, to work, and in the fullest sense of the word to live, is only to be looked for from yourself, not from explanation others can give you.

With kind greetings and best love from Mary, who will finish and send off her letter to you to England.

Yours very sincerely,
CONRAD FIEDLER.

(b)

FROM JOSEPH JOACHIM

(*Translation*)

Berlin : March 22, 1888.

Honoured Miss Smyth,—I have been here for a couple of days conducting a Memorial Festival and return to London to-day. I had been unable to try over your Trio there, but ran through it here yesterday, as far as it is possible to play such a difficult piece at first sight. I am sorry to say I have gained no other opinion to that I gave you in Leipzig, either as regards the Trio, or the Sonata, which I played through again with Miss Davies. In spite of talent here and there, many a clever turn, and a certain facility, candour compels me to say that both works seem to me failures—unnatural, far fetched, overwrought (' *geschraubt* '; *literally ' screwed-up* ') and not good as to sound. . You say you wonder whether I am ' in the same boat with Bernsdorf '; [1] to that I can only reply that I am not acquainted with that gentle-man's æsthetic standpoint, but when two people act similarly it is not always the same thing though it looks like it : ' Si duo faciunt idem non est idem ' fits the case perhaps, but as I say I do not know.

I hope you will not bear me a grudge for my lack of assi-milative power. If your creative instinct is genuine it will not perish on that account ! Which reflection consoles.

Yours sincerely,
JOSEPH JOACHIM.

(c)

FROM MY MOTHER

(1)

[After my return to Leipzig in 1886]

September, 1886. My darling,—Your delightful long let-ter written the day after the dear first one gladdened my heart more than any words could convey ; it so completely fulfilled my hopes of what your pluck, resolution and healthy tone of mind would do. You WILL win in the end . . . I called on Mrs. R. yesterday ; she made many enquiries after you and was almost genial, full naturally of her ' sweet G.'s ' engagement, of the L. diamonds and lace, of the adopted mother's diamonds, the lovely estate in prospect, the bijou house in St. James's, etc. ; it was quite nice really to see them so happy. . . . My wedding present to Nelly will be the onyx set and my blue enamel and diamond snake bracelet, as I am going to divide all my jewels among you soon, except the pearls, diamonds, and rings which I will wear to my ' dying day,' dividing them by Will. You, dar-ling, have the sapphires, the best thing I have next the dia-

---

[1] A specially venomous Leipzig critic who had been very scathing about my Sonata.

monds, Alice the pearls (that *are* hers already) and Bob the diamonds. The lace I also keep to the last. Give my kindest compliments to all your friends (*here follows list*) specially your present host and hostess [1] and always think of me as your devoted mother.

N. SMYTH.

(2)

Autumn 1886. My Ettie,—I don't half like addressing you to this new place. I did so love your old rooms with the garden opposite; I could always *picture* you to myself there and call the dear image up whenever I liked and now I can't. Do, darling, send me a sketch of the rooms. I am sending you another photo of Bob which I like much better than the Slave-driving one with the cigarette. Have you a pleasant lodging-house keeper where you are? Write me full particulars as soon as you can, as I feel restless till I know all about those new quarters. . . . Nelly is going up to Alice, as at the best the marriage cannot take place this year, and this constant meeting is not fair upon anyone concerned. What with one thing and another the uncertainty of his plans is becoming rather a worry.

We went to —— Church to-day to hear Mr Z. preach. I had never heard him before and was much impressed. He is very powerful but of this earth earthy. I mean that where he is most masterful is in depicting the way we are so easily led into indulging ourselves through shortcomings, or rather superabundance, of fleshly tendencies; and though he is grand in pointing out the remedial and rewarding effect of self-denial for higher aims, his *strength* seems to lie in his wonderful knowledge of the power of temptation over poor human nature and all the wily traps we set ourselves for satisfying or silencing conscience every now and then. I should like you to hear him but I think him too *cru* for general use. [2]

Do send me word as soon as you can about your dresses;

---

[1] The Limburgers.
[2] The clergyman in question, a popular London preacher beloved of the Smart, shortly after went under in connection with a terrible scandal.

they are quite ready. Would you like anything else put in the box, your plush mantle for instance? Addio carina, *send me the sketch.* . . .

(3)

February 1887. My own darling,—Papa came back yesterday night from seeing our young couple off in the *Euphrates* and brought back a glowing account of everything, a magnificent ship, the cabins so lofty that he could easily stand upright in them with his tall hat on (*here follow three pages of details*). Poor dear things, I do hope they will like India; and now to-morrow Bob starts in the P. & O. ship *Khedive* from Gravesend. Papa takes him down to introduce him to the Captain and I have written to——and ——to be kind to him at Malta and in Cairo. . . .

Alice says she never saw a young couple start for India under such favourable auspices as Hugh and Nelly. What that dear Alice has been, advising and packing for the travellers, whose needs she is so well acquainted with, it is impossible to describe—so practical and clear headed. Poor darling, she was nearly voiceless when she arrived, and though that improved she was still very weak and looked very wan and tired when she left us, but I had a letter from her to-day saying she was none the worse and found both her boys better, so I hope her unselfishness will have no unhappy results. If all this last trying time had done nothing else it has shown me more and more what dear, dear good children mine are—what a Darling you were and are to me in all this, so kind, so thoughtful for everyone! and *how* joyful I shall be when I see your dear face again! . . .

(4)

February 1887. My own darling,—I have been waiting since last Wednesday to write to you hoping to hear from Malta of the safe arrival of the travellers and the letters only came this morning. . . . Bob evidently has, like you and Alice, another sense for travelling. . . . Are not these earthquakes terrible in France and Italy? Fancy Lady X [1] driving one day at the Feast of Flowers at Nice in a Victoria all made of (or covered with) forget-me-nots—harness, reins, vehicle, everything the same—she herself reclining all in moss green in it; and the next day flying in abject terror from Nice in a sable-lined cloak over her nightgown!! Your delightful Sunday letter warmed the cockles of my heart; in the first place it was so dear of you to write, tired out as you were, and in the next place it is such a real joy to me to see how you enjoy the possession of the sapphires, and that you have preserved that rich old French setting. I should have liked to *see* you that night, my Darling, at the ball!

We are rather amused with the M.'s just now; you know he is High Sheriff now, and they were both most fearfully offended at Mrs. H. having asked Nina to collect subscriptions from the women of the village for the Jubilee instead of, as he told Nina, asking *the High Sheriff's wife*. Nina aptly answered she supposed it was because they thought Mrs. M. as *High Sheriff's wife* would be fully occupied otherwise; she Nina wished personally that Mrs. M., as being so much the more active of the two just now, *had* been asked! (I don't mean she made this last remark to Mr. H. of course).

Good-bye, my Darling, this hard frost has made my hand stiff again. . . .

(5)

June 1888. My darling, darling child,—What a lovely birthday present that old silver handle is! I never saw such a beautiful, rich, clear design—those dear little cheery dancing men—it makes one's heart light to look at them! I won't have it put on an umbrella till you come, as Papa keeps saying they must *drill a hole* through to make it firm and the bare idea makes me shudder! . . . I think you are quite right to refuse that musical suggestion. You can't afford to write musical jokes till your name is known, besides which the ordeal of mind and nerves you have gone through

---

[1] Our exceedingly stout neighbour of the curious household, whose husband had meanwhile died, and who had married the clerical Peer—at last a widower.

the last two years is not calculated to qualify you for light compositions. . . . I shall, we all shall, be so overjoyed to have you *really* with us, *here*! Nearer our hearts you cannot be, but there is something in feeling tangibly that you are! . .

CHAPTER XXXIX

SUMMER 1888 TO SUMMER 1889

THAT year I left Leipzig late in June with every intention of going back there for the following winter, but as the summer wore on it became evident that my mother was dreading the emptiness that would soon possess the house, for Bob, her Benjamin, to whom she was specially devoted, had finished his Militia training and was going to yet another crammer in July. Realising her feelings so wrought on mine that I determined to try a winter in England. I had lots of work waiting to be shaped and plenty of rooms to choose from, so the schoolroom became my Studio. . . . There was one dear face at Leipzig that in any case I had never hoped to see again. Frau Röntgen had long been failing under a mortal disease, and in July 1888 she died leaving a tenderer more ineffaceable memory in my heart than many with whom I stood in closer relations. Such is the mystery of personality. . . .

It was in that summer that I got bitten with the genealogical craze and started researches that proved to me how useless it would have been, even had the funds been available, to put the Royal College of Heralds on to the job. Nothing shall persuade me that you can expect from outsiders the perseverance necessary in these cases to following up clues, nor conscientiousness enough to refrain from pressing them unduly. Again, none but a member of the family is in a position to collect and exploit the valuable indirect hints that fall from the lips of the elder generation. I used to astonish my father by asking him if he could tell me anything about some half-forgotten great-uncle of his I had found an allusion to somewhere; and as both he and two of my aunts had memories that responded to stimulus, and were not addicted to romancing, the results were sometimes surprising. Nevertheless it took me two years and a visit to Ireland, including hours upon hours spent in the Four Courts at Dublin, to establish a certain missing link in the seventeenth century, and incidentally I discovered that our line was literally held together by Church dignitaries. My relations with Lambeth and Windsor were evidently more in order than might have been supposed, and I was altogether delighted about our Bishops, having a strong natural affection for the Anglican Church which neither personal scepticism nor an ancient predilection for a celibate priesthood undermined.

Why it offends one if a Bishop's wife insists on having rice pudding placed within reach of her husband lest he should wake up hungry in the middle of the night, whereas the same action on the part of a Cardinal's body-servant would strike one charmingly in a biography, I do not know . . . but so it is. It was therefore with pleasure that in the course of my researches I lit upon evidence proving that an ancestress of ours had been equally doubtful as to the advantages of the Anglican system in that respect.

It appeared that a certain Irish Bishop who had married a Miss Smyth was about to embark on a controversy concerning the Celibacy of the Priesthood with a well-known Roman Cardinal, but just as he was collating his notes for the printer his wife seized them and threw them into the fire, remarking that a man weighed down by the cares of a large family was ' no fit antagonist for a nimble-minded unencumbered Cardinal.' One wished this very sensible woman had framed William III.'s Laws concerning Catholics instead of her cousin.

My correspondence with unknown relations in Meath, Westmeath, and Queen's County would fill a bonnet-box, and there was one particular Smyth, head of the X. branch, with whom I had a particularly friendly interchange of letters, taking pains to make it on my side as little dreary as the depressing nature of the subject permitted. After this had gone on for quite a year, he having repeatedly said how agreeable it was to find he had such a pleasant kinswoman (sixteenth cousins we may have been) I set sail for Ireland and was invited by him to come and inspect the family portraits. Never shall I forget my surprise and chagrin when towards midnight, after much delightful Smyth talk, settling down comfortably in his chair with pipe and grog handy he suddenly asked : ' And now tell me, who the devil *are* you . . . *really* ? ' . . .

It was not a relation, however, but the then Bishop of Down and Connor who called my attention to a gratifying point already referred to ; in fact he got quite keen about our ecclesiastical record and said it was ' really amazing to see how generation after generation had produced men remarkable for piety and learning.' No suspicion as to other possible reasons for my ancestors' consistent preferment seemed to have crossed his mind—or perhaps he was too polite to mention them. Anyhow it was nice to feel one had piety and scholarship running in one's veins, however little there was to show for it ; better still to learn ' the Smyths seem to have made it a habit to intermarry with attainted families ! . . . ' After all then I had every right to be a rebel !

At length the great Genealogical Study was ripe for printing by subscription and I confess to being prouder of this opuscule than of most things I have attempted, furnished as it is with pedigrees, catalogues, original documents, and many interesting forgotten facts; moreover of an intrinsic quality to challenge fifty Colleges of Heralds and win me any lawsuit founded on its evidence.

It is a strange thing, this passion for running a heel line after some ancient defunct rabbit such as John Smyth, nonentity, deceased 1702, brother of the most ill-advised Bishop on the whole Episcopal list. An American singer once said to me : ' You wouldn't believe it, Doctor Sm*eithe,* but I was twenty-three years of age before I knew where my diaphragm really *warze,*' and I thought the remark quite mad, holding that no amount of anatomical knowledge will turn a bad singer into a good one. But how much madder this two years' effort to answer satisfactorily Smyth of X's immortal question, ' who the devil are you, really? ' . . . Nevertheless I thoroughly enjoyed the hunt, and in due course neatly bound copies of the result were forwarded to subscribers and other interested persons, from whom I expected and received much praise. . . . But there was one exception ; a cousin, member of the ever-critical J. clan, drew my attention to the fact that I had wrongly stated the initials of his grandmother (not a Smyth) as also the date of the birth of one of his nephews (also not a Smyth). I replied that I knew there were other minor errors of this sort besides those he mentioned, and was tabulating them in a page of *Errata* to be placed in all copies ; whereupon he answered : ' *Errata* indeed ! better call it Ethel's st*oo*pid mistakes !' We were amused at this remark but exclaimed in chorus : ' *How* like a J. ! '

. . . . .

Having brought the story of these activities of mine to a conclusion, let me go back to the year in which they were initiated.

In the course of this summer (1888) Lili Wach wrote that at last there had been a satisfactory meeting between her and Lisl, who was evidently suffering bitterly under our separation. Frankly I did not believe this. Given her overwhelming desire for harmony, and also the curious humble strain I have spoken of, I felt certain that she must be unhappy under Lili Wach's gentle, inflexible condemnation, and in my answering letter remarked that the Vox Humana stop had probably been pulled out, though of course without conscious hypocrisy, for the other's benefit. The reply I received may be quoted as one more illustration of an eternal tragedy—that good advice always comes either too soon or too late. The deep wisdom of that appeal to stifle feelings which evidently were obscuring my memory of Lisl strikes me now, but then it fell on deaf ears. ' No fresh flowering of a life,' she writes, ' can be hoped for in such soil, and believe me, the spirit that tempts you to heal your wound by nourishing bitterness against her personally, and against her attitude in such a difficult situation, is no good spirit. Would it not be better to hold these years of incomparable intercourse, for the loss of which I well know nothing can console you, in sacred remembrance? Granted that a higher love would have stood by you, cannot you say for her what no doubt you have often said for yourself as regards your own shortcomings: " les détails d'une faute réconcilient avec elle "? '

This appeal produced a certain effect for the moment, but as the months passed and nothing further happened, I reverted to my conviction that Lisl's ' sufferings ' were mythical.

And yet in a letter from Mary Fiedler, with whom I had now re-started a fitful correspondence, I find mention of an incident so curious, though at the time it made little impression on me, that one can only say once more the psychology of Lisl defies analysis. It appeared that some six months after the ' Berlin Congress ' Mary had again seen the Herzogenbergs at Berlin, just at the beginning of his illness. She had found him lying in an armchair in constant pain, and had been greatly shocked at his appearance, and still more at Lisl's apparent gaiety and obliviousness. In the stress of conversation she would even strike his knee rather hard—a frequent gesture of hers when animated—causing him to wince with pain and cry, half comically, half reproachfully: ' . . . but *Lisl!* ' Whereupon she would embrace him, ask his pardon, call herself a brute . . . and presently . . . do it again! Mary thought to herself ' is she blind? is she heartless? ' but when Lisl went with her to the door she suddenly burst into tears, flung her arms round Mary's neck and said: ' O what . . . *what* is the matter with him? No one knows—what can it be? ' Coming across this incident in that old letter, who, I asked myself, shall say what was in the heart of this strange woman throughout those years with regard to me? As she had said of Julia ' Who shall explain her? '

.   .   .   .   .   .

In November I went on a delightful expedition to the Sologne to stay with a sister of H. B.'s whom I had met in Florence and seen once or twice since in Paris, whose husband kept a pack of hounds. The French describe our hunting as ' de l'équitation,' and certainly the experiences I was about to partake in were, as Allen would have put it, quite a novelty. The hounds were bred larger than fox hounds and hunted roe-buck and wild boar indiscriminately. We were generally out all day, pursuing the same animal perhaps for hours and hours, and not in the least averse to giving it a thorough rest while we ate the excellent luncheon that had been following us in a cart all morning. If you had a good run so much the better, but the most exciting chase was unanimously considered a dismal failure unless you killed. The whole thing took place in forests, with very occasional short-lived bursts in the open, and there was much galloping up and down rides, still more crawling and standing about in rides, no jumping to speak of, and interminable jogs home in the dark. This sounds deadly dull, and so it would be but for the fact that in France every hunting man or woman gradually becomes an expert, understands the whole game, is familiar with the habits of the animal they are chasing, and can detect, stooping from the saddle at a gallop, marks which I could not see even when down on all fours, staring with all my eyes. Further these supernumerary huntsmen and women were able to tell from the footprint what the age of the animal was, the hour at which it had passed that way, whether it was the original quarry or not, what its exact state of mind was at the moment, and other details I have forgotten.

But what astonished me most was, that totally unmusical people like my hostess had no difficulty whatever in distinguishing the many exquisite calls on the big curly French horns carried by the master, the hunt servants, and one or two privileged members of the field. I used to make M. de Terrouenne blast these calls at me after dinner, to the horror of Marco, who didn't get on with the hounds and was not popular in a château with parquet floors like Villiers. But in spite of taking notes and studying them in bed with a view to to-morrow's hunt, I always mixed them up when the time came. Mr. Ewing had once told me that tone-deaf and exceptionally stupid soldiers were far better at learning the bugle calls than he himself, so I suppose my musical proclivities were against me.

Many people have said that to hunt down a wild boar seems a meritorious action at the time, so strong is the repulsion that animal inspires, and this I can endorse. On the other hand, though our pack didn't hunt deer I rode with one that did, and shall never forget my distress at seeing a magnificent stag come blundering exhausted out of a thicket and fall headlong on to the road below, to be torn at by thirty couple of hounds. Never again, I said to myself as I turned hastily up a ride, would I risk witnessing such a spectacle. But presently someone came galloping after me, the ' Hallali ' was about to begin and I must come back at once. By that time they had put the stag out of his pain. He had struggled across the road, and lay, a noble and piteous sight, in the centre of a curiously regular circle of trees, on which the sparse leaves, nipped scarlet by frost, hung like drops of blood in the setting sun. While my forehead was being dabbled with real blood—I did not mind that part at all, it hurt neither me nor the stag—the field grouped round him, and then four individuals in green and gold, one of whom was the Master, and another, perhaps unknown to himself, a very fine musician, gave us a specimen of music in one of its most moving and heavenly forms—horn calls in four parts. Let anyone ask for the gramophone records (not to be had in England perhaps) of Rossini's ' Messe de S. Hubert ' and judge if this sonority, which comes out well on the gramophone, can be surpassed for beauty. . . When I went back to England it was with the secret feeling that compared to this sort of thing, our hunting, however delightful, is sophisticated and artificial . . . in fact ' de l'équitation.'

Of course my host and hostess were all-round sportsmen, and Kate Terrouenne, an excellent shot, went out regularly with her own dogs; but even if I were a good shot instead of a vile one, I think I should always hate shooting, especially waiting about in woods, and waking up out of a reverie to fire at the recollection of the animal you have just seen crossing the ride. In the Sologne I expended exactly 114 of poor M. de Terrouenne's cartridges and secured ten head of game, including an invisible woodcock, brought down at word of command in what seemed to me pitch darkness.

One trivial incident connected with that visit—a trenchant criticism of the kind you never, never forget—I cannot refrain from mentioning. Wishing to do myself credit on the French scene I had ordered a new habit, and during the last fitting, seated on the saddle, my eye on the mirror, expressed a fear that my shoulder blades stuck out rather. The artist's reply, uttered with great decision, was : ' You have a magnificent back, Madam ; *I only wish you had a front to match.*'

.   .   .   .   .

While I was in France Nelly and Hugh came back from India, and that Christmas there was a forgathering at Frimhurst of the six daughters, the five sons-in-law, and the only son of the house. Hugh Eastwood being a typical John Bull in every fibre of his being, my loudly advertised appreciation of other countries would sometimes get on his nerves. He was then already a young father, and one day remarked that if, later on, any of my foreigners should wish to marry one of his daughters he would consider it a piece of d—d cheek. I enquired why on earth some charming French or German officer (I carefully kept to the army) should not aspire to the hand of an English girl, and Hugh answered, with a gentle smile : ' Why not a gorilla? ' . . .

At this stage of my story it seems superfluous to relate

that after Christmas Charlie Hunter, whose brilliant business faculties were turning a poor man into a rich one, mounted me as usual, besides which Mary gave me many a day on her own horses. No brother-in-law was ever more generously disposed as regards his stables, or more unreservedly delighted if you put the powers of his animals to severe tests —which, after France, seemed emphatically the legitimate course to pursue in England. It is also needless to add that I afterwards went on to beloved Muirhouse, but before speaking of that particular visit, a certain subject must be touched on that connects with it in my mind.

Though my intercourse with Mrs. Benson and the Windsor Davidsons tended to a renewed interest in the Anglican position, my views on religion had remained as before. Concerning these, wild ideas had obtained in my little world at the time of my flight to Leipzig and after. One of poor Mr. Ewing's crimes had been introducing me to Max Müller's studies on the Eastern Religions, and owing to what was in reality a very slight acquaintance with Grecian philosophers I was credited with leanings towards many a mysterious form of paganism. For instance on one of my recent returns from the Continent a light-hearted cousin of mine, Lily Milles, had remarked between two games of tennis : ' Now do sit down and tell me all about your religion; I believe it's awful and that you got it from Aristopheles.'

As a matter of fact I simply disbelieved in God, greatly to the distress of dear old Mr. Davidson with whom on this particular visit I used to walk about the woods discussing the subject almost daily. I remember his begging me nevertheless not to abandon prayer, and to begin thus : ' O God, if there be a God,' should that formula be acceptable to me— which it was. He also insisted on my going to hear the Presbyterian Minister, Dr. MacGregor, and we sat under him that Sunday morning in such a literal sense, our pew being right under the pulpit, that I left St. Giles with the stiffest of all the many stiff necks I have endured in my life, not having moved my head or taken my eyes off the preacher for an hour and a half. Being intensely refractory to sermons, and indeed to all things that involve sitting still for prolonged periods, this may give some idea of Dr. Mac-Gregor's performance.

I wish I could describe his style as preacher—the rolling of the r's, the prolongation of certain vowels, the frequent use of long sonorous words, the gesticulation, the incredible emphasis that never suggested ranting. One of his peculiarities was breaking away from what he had evidently set out to say, and branching off into something that had suddenly occurred to him. Ernest Davidson, Harry's younger brother, once told me about an impassioned outburst he had just had the good fortune to listen to : ' Why don't you read your *Bibles?* ' Dr. MacGregor suddenly asked : ' You read your Shakespeares, your Miltons, your Donnes, your Shelleys, your Tennysons . . . splendid poets all of them, God bless them ! But why don't you read your *Bibles?* Isaiah, Jēremiah, Hēzekiah . . . . gr-r-rand old poets, everyone of them ! . . . Listen to this ! ' (here a tremendous passage was read out) ' and this . . . and this.' And as he rolled forth one sonorous phrase after another, the leaves of the Bible before him were dashed over in such fashion that Ernest thought they would surely come fluttering down from the pulpit in fragments.

But his praying was, I thought, even more striking than his preaching—the wonderful lava-like outpouring, the vivid, nervous language to which his Scotch accent seemed to lend what in this case was not needed, an extra ring of sincerity. Not even an extensive acquaintance with the Bavarian peasant class quite cures one's tendency to confuse dialect with purity of heart. There is a dreadful man in London—accepted for his great wealth's sake by people who ought to know better—who drops into the quay-side low Scotch of his early days whenever he wishes to ingratiate himself with persons of social importance I have heard him do it and seen his interlocutor unbend more than once. But Dr. MacGregor could no more have divested himself of his accent than of his limp, and as he was said to talk Spanish admirably I often wondered how that language fared in the struggle.

He was a curious looking little man—misshapen, sallow, with the religious enthusiast's burning eyes—and in his company, too, I often walked the Muirhouse woods, discussing religion, moral effort, regeneration, and kindred themes. I remember one day when we had passed from serious topics to Spanish literature, his complaining bitterly of Anglo-Saxon mispronunciation of that fine name Don Quixote: ' The way to pronounce it,' he cried, ' is Don Kee-*hott*-tay; now say it after me carefully, Don Kee-*hott*-tay ' and I obediently echoed him to the best of my ability. But he was not satisfied : ' No, no, that's not it at all; try again—Don Kee-*hott*-tay . . . Don Kee-*hott*-tay,' and we wandered along, crying ' Don Kee-*hott*-tay ' alternately, as if reciting some demented litany. Gradually his voice died away, and though he still murmured the magic syllables I saw his mind was elsewhere. ' *Ehm*-hi,' he suddenly thundered, and thinking this was another Spanish word reconstructed for my benefit, though it sounded to me more like Hindustani, I repeated, also with great emphasis : ' *Ehm*-hi '; whereupon Dr. MacGregor pulled up short, stared at me in astonishment, and said very earnestly : ' I say to you, dear young lady, as I say to all poo-r-r sinners, and preëminently to myself, whatever ye do . . . *ehm*-hi '—and I perceived he had relapsed into the former conversation, and unlike Mr. Alfred Scott Gatty was imploring me to aim high.

In later life, taken up enthusiastically by Queen Victoria, I believe that ' wee MacGregor,' as his countrymen lovingly called him, lost some of his unsophisticatedness—the inevitable result of keeping high company. If so, I am glad I never saw him again.

CHAPTER XL

SUMMER 1889

THROUGHOUT all these years, from 1886 onwards, the main-stay of my life had been Mrs. Benson, and needless to say no one could have striven harder than she did against the long cold night of the spirit that fell upon me when all hope of a reconciliation with my friend had to be abandoned. In a book which turned out to be by a Benson under a pseudonym—' The Memoirs of Arthur Hamilton,' by Christopher Carr—I lit on a phrase that arrested me about its being ' a pity to miss the chance of facing a hopeless situation,' but I did not know how to do this. . . .

Meanwhile I had become acquainted with the rest of the clan, meeting them occasionally in a fugitive manner at Lambeth, and more satisfactorily at Addington. Everyone knows what an unpermissibly gifted family they were. I say ' were,' thinking of the five who have since passed away, the last to go being the mother—that wonderful woman, whom to call ' Ben,' as her intimates, did, seemed as fitting when she was over seventy as it did when first I knew her thirty-three years ago. Be the void she has left what it may, I am thankful that to the last, in spite of failing bodily strength, there was no other change. One could not have borne to see her slower at the uptake, less deadly in repartee, less amused at the infinite comicalities of life.

It is a curious fact, and one that proves the richness of her equipment, that though she was one of the many ladies pronounced by Mr. Gladstone to be ' the cleverest woman in England,' her master passion was undoubtedly the cure of souls. A great part of her life was consecrated to her patients, as I used to call them, who when bereft of her physical presence were kept going by words of counsel and comfort written on letter paper so diminutive that it inevitably suggested a prescription. I really think the spiritual or moral dilemmas of Mrs. Jones the curate's wife interested her more than what Lord Salisbury said last night at dinner, and fancy the position she occupied, involving automatic and effortless contact with the most distinguished personalities of the day, gave her no great satisfaction. Speaking of her astonishing unworldliness, I once said as much to a very worldly old peeress, who thoughtfully answered : ' Yes, poor thing, you see she has *no precedence.*' I remember once walking with her through the huge dining hall at Lambeth when the table was laid for some state banquet ; appalled at the solemn spectacle I asked whether champagne was served on such occasions, and this amazing hostess's reply was : ' I haven't the faintest idea ! '

At a given moment of my life we differed violently on an essential point of conduct, and during some years met but seldom. But even then a link was her deep admiration for H. B.'s books, one of which, ' Theories of Anarchy and of Law,' was answered by Maggie Benson in one of the Reviews. But Mrs. Benson's favourite was the exquisite ' Prison,' which she once told me accompanied her everywhere ; it and the Bible . . . strange travelling companions !

One passage in her last letter to me (June 1918) is so characteristic that I may be forgiven for telling its story here. I had just come back from abroad and wrote asking if I might go to Tremans, her Sussex home, some time in July and endeavour to efface the recollection of our last meeting there a year previously. She was so game, such a gallant fighter, that one sometimes forgot she was no longer a vigorous woman in the prime of life, and on that occasion I had inveighed against the Church's attitude throughout our struggle for the vote with such violence, that shame and remorse overcame me whenever I thought of it. (Remorse, that is to say, for the brutality of my controversial methods, in no wise for the views expressed.) Her reply was : ' Now you speak of it I *do* remember a few stormy moments in the Shelter that day, but my dear, you never *were* given to understatement, were you? ' Alas ! that expiatory visit never took place, for before July came she was dead.

Among the boys the one I knew best was Fred, of whom I was always fond because he was such a dear at home, not to speak of his intense funniness and proficiency in games. Arthur Benson was already an Eton master and I seldom saw him at Lambeth, but we once had a spell of intimacy of a moral or intellectual order—I'm not sure which it was—charming while it lasted, but all too short. For various reasons I knew Maggie less than I could have wished, but her extraordinary intellectual power, though devoted mainly to subjects I was quite at sea in, such as political economy, philosophy and other abstractions, could not escape the attention of even the most ignorant among her acquaintances. Meanwhile the way she dropped on any flaw in one's argument was convincing enough. There was a pure, aloof dignity of spirit about her which reminded one of Alpine peaks and all things majestic and not easily accessible, yet . . . there were distinctly passionate possibilities too. No storms are more terrible than those that rage in high altitudes, and I often wonder exactly what inner conflicts brought about the final clouding of that wonderful brain.

The one of the family who eventually became my particular friend was Nelly—take her all in all the most remarkable of the younger generation as personality, in my humble opinion ; but as she died on what is merely the threshold of life for women of that calibre one cannot be certain. Re-reading her letters, penned in easy profusion, the handwriting so identical with her mother's as to baffle one again and again on the envelope, I realise that in a wonderful collection of correspondence I have nothing to touch this particular blend of humour, profundity, and high spirits. There is the same fastidious literary quality as in Arthur Benson's writing, *plus* something indescribable that may be called genius for life. Nelly was the only close friend I ever had to whom games and adventure meant exactly what they do to me; a bond as great as our other link, a twin taste in humour.

Yet twins have dissimilarities! For instance I remember Mrs. Benson once saying it was inconceivable to her that anyone could be amused at a tipsy man, and Nelly added : ' No decent being could be '; whereupon the confession had to be made that on occasion I had found tipsy people intensely funny.

Barring this limitation, which in all probability applies only to the female members of the party, to write the word ' humour ' is instantly to think of a Benson. I never met a family in whose existence that blessed element played a greater part, whose domestic wrangles made you long so intensely for a pocket gramophone recorder, especially if you have a bad memory for verbal felicities; in short one's prevailing state of mind in their company was : ' What made you so awfully clever? ' Hugh I knew less well than any of them and instinctively liked him the least, mainly for the frivolous reason that when he was his father's chaplain he used to flit up and down the corridors of Lambeth in coats the skirts of which almost swept the floor—a common foible of short men. I never saw him after he became a Roman Catholic, but it was a relief to think of him safe in a cassock.

Of the Archbishop I stood in deadlier awe than of anyone I ever met in the whole course of my life. To begin with there was the beauty I find so disconcerting in a man; then his office, which deeply impressed me; and lastly and chiefly the fact that like many hyper-sensitive people he was seldom quite at his ease—a state of things that in my youthful days utterly deprived me of my means, as the French say. Watching the progress of our duologues from her end of the table, with the particular look of devilment one knew so well on her face, Mrs. Benson would afterwards declare that the

mouselike voice which replied to the Archbishop's remarks
was a very beautiful thing to listen to. The sight of his
majestic form approaching the tea-table scattered my wits as
an advancing elephant might scatter a flock of sheep. I
never did quite such stupid things with other people; nothing
but sheer nervousness can have induced me, for instance, to
contribute a certain anecdote one day at luncheon, for I could
read the domestic storm signals and guessed that the Archbishop was not at his most serene that day.

After a few bad moments the conversation had turned to
printers' errors—as well it might in a family, six out of the
seven members of which were authors—and I had got as far
as saying I had recently read about a printer's error, merely
the omission of a final ' d,' that really was . . . and here I
stopped, overcome with misgiving. But there was no dis-
obeying His Grace's acid-affable : ' Pray let us hear the case
in question,' and with death in my soul I told them how a
local newspaper had stated in connection with a recent visit
from General Booth, that after his train had left the station
a large crow remained on the platform for half an hour singing ' Rock of Ages.'

Whether at another moment, or given another narrator
than myself, His Grace would have been amused, and let this
very innocent specimen of joking on sacred subjects pass, I
do not know; what happened then was, first silence all round,
then someone tried to laugh, then Mrs. Benson said cheerfully : ' A fine athletic performance anyhow ! ' and instantly
asked the Archbishop whether the Dean of Rochester had
spoken well at the Meeting that morning? . . . ' But it
really *was* a funny story,' I afterwards pleaded to Nelly who
had not been present. ' Funny ! ' she replied gloomily, ' of
course it was funny, but what on earth has that to do with
it? ' . . . what indeed !

But the worst was to catch oneself raking up scraps of
antiquated schoolboy slang in one's disorder—expressions I
had neither used nor heard since the Sidcup days. I remember one occasion, someone having diabolically repeated a

foolish remark of mine about Händel's music reminding me of a Mothers' Meeting, when the Archbishop who of course adored our great English composer demanded with some dignity to hear my reasons for such a statement. After listening in silence till a halting explanation had died away on his interlocutor's lips, he remarked : ' Are you aware that you have used the words " that sort of thing " seven times running? ' He must have loved Händel even more than I knew. Eventually, for a very brief moment only, we became quite good friends, the basis being stately semi-jocular indulgence on his side and terrified gratification on mine; but of this interlude I will speak later when the time comes.

Apart from the fact that as Mrs. Benson once put it : ' We all realise that you and the Head of the Church are *not* two dewdrops destined to roll into one,' my relations with the Benson family though enthralling—to me, at least—were rather tempestuous, most of us being more or less aggressive and cocksure. The word used for our frequent collisions was ' jars,' and out of it sprang the only riddle I ever made—one of which I am still proud : ' When is a jar not a jar?—When it's *adore*'[1] (by which I hope to convey that though I fought with them I loved them dearly). To my mind the women of that family had not an ounce of artistic blood between them, and though I delighted in the reason Maggie gave for not going to hear the Passion : ' I don't like Bach because he is so very ugly,' this difference of breed was no doubt the main source of the jars. People who only admit one view of moral law—that of the Church—can hardly mix at bottom with those who see life through an artist's eyes; not at least unless artistic kinship is there to bridge the gulf between them. When first I knew the Bensons—the time at which I was closest to them—the artist was in abeyance, and though I was not a believer our outlook was more or less the same; but even then the dissimilarity of grain made itself felt. Sometimes I am glad Nelly

[1] Original : ' When is a door not a door?—When it's *ajar*.'

died before I left their road and took my own; we could never have become alienated, but there would have been bad moments, and we should both have been very unhappy.

My friendship with her—the only one of his adoring children, by the by, who was completely at ease with the Archbishop—sprang up, strange to say, on the cricket field. During the summer of 1889 the cricket mania possessed all the young women of my acquaintance, the fountain-head of inspiration being the celebrated White Heather Club, of which Talbots, Lytteltons and Brasseys were the moving spirits. This club was the Zingaree of women's cricket and sported the prettiest colours I ever saw, a yellow, white, green and black ribbon with a faint line of pink in it. In the light of her subsequent career, and also apart from any such considerations, I am proud to say that my particular friend was Meriel Talbot, a cricketer compared to whom most of us were impostors. We all quite realised the fact, our feelings towards her being akin to those of schoolboys for W. G. Grace; and however that great man may have treated neophytes and other inferiors, I can only say that Meriel met our incompetence with the gracious indulgence of a true artist. In one respect only, rapidity of movement, were some of us her superiors, but as she made most of the runs for her side she had every right to make them at her own pace—a curiously majestic one. The Club spread its net wide; thus it came that my sister, myself, and Nelly Benson were members, and have played cricket under the very eyes of demigods such as Edward and Alfred Lyttelton and Jack Talbot.

Fortunately people who love games are almost sure to possess qualities which redeem other deficiencies, for it is not always easy to beat up eleven wholly sympathetic young women. The White Heather of course could afford to pick and choose; not so certain smaller clubs we played against, whose members were sometimes more competent than socially satisfactory. Once there was a celebrated match at Falconhurst, on which occasion Meriel's father, Mr. J.

Talbot, gave a sumptuous luncheon to both elevens in a marquee, and the visiting team, whose behaviour had been rather rowdy all morning, now began hacking strands off the beautiful ferns that stood along the centre of the narrow tables, the idea being to gain easier access to the lobster salad.   At this point Meriel rose in her place, and no one who had the privilege of hearing her utter the words : ' Leave those ferns alone, please ! ' could question her fitness for the posts of command she has since occupied.

Another time a match actually took place at Lambeth, the Talbots bringing a team against one raised by Nelly, for whom I played on that occasion.   We thought the other XI were going to have a walk over, and in spite of their civil efforts to disguise the fact, such was evidently their own expectation, but strange to say we beat them by three wickets.   Mr. Talbot, who was attending the Diocesan Conference in the Library, came out to watch the match, which was pretty well, I thought ; but the surprise of the day, to me at least, was the Archbishop's almost boyish delight in our victory.   It was just these human rays, shooting out unexpectedly from behind clouds of awfulness, that made him such a nerve-shaking acquaintance.

When golf arrived in England, the cricket mania, which involved a certain amount of restlessness, was superseded as far as I was concerned, but it was a very jolly mania while it lasted.

.   .   .   .   .   .

All this time, though I had been working steadily at orchestral composition as Tschaïkowsky had advised, it was becoming more and more clear to me that unless my musician's soul was to be lost I must go back to Germany ; back to a country, to mention one point only, where friendly conductors give one a free run-through of one's first orchestral attempts—a thing impossible, of course, in mercenary England.   But apart from this I now knew, after giving it a long patient trial, that to live an artist's life at Frimhurst was an

me hear my orchestral pieces and where I should see the
Fiedlers, whom I had not met for two years) and after that
go on to Vienna which Tschaïkowsky had described as the
musician's Paradise.   We started *en masse* for Paris in September, all of us at the last stage of penury except Herbert
Hollings, who, never addicted to extravagance, and much
put to it to keep Nina's quite opposite tendency within
bounds, was firmly decided to cut their cloak according to
our cloth.   And throughout that expedition another familiar
appeal to his wife : ' I do hope you will do nothing to make
yourself conspicuous ' was launched on every possible occasion with the usual stimulating result.

We installed ourselves in one of those hideous plaster
buildings, shaped like elongated cubes set on end, that kept
springing up overnight all round the Exhibition enclosure for
the benefit of ' les étrangers,' and found ourselves amidst a
floridly dressed crowd who criticised the food at the top of
their voices all through dinner.   As Bob remarked, it was
strange that people who be-hung their bare necks with the
chains of the chandeliers should have such a fastidious taste
in cooking.   Marco, one of our party of course, was the
great problem.   He disliked and was unaccustomed to being
left alone, and on the other hand could not possibly accompany us to the Exhibition, so had to be locked up in my
room.   Returning at night we found the floor littered with
plaster ; true to the traditions of prisoners he had endeavoured to scrape a hole through the wall into the next room
and very nearly succeeded.   We swept up the mess into a
newspaper, stowed it away in my trunk, and masked the
excavations with a heavy chest of drawers.

During our short stay in Paris every bit of furniture in
that room was gradually shifted for the same reason ; but as
the authorities said not a word, we hoped that what with
guests continually arriving and departing, and the prevailing
famine in chambermaids (our own had been generously tip-
ped to start with) the matter had escaped notice.   Vain hope ;
while accounts were being settled, a long bill headed
' Dégâts causés par le chien ' was suddenly handed to me

by the tight-lipped proprietress, who thereupon folded her arms and stared into vacancy. I said I would consent to meet her half way, and in the course of a heated altercation I remember one lapidary phrase of hers : ' Ce n'est pas votre adresse, Madame, que nous voulons—c'est votre argent.' But troops of fresh clients were pouring in, and whether from hurry or boredom the compromise was accepted.

One feature of that Exhibition specially remains with me, the native band that played at the Roumanian restaurant. At that time the stream of gipsy improvisation that so often inspired Brahms had not been muddied by industrial exploi- tation, and I then realised with stupefaction the musical genius of these people of the Near East, the infiltration of which accounts for the matchless quality of Viennese orches- tras. Every day we either lunched or dined *chez les Rou- mains,* and became, perhaps not wholly owing to our artistic support, tremendous favourites with the performers, who thoroughly mastered our individual peculiarities and referred to Herbert—the type of man who always wants to get on to the next item on the pleasure-list—as ' ce monsieur qui est toujours si pressé.'

Finally, at the end of all things, came one of those poig- nant little incidents that throw a chance light on an imme- morial situation. While we were all shaking hands effu- sively with the band and endeavouring to express our senti- ments with a sincerity which I hope drove a way for itself through the strange French of some of our party, a little Roumanian girl—she may have been sixteen perhaps—with black eyes and golden hair, drew Violet apart and shyly asked her whether she perhaps knew Monsieur Henderson of London? Violet said she knew two or three Monsieur Hen- dersons; what were this one's initials and address? But on these points the child could give no information, merely say- ing it was the Monsieur Henderson who had visited the Ex- hibition last month and would she give him this letter? . . . after which she flew back to her comrades. Of course it was hopeless to look for this needle in the bundle of London hay, and Violet says she destroyed the note unread—which, given

Lisl's, having in spite of Conrad's aloofness from Wagnerism become an intimate of Wahnfried. In various little digs at the Herzogenbergs and the limitation of their outlook both in Art and Life, in remarks about coteries of manacled spirits congratulating each other on the purity of their little ideals, and carefully keeping out every breath of fresh air, I at once recognised the voice of Cosima.

This wonderful woman was far too clever, far too much a woman of the world, not to appreciate the decorative value of an occasional and carefully selected heretic in her inner circle; hence she had no objection to a man of distinction, such as Conrad Fiedler, declining to fall flat on his face before ' Our Art,' or even questioning, as he did, its fundamental principles. Besides which Conrad was wealthy—in her eyes a supreme merit. Similar heterodox views on the part of Hildebrand, a still more famous man, were put up with for analogous reasons, and meanwhile both men did ardent homage—as well they might—to her genius. But what she could not tolerate was, that eminent personalities in the musical world such as the Herzogenbergs should recognise Wagner as one recognises Anarchy or any other destructive force, the while worshipping Brahms as the true god. In after years two staunch satellites of Cosima's told me she was never more magnificent than when denouncing the Herzogenberg crew; thus I was rather surprised, on meeting her for the first time in my life at Berlin, to learn from her own lips that the premature death of Elisabeth von Herzogenberg, one of the glories and graces of Germany, had caused her heart to bleed. Suddenly I recollected that our hostess, who was standing close by, *and had adored Lisl,* was a power—in fact, one of the greatest ladies in the German Empire! Whatever her faults may have been Cosima did nothing by halves.

To return to my journey; it was not, therefore, a fear of finding my wrongs still obscured by the glamour of Lisl that agitated me as the train banged along southwards, but the knowledge that while I had been at the Exhibition the Fiedlers and the Herzogenbergs had been meeting in the mountains. I longed to know how Herzogenberg really was, if his illness had told upon her physically—over-strained her heart, or even dimmed the brightness of her hair (a frequent result of prolonged anxiety). For some people the outside shell counts a great deal; I think I would rather become deaf to my friends' voices than blind to their faces, their gestures, and the little physical ways that exteriorise personality. Lisl, for instance, had a very characteristic way of holding her head a little on one side and nodding gently as she spoke. . . . All down these later years nothing had given me more pain than the way some flowers nod . . . or again, sometimes walking along a road in the dusk, my mind on music and all else forgotten, a tree top would suddenly bend towards me with the old familiar gesture and wring my heart as if put there on purpose to do it. . . .

I remember that on that journey the words of a recently published poem were running in my head—not very grand poetry perhaps, but the cry of a man sorrowing over a broken friendship. I can repeat one verse even now :

' I had but to utter his name, and my youth
     Rose up in my soul, and my blood grew warm,
And I hardly remembered the broken troth,
     And I wholly remembered the ancient charm.'

But this gentle mood was doomed to find scant nourishment at Munich, Mary's sentiments for Lisl having passed from indifference to something very like contempt—and that for a reason which rather amused me, though it was a legitimate one.

There is one manifestation of German ' Gemüth ' [1] which I have always detested. If two husbands are friends and call each other ' du,' the same relation subsisting between the two wives, there may always come a moment—generally after supper—when someone suggests a general stir-about,

---

[1] Untranslateable : between ' feeling ' and ' sentimentality.'

and everyone begins calling everyone else ' du.' . . . You may regret it next morning, but there it is, a fact not to be gone back upon. I always classed people by their behaviour on this point. For instance the Fiedlers were lifelong friends of the X.'s, the couple that turned the scale against me at the critical moment, but there was no indulgence in this unpleasant promiscuity; on the other hand, as it appeared, a great alliance had now sprung up between the X.'s and the Herzogenbergs, resulting in ' du ' all round ! If the Fiedlers were rather disgusted, I was both disgusted and bewildered, for no one had loathed and inveighed against this abuse more than Lisl. I also learned, with bitter rejoicing, that, the X. husband being the interesting one of the two, Frau X. had soon fallen away from her first enthusiasm, and now maintained that Lisl was ' die raffinirteste Egoist in der Welt ' ! (the most subtle egoist in the world). . . .

But what made the deepest impression on me was that Conrad, who unlike his wife was inspired by the kindliest feelings towards my former friend, told me that in his opinion the real trouble was . . . lack of depth of feeling. He hastened to add that Lisl had said how greatly she envied their being free to see me, whereupon Mary ejaculated : ' That was said to save her face ! ' and in answer to Conrad's remonstrances she added : ' *thou* thinkest it. . . . *I* say it ! ' (It is only fair to add that a couple of years later, when Lisl, evidently a dying woman, stayed with the Fiedlers on a journey south from which she never returned, she completely recaptured Mary's sympathy—a fact for which, when the time came, I was deeply thankful.)

And now I began definitely to hate Lisl. I felt, perhaps with some justification, that during these last years some subtle deterioration of character had been going on, reflected fiercely that such is the fate of all traitors, and . . . was more miserable than at any other period of my life.

. . . .

All this while, indeed throughout our short-lived friendship, from August 1889 till her death in November 1890, I was in constant enchanting correspondence with Nelly Benson, and it is curious to see how she too, like Lili Wach, and later H. B., combated the idea of a callous, light-hearted Lisl, on the ground that it would not rhyme with those seven past years. ' Does the nature of the case,' she writes, ' quite forbid you to believe that envy of the Fiedlers for being free to meet you *is* in her mind—kept down, suppressed, anything you like, but there? Of course the compelling force of circumstances upon her has been awful, but how could things have changed like this? How can one believe she has not suffered? ' . . . But as in the other cases this plea left me unmoved—the time had not come yet.

.   .   .   .   .   .

I have often noticed that when Fate has a phenomenal run of ill-luck in store for you, she begins by dropping a rare piece of good fortune into your lap, thereby enhancing the artistic effect of the sequel. Later events will show the bearing of this remark on the fact, that when my short visit to the Fiedlers was over I instantly lit upon charming lodgings —a great point just then, for a spell of hard and hurried work was before me. That summer I had made friends with Manns, the conductor of the celebrated Crystal Palace Concerts, and after seeing a String Quartett of mine he had held out hopes of producing one of my orchestral pieces in the spring of 1890, provided I could let him have the score and parts by January 1. Now I had never yet written for orchestra, and foresaw that after hearing my work there would be various improvements to be made—and what that involves only composers know ! Unfortunately the hearing could not take place yet awhile, for a sort of minor Wagner Festival was coming on, and given the endless rehearsals Levi insisted on, I knew that the sight of a new MS. on their desks, to be run through by favour, would be more than even his orchestra could bear. So I just let him know I had arrived, and why, begged him now and again to give me a free pass to the Opera, and proceeded to make my first real acquaintance with Munich.

Because of what was to befall me there, for many years I shrank from the very thought of Munich; scene, as occurs to me while I am writing, of the bitterest disappointment of my life twenty-six years later . . . the ideal production of the ' Wreckers ' annulled by the war ! . . . At first the place put a spell upon me; I even appreciated the strivings after the architecture on the far side of the Alps which some people find so ridiculous. But the chief fascination lay in the Alps themselves—on certain days apparently not more than ten miles off (really forty)—and the fiercely rushing green Isar, which brings you still closer to the glaciers for which the heart of mountain climber ever yearns. Marco hurled himself daily into that icy river after sticks he seldom succeeded in timing properly, so violent is the current; realising which he took to rushing on ahead and plunging in long before I reached the bank, to be swept backwards down stream, his eyes passionately fixed on my right arm. . . . O he was a gallant dog ! . . . Another sympathetic feature was that town and country seemed far more intermixed than elsewhere; peasants came to market in costume, and not having yet learned that the Bavarians are the least reliable race in the world, I was captivated by what seemed to me their simplicity and bluff good humour. Here too one at last found traces of religion on a German scene. Even in the town the Churches were thronged by men as well as women, and in the rural districts there was a certain fantastic element that Roman Catholicism seems to bring with it, which redeems village life from the unutterable flatness of Lutheran and free-thinking communities in North Germany. Finally, to crown all, Munich owned a town-witch, or had till four months ago, when owing to irregularities in money matters she had been banished to an outlying village. But her enormous *clientèle,* many of them people of high rank, remained faithful, and were in the habit of going out quite openly by train to have their horoscopes cast.

During that winter I had many interesting discussions with Conrad Fiedler, who was a really deep and independent thinker, and recall one about the total absence of religious feeling among the cultivated in his country. Figures like Mr. Gladstone, Lord Acton, and other men on the first line intellectually yet believers, are quite unthinkable in Germany, for which reason it came natural to all to suspect poor Wach of insincerity. Mediatised princes, whether intellectual or the reverse, were ostentatiously devout, but as this was part of the ' durchlauchtige ' make-up it was discounted. I remember that Reuss, in spite of his respect and affection for the Herzogenbergs, once read them a little lecture for referring unbecomingly to the Athanasian Creed before the servant. They accepted the reproof meekly, considering themselves guilty of a breach of manners, but nothing would have persuaded them that an intelligent fellow like Reuss could really take religion seriously. This contemptuous attitude towards belief induced, so I argued to Conrad, a dryness of spirit in which I saw no proof of superiority, and I remember his replying : ' Perhaps you are right, yet I confess that to us it seems impossible to look upon religion as anything but the fad of lunatics and women.'

In support of his thesis he told me a wonderful anecdote about dear Johanna Röntgen, Line, and Line's *fiancé*, who had passed through Munich that spring on their way from Italy—the girls still under the influence of an afterwards celebrated Lutheran pastor with beautiful eyes, whose coming to Leipzig I had assisted at and whom I considered a *poseur*. It appeared that our friends had gone to St. Peter's on Easter Sunday, and while the congregation, to quote Johanna, was revelling in pagan orgies below, the three Protestants scaled the Dome, and standing in the outside gallery clasping hands, sang Lutheran chorales at the pitch of their voices to the roofs below. They related this achievement with triumph to the Fiedlers and were more surprised than offended at the result, the *fiancé* asking wonderingly : ' But what is there to *laugh* at? '

The soul of honour, politeness, and refinement, Conrad's

spirit of detachment tried me a little at times. Even at my present age I find it difficult to really enjoy intercourse with people whose characters I disapprove of, and Mary, the most instinctive of beings, was of my way of feeling; but Conrad would tell her that Lisl's character was not her business, that you can't blame people for acting according to their nature and so on. This fair-mindedness and caution, accentuated in his case by lack of temperament, are very Saxon traits. By degrees I picked up details concerning his championship of me against my traducers; how he told Lisl it was her duty to contradict the reports her mother was spreading; how Lisl had protested : ' But I can't proclaim my mother a liar '; how he had replied : ' But if she is, you must,' and almost broke with her about it.

At the same time he was still in transports of admiration at Frau von Stockhausen's elemental nature; ' Why,' he said to me, ' if she could, she would torture you physically, and not able to do that, she tortures you otherwise '; and when I pointed out that the real reason of this fanatical hatred was not, as might be supposed, the ills I had brought on them, but jealousy about Lisl, he declared this to be a fine and typical example of maternal instinct. Much as he regretted her lack of other qualities, nobly as he had thrown himself into the breach, he nevertheless applauded this ravening mother from the stalls.

I went to see one or two of the mad King's castles, also the lake where, frantically struggling, locked in each other's arms, he and his doctor went over the edge; and there I remembered that a delightful old man (I was passing through Munich when the tragedy happened) had remarked : ' Nur eins freut mich, dass endlich einmal der Arzt vom Pazienten umgebracht wird ' (Anyhow I'm glad that for once the patient has killed the doctor). Fiedler had a curious collection of prints showing the King's activities as architect and upholsterer, among them villas and interiors designed and provided by him for Wagner's mistresses. That great man's muse was notoriously dependent on *le décor*, and the King was determined stimulus should not be lacking during his sojourns in these places. Can sympathetic patronage go farther?

Early in November I made my first acquaintance with Bavarian slipperiness, my landlady suddenly informing me that the owner of the house—the omnipotent ' Hausherr '—had threatened to give her notice unless she turned me out immediately, the flat having been let on the express understanding that there were to be no female lodgers. Learning however that my rent had been prepaid up to December 1, he had graciously consented to tolerate my presence till that date. I wondered if the Hausherr was a woman-hater, a lunatic, or what, but there was no time to take further action just then for a note arrived from Levi bidding me present myself with my Scores next day : namely a Serenade in four movements, and an Overture to Anthony and Cleopatra.

The result was eminently satisfactory—according to Levi —but I saw that many details could be improved and that to get these done by December 1 would take me all my time, so the search for other quarters had to stand over for the present. . . . And now came further acquaintance with Bavarian reliability; copyist after copyist accepted the job, and two days later, being mysteriously stricken with illness, found himself unable to go on with it—each man writing an endless letter to explain how painful it was to his own feelings to break faith with me. Eventually I had to do nearly the whole thing myself, for a fortnight working twelve or thirteen hours a day, eating horrible food, and taking next to no exercise.

.   .   .   .   .   .

Meanwhile disquieting news arrived from home. Bob had just scraped through his examination, being last on the list of successful candidates—a far more promising situation than being first, for evidently you must be a favourite with Fortune to have got in at all. But this meant qualification for the cavalry only, and as another time he might fail altogether, it was decided to put him into the 21st Lancers (then

Hussars)—a regiment reputed to be quiet (!) and stationed
. . . alas ! poor mother . . . in India. Indian pay is
double pay, nevertheless an allowance that in those days
would have done well enough in the Rifle Brigade would
certainly not be sufficient for a cavalry officer, and I gathered
that for the first time our optimistic father was seriously
troubled by the financial situation of the Smyth Family
Robinson. And here was I, draining the estate of £120 a
year ! . . .

I think I have not yet said how generously and uncomplainingly this allowance was bestowed, for by now even my
father believed in me, and my ' success ' was the dearest
wish of my mother's heart. As a matter of fact enough
could have been saved in six months at Frimhurst to keep
me in affluence for a year in Germany, but the point was that
living at home I should cost them relatively nothing. Nelly
Benson argued that I ought to look upon myself as an inevitable burden, much as if I were a cripple, and accept the
position philosophically ; which perhaps might have been
achieved had I not been feeling so extraordinarily ill and
unlike myself—above all haunted perpetually with visions of
mother bereft of every single child. . . . I mentally decided
that when the time came for quitting my present lodgings I
would live in one room only and reduce my allowance by a
sixth.

In spite of work I managed to go to the Opera occasionally. When it was too late to claim the opulent seats Levi
placed at my disposal I used to sit, or more often stand, in
the gods, and as there was little time for correspondence at
home I once began a letter to Nelly up there, standing and
holding the writing block in mid-air. Presently a nice ugly
young man who was sitting just below me turned round and
said : ' May I offer you my back as desk ? ' and bent forward
to put himself into position. In common gratitude the letter
had to be a short one, but remembering this sympathetically
German incident, which caused no sensation whatever in the
gods, I see that life at Munich was not without poetic charm.

On another night I had a stall for a Lohengrin performance, and, looking round the house, to my surprise caught sight of some English faces I knew in the Dress Circle—Lady Trevelyan and two of her daughters, friends of Mary Hunter's whose acquaintance I had made in London during the summer.

The Trevelyans were inexplicable people, as absolutely musical, and what is more, as completely at my own standpoint in matters of art, as any of my friends abroad. And though Lady Trevelyan was Irish one cannot say that explains everything, for Sir Alfred was of course English, but as unlike the ordinary Englishman in his views and tastes as the rest of the family, and incidentally one of the most original and delightful of personalities. The girls had studied music in Germany and like their mother not only felt, but knew and judged. Absolutely unworldly, not caring two straws about society, they thought for themselves and belonged to no set in particular, which is perhaps the only receipt for keeping a really fresh mind. Though it is impossible to think of Trevelyans being standardised, it may have helped matters that they were Catholics, devout Catholics, but of the old English type—in fact I think Sir Alfred was a bit of a Gallican—consequently the main idea of the Manning school, the conversion of Anglicans, played no part in their scheme. This much it had been possible to glean in the one or two meetings achieved in London, also that Pauline, the eldest girl (there were no sons) was probably the most musical of the party, anyhow the chief executant. But little did I dream that when all else had failed, when, with the cheapening of what had been my great treasure, life seemed almost worthless, a miracle would be wrought by what one calls chance . . . and that the agent, humanly speaking, was to be Pauline.

At that moment only Lady Trevelyan and two of the other girls were in Munich, Sir Alfred and Pauline turning up for the ' Ring ' later on. After that we had ' Tristan '—inexorably, without one cut—and as we left the theatre, Sir Alfred, who had been deeply bored, remarked : ' I am glad they

cine. Now if a Minor Canon of Canterbury Cathedral were
similarly inspired, if the whole scandalised Close rose against
him, not to speak of envenomed medical opposition, I
imagine even the Archbishop himself would be powerless to
affect the situation. But things are otherwise ordained in
Catholic countries; Kneipp's Bishop not only broke down all
opposition, but later on, when the system became famous,
got him permission to hound away would-be hotel specu-
lators, on the principle that none but his own peasants ought
to profit by visitors' money. As for what the accommodation thus provided amounted to, I again refer to my remarks on Aibling.

At first, but for his strong wonderful old face and the virtue that went out of him, you might have fancied the Pfarrer
was a charlatan, for when you began to describe your symptoms he waved his hand and said : ' I know . . . I know,'
hardly honouring you with a glance, and proceeded to give
rapid directions to his stalwart niece, Fräulein Marie, who
looked after the female patients. But when Pauline presented herself he instantly put his finger on a certain spot
and asked : ' How long have you had constant pain here ? '
(At that time I never knew she had pain anywhere, nor did
anyone except her family.) Kneipp's gifts, including this
lightning diagnosis, had by now gained him a solid reputation ; we knew that great doctors sent him hopeless cases—
doomed and gangrenous limbs for instance (a speciality of
those parts) ; also that he cured even cancer if taken before
operation. Nevertheless this incident with Pauline was an
eye-opener.

The *Etablissement* consisted of a few rough sheds, for
men and women respectively, into which the patients were
herded four at a time, and having once been shewn what to
do treated one another. Each stripped in turn, went down
on all fours in a flat tub, and cold water was poured out of
a can over a given section of the body. These pourings,
called ' Anwendungen ' (applications), were varied every
three days and in our case Fräulein Marie did the libations,
but Sir Alfred and Chorinsky officiated for each other. You

then got, dripping wet, into your clothes, the thermometer being well below zero, and walked about briskly for a quarter of an hour, by which time your clothes were dry and you yourself in a wonderful glow. Incidentally the Trevelyans believed they must have been the Pfarrer's first English patients, for when Madeleine mentioned that they all tubbed daily he exclaimed in astonishment : ' täglich dieselbe Anwendung? . . . *das* versteh ich nicht ' (the same application day after day? . . . *that* I cannot understand).

There were other heroic features about the Kneipp system. On arriving at Wörishofen the first thing that met my gaze was Sir Alfred, his hat rather on the back of his head, his face wearing its usual half-bored, half-amused expression, walking about barefoot in the snow with a pair of laced boots dangling from his arm. For a moment I thought he had taken leave of his senses, but learned this was an essential part of the cure and did the same myself later. And meanwhile the Pfarrer stood or rambled all day between the huts, with nothing under his thin old cassock but one linen garment ! . . . There was also a Convent attached to the community in which the nuns brewed simple herb medicines under the Pfarrer's directions ; but though they adored him they lived in perpetual dread lest the cure should be prescribed for them too, and carefully kept their little ailments to themselves. Of the rich, Kneipp had the greatest horror, taking from them only just enough to keep his sheds and cans going and enable him to treat the peasantry for nothing. One man, a peasant proprietor whose arm he had saved after a month's treatment, wept because his benefactor would only accept one mark, declaring he was rich and could afford to pay more (I must add that no one who knows them would credit such a trait in a Bavarian peasant, but this happened while we were there). At last the Pfarrer yielded : ' Well,' he said, ' if you really are rich I will take 1 mark 50 pfennigs.' In fact, as Sir Alfred said, Wörishofen was the only place he had come across where money was powerless— and this, he added, was the real point of interest, not the cure.

As far as I know, religion played no part in the system, but what with his rugged simplicity, his power, and his passionate faith in God, the Pfarrer always reminded me of an Old Testament figure with the quality of the perfect Christian thrown in.   He needed all his faith just then, for during our stay he had a little run of ill-luck; perhaps I brought the microbe with me.   First there was a monk, a visitor from afar who lodged at the Pfarrhof.   Kneipp saw at once that nothing could be done, and was about to send him back to his Monastery where he could be properly tended, when he suddenly died, and the whole village accompanied the coffin to the parish bounds.   He had had no ' Anwendungen ' and obviously the Pfarrer was not to blame; nevertheless he took the matter greatly to heart, and the peasants, who worshipped their prophet but as usual had stones in reserve, were inclined to throw a few now.   Yet the amazement on all sides at this misfortune bore out their everlasting boast that though, of course, all could not be cured, no one was ever the worse for coming to Wörishofen.

And then followed another sad incident.   A day or two afterwards my landlady met me, a touch of triumph in her manner, with the remark : ' Heute ist wieder Einer gestorben ! '   (Another has died to-day); and this time it was difficult not to connect the cure and the disaster, for while water was being poured over the patient's shoulders he had had a stroke !   He lived long enough for the last rites to be administered, and I can still see poor old Kneipp's tragic face as he said in his deep, steady voice : ' Gedankt sei Gott für sein seliges Ende . . . aber ach! es ist ein Jammer . . .' (then a terrible sigh) ' aber gedankt sei Gott ! ' . . . (Thank God for his blessed end . . . but oh! how sad it is . . . yet God be thanked).   And meanwhile, for I was calling at the Pfarrhof, there stood cheery Fräulein Marie awestruck and miserable; the little great-niece was rushing about claiming everyone's attention for her new doll, and the Pfarrer's horrid little ' Spitz ' shrieking rather than barking at Marco, its master not even telling it to be quiet. . . . When I got home my landlady and her friends were still gloating over the tragedy, agreeing that probably the cure was very dangerous, that to pour cold water over people at all, especially in the winter, was ' gegen die Natur ' (against nature) and so on. One thought of this man who had dedicated his life to others—rejecting money, promotion, honours, everything—and wondered if he feared that perhaps God was forsaking him in his old age. . . . Nothing in my life has brought home to me more painfully how cruel and ungrateful human beings can be, and I scored it up, perhaps unjustly, against the Bavarian peasant for ever.

CHAPTER XLII

WINTER 1889 TO SPRING 1890

DURING these weeks began what, as I have said, was destined to be an eventful relation, my friendship with Pauline. Wondering how to give some idea of her personality I remember a remark Lady Trevelyan once made to me at Nettlecombe, their home in Somersetshire : ' If I were to go into Pauline's room,' she said, ' and find she had suddenly vanished, melted into air leaving no trace, it would hardly surprise me.' There was neither sentiment nor apprehension in her manner, it was merely a characterisation that conveys what for lack of a better word one might call the unearthly element about Pauline. Her extreme gentleness and delicate beauty had something to do with it, but these were only the garments of her soul. Full of enjoyment of life, a grand laugher—and this I think stands high on the list of merits—there was yet the abiding suggestion of a visitant from another planet lent to this world for the time being . . . and as it turned out not lent for long.

It was strange to realise that this most serene and contented of beings had been acquainted with physical pain from youth upwards, indeed was seldom free from it ; here then was one key to her saintliness. But on another point enlightenment of a less distressing kind awaited me ; it appeared that every man she met fell in love with her—generally two men at a time—and the lives of her mother and sisters, so they said, were sometimes made a burden to them by Pauline's disconsolates. Yet nothing in her demeanour would have led you to suspect she was the object of embarrassing homage—surely a rare and exquisite trait.

There are certain people who, without exactly insisting on their conquests, mysteriously impel their surroundings to raise them a pedestal, once placed on which, the fact that they are universally sighed for becomes manifest to all. The thing develops into a tradition, a legend; one man catches the disease from another and passes it on to a third, and half the victims succumb before their eyes have met those of their enslaver. I do not believe that Helen of Troy was more beautiful, more admired, more desired, than thousands of other women, but each lover and friend felt moved to contribute a stone to the solid, soaring Cheops-Pyramid from which she dominates the ages, and to which each passing generation adds its quota. And I feel convinced too that Helen was aware of and delicately encouraged these architectural promptings.

Well—among women thus formed, as Mr. Mantalini would have put it, to distract the senses of men, I know of one only, Pauline, who ignored and took no pleasure in her power. She must have listened to each inevitable declaration as if such a thing had never met her ears before, and having no doubt behaved with just the right blend of kindness, tact, and firmness, will have gone back with a sigh of relief to her twin realities, religion and music. Indeed I heard of a case, no doubt a specially painful one, when simultaneously with the bang of the front door of 74 Harley Street, a shower of scales from Pauline's piano rent and refreshed the air. This sounds rather heartless, but if you are absolutely free from vanity and absorbed by two master passions, unsolicited love may well be a nuisance. No one's store of sympathy is limitless and there are only twenty-four hours in the day.

I often noticed how, quite unconsciously, she imposed her ways on all around her—merely by the penetrative strength of ' a gentle noble temper, a soul as even as a calm.' The quality of her spirit sometimes put her beyond one's reach; I did not always understand her, but was invariably and per-

fectly understood.   There seemed to be no limit to her instinctive grasp of life and its intricacies ; essential rays that
got broken and dispersed on the rough surface of other minds
passed easily and unbroken into hers.   You could have been
silent with her all your days and yet know you had become
part of her mind.   Assurances were neither given nor needed
. . . her quiet reticence bred a faith that nothing could
trouble.

I loved Lady Trevelyan, who worshipped and in many
ways resembled Pauline, with the same kind of affection—a
feeling from which her intense reserve and shyness would
have made her shrink had she realised its existence.   A pure
bred Milesian, she found Anglo-Saxon placidity rather a
trial, as did my mother, and once remarked : ' So many English people seem to live at such a *low ebb* ; they speak so
softly you can't hear them, they enjoy so discreetly that
you'd never suspect it.'   And I also remember her declaring
that she didn't want the United Kingdom or any other
country to prosper as long as men disregard God's laws and
look upon immorality as a thing that goes without saying;
as long as tradesmen hold that only by sharp practice can
you make a fortune; as long as advertising a performance
is considered more important than the performance itself.
Gentle, wise, subtle, and yet infinitely simple and single-
hearted, it was this underlying passionateness that I loved so
in her.   I once told Pauline I would rather confess to her
mother than to any priest on earth, and pictured to myself
with amusement how she would turn white with horror at
the thought and flee upstairs, gently muttering prayers for
herself and me.

Needless to say Lady Trevelyan had a great sense of
humour—as essential a note in the ideal confessor as saintliness or anything else—and musically speaking even a greater
critical faculty, perhaps, than Pauline.   You had to finesse
to get her opinion, but any amount of trouble was worth the
deadly hitting on the nail that followed.   Pauline had the
same dislike of categorical statements, and in her case matters were further complicated by the side I used to call ' Mrs.

Winslow '—the Irish side. As she was intensely absent-minded (a very delightful quality) the soothing syrup would sometimes be administered hastily in a spirit of propitiation before the matter in hand had been fully grasped, but there was never any doubt as to her ultimate opinion. Another trait the two had in common—a curious one in such gentle people—was a faculty of getting white with anger; I remember first noticing it in Lady Trevelyan when we were talking about people who won't take care of their health—a form of tiresomeness she had no patience with. The whole family were more or less on the same lines, and I have the impression that you might search in vain for their prototype outside the Roman Communion; to be honest I must add that these were among the very few devout Catholics I have met who struck me as full-fledged, responsible human beings.

What a simplification of things it is to speak the same language! I never realised this more strongly than in my relations with Pauline, who was fated to walk with me through a stretch of life in which we did not see eye to eye. By one short phrase in music, by a note sometimes, you can convey more to a fellow musician than by endless words; not specific things, of course, but lights and shades—subterranean movements of the soul, the memory of which plays in and out of your mutual consciousness and saves the situation just as you are on the verge of a deadlock. It was the lack of any such mitigating medium that made itself felt between the Bensons and me, its presence that lifted my intercourse with Pauline high above rocks and brambles into hitherto unexplored regions of serenity.

.   .   .   .   .   .

We all went back to Munich in the middle of December; two days later the Trevelyans left for Cannes, and then came the worst nightmare of my life. I say it deliberately, for when the breach with Lisl had taken place I was well in mind and body and had never yet had to call up my reserves; now I was ill and morally at the end of my tether.

The search for lodgings was begun in appalling sleet and slush, and then, not till then, did I discover what Fate, in permitting me to drop at once into ideal quarters two months ago, had purposely hidden from me till the weather became impossible—namely that furnished rooms for lady students of my type do not exist in Munich. The lunatic landlord had merely been a normal Munich burgher! If you were respectable you lived at a pension (and as lady composers were scarce in those days, pianos on every floor were I suppose considered no deterrent), if you lived in rooms like a man you were disreputable. . . . Quite simple.

Hounded from pillar to post, I at last found a room on the ground floor—situation hateful both to Rheumaticks and lovers of light; but as the landlady assured me there were no pianos, that all her other clients were students—that is lodgers who are never in the house except from 2 A.M. to 10 A.M.—and that the baby I heard crying was her great grand-daughter whose Mama was on a two days' visit, I engaged the room. It afterwards turned out that one of the students had a lady with him—a lady who called the filthy maid of all work ' Fräulein,' which gives an idea of the class—and that the baby was hers and the student's property. I had to fight for a table to write on, for a vanished armchair I had seen a few days back when engaging the room, for firewood, for briquettes, for everything, and was soon off again, rheumatism all over me, once more facing the same sleet and slush, the same insulting refusals to take in single ladies. Eventually I found another miserable room; again I was told there were no pianos in the place, and asking what the tramplings overheard might mean, learned it was only preparations for the Christmas tree. By this time I believed less and less the accounts given by landladies of their establishments, but how test the matter otherwise than by taking the rooms? A few days previously I had gone to call on Levi, with the idea that his influence might induce some decent owner of furnished rooms to admit me in spite of sex disabilities, but arriving at his door I had learned that he was ill in bed, with high fever and pains in his limbs. . . .

Because the incidents that now follow proved to be a turning-point in my life, because too, strange to say, contemporary words tell a personal story almost impersonally, I shall again let one of my letters speak for me. It was written to Nelly Benson on December 21, the day before I fled from the vicinity of the student, his lady, and their ever-squalling infant. I will not even correct mis-spelt words and weak-backed sentences—points which certainly did not escape the notice of my correspondent, who periodically drew up lists of words she could no longer bear to see massacred, and would have been incapable herself of literary slovenliness even at the point of death.

' . . . Yes, you are right, I am ill; that is one reason why my letters have flagged; possibly too the cure at Wörishofen was *not* a happy thought. But all the same I'm glad and thankful I went there for that stay has revealed to me certain things about myself. Seeing what the Trevelyans' relation to God and the world is, loving Pauline at once almost as I did (I swear to you chiefly because of that but also because of herself), feeling so broken-hearted when they went away, finding my vaunted strength and calm gone, coming back to this miserable lodging . . . all this brought about a crisis.

' And now let me tell you a detail. Pauline had left a little " Imitation de Jésus Christ " at her Hotel here and asked me to claim it for her; not to send it but to give it back when I should see her next. She said she had another but prized this one because her mother had given it to her. So I went to the Bellevue; nothing had been handed in at the Bureau, but their apartment was still unlet if I would like to take a look round. . . . I wonder if you can guess what it was going into those desolate rooms where I had been so happy? . . . To my joy I found the book under the sofa cushion, which will give you an idea both of Pauline and Bavarian housemaids, but struggling against the awful wind and snow from the mountains it must have got jerked out of my pocket, and when I got home . . . it was gone! I was in despair. I had thought perhaps in her heart she had wanted me to keep it hoping I might read it, though as you can imagine I didn't ask her if this was so. Anyhow I had meant to . . . and now it was lost ! . . . Well, I advertised, and O Nelly, last night it came back, almost like a message from him whom the book is about, but I have no time for reading now, for I clear out of this place to-morrow.

' I can't tell you what these days have been. There *is* a piano in the house after all, though a long way off, but the faintest sound of a note makes me tremble all over. I have lain for hours on the sofa, powerless with fear of life, feeling that I am broken and done for. I thank God for two things, that Mary Fiedler is here, and Marco, for I know but for these two I should have killed myself. I felt I was going mad, losing control, yet hated the idea of leaving such a horrible legacy to the dear Fiedlers . . . and still more the thought of poor lonely distracted Marco ! Then this book came back and I feel as if I had been purposely driven into my last entrenchments. I give in and am ready and longing to try and learn there is another refuge and strength than human love and my own powers. I know it will take long but I believe it won't be denied in the end.

' You will wonder how all this came of the Trevelyans. Well, you see they are very " artistic " people, real artists at heart, all of them, and one, Pauline, has, as I told you, suffered much and will suffer more. These two things somehow made a way from her inner life to mine though we talked directly about it but little, and I don't think she has a notion that she reacted on me like that.

' I cannot tell you how good Mary F. has been. I went to her yesterday to ask the doctor's address and broke down ; she has a pitying way with me that does upset my fortitude, but perhaps it does good afterwards. She sees how my nerves are all weak and jarred, and is so unutterably dear to me. I told her all, why life looks so black, &c., and she made me swear if I felt like that again to send to her, which I will do. Of course she urged me to go and stay with them for a bit, but that is not what is wanted ; I must, must stand on my own feet and this she understands. She told me that, as I knew, she always gives me a handsome present at Christmas (she is well off and loves giving) and that this year she means to give me money—that we had known each other now for ten years and she supposed I couldn't be proud towards *her*. Nor can I. If ever I am rich I shall do the same; when you know people are thinking not even of shillings, but of pence, what is the good of giving them jewellery and so forth?

' I think she has a perfect horror of Lisl since she realises things more, I mean how my life was rooted in them, and also that owing to dear old mother it can't take root in England. Ah! how Lisl spoiled me for this sort of thing . . . but what I realise more strongly than anything is, that if I were rooted elsewhere I shouldn't mind it all as I do. O! and I have been so unwilling, so caring for other things. . . . But I will stop this account of my troubles. I don't know but what you are too young to write such a letter to at all.

' By the by the Pfarrer was not really upset in the depths of his soul by his patient dying, and when I left was full of two wonderful cures he is bringing about; one a man who has been in agony daily for ten years from a railway accident (concussion) and whom he has cured in six weeks; the other a blind man who is beginning to see.

' While I have been writing Marco lies slumbering peacefully at my feet, little knowing what a definite part he has played in my career. The thought of him . . . nobody's dog . . . (he is awfully nervous) or even travelling alone to England, moved me . . . ah me, what was it? Marco, for one thing, and other things too. Thank God it is over and done with now.

' Finally, to sum up the situation : (1) My life seems smashed up, for I don't think I can stand Germany without Lisl. (2) You know why England is out of the question. (3) I know the music in me isn't dead, only cowed into silence. (4) I at last believe—with relapses, but still believe —that a way may be found for me.

' Farewell. E. '

Looking through some 150 letters addressed to her it is a relief to find that on two occasions only, both of this epoch, was poor Nelly harrowed in this way! but it is strange to see how little I seem to have realised what an enormous amount of courage is necessary to the coward's end.

Next day I moved into the new lodgings, of which I had a latchkey and where the tramplings raged overhead as before. I had specially begged that the room be very warm, but the stove was out and not a soul in the place. As I had found elsewhere, there was no service, no machinery to meet my case—I was a waif and stray; the sort of ladies who inhabit furnished rooms have maids, and as I said, students are never at home. So I went into the kitchen to look for wood and noticed a letter addressed to me lying on the table; it was from Conrad to say that, like Levi, Mary was ill in bed, with pains all over her and a temperature. . . After seventy-five years of quiescence the influenza epidemic, unrecognised as such for the time being, had again put in an appearance!. . . For the first time in my life I should spend Christmas alone, . . . and in this place!

That night in bed I read a few sentences in the 'Imitation,' as one might finger a shilling or two of a fortune which may, or may not, turn out to be meant for you, all the while possessed by a not unreasonable presentiment that the worst was yet to be. Next morning I was awakened at 5.30 by what I was told was the sweeps, and as the days of closed shops were approaching went out to buy a few necessaries. I remember coming back at midday and falling with a flop into the armchair; then, crash, bang, as if to welcome me home, with a few violent well-known chords a stentorian voice on the floor above launched into the recitative of a celebrated scene in what we English call ' Grand Opera.' . . . I rushed upstairs and was informed that the new tenor of the Hof Oper, Herr So and So, had taken the suite overhead for six months! . . . That afternoon, although in this case I had been obliged to prepay a month's rent, the frantic hunt for the non-existent was taken up again under the usual weather conditions, and continued till long after sundown,

by which time I was well in the grip of familiar symptoms—
burning heat and shivering fits; and when I came home the
tenor was still studying his new part.

Next day was Christmas Eve. I lay on the sofa, far too
ill to go out room-hunting, and again opened the ' Imitation.'
The tenor boomed away overhead but presently I ceased to
hear him, reading and reading throughout the day . . .
reading at the restaurant where I tried to eat a midday
meal . . . reading on into the night . . . awaking after an
hour or two to light my lamp and begin reading again. If
I did not remember that it was Christmas Eve it would seem
to me that I read ceaselessly for days and days. . . . Now
all was clear to me; I had always thought of myself, and of
nothing else . . . of what I had to achieve in life, of what
my duty to myself was . . . always myself. No wonder I
had failed; no wonder all I had touched, no matter with what
excellent intentions, had turned to dust and ashes; no wonder
that even Lisl was lost to me and that I had gone into the
Desert in vain. . . . Now my path was clear . . . music
must be thrown overboard too; there was only one road to
happiness, renunciation. The Prior had said it would take
many, many years to learn that lesson, but life had moved
swiftly and violently with me, and in five I had learned it, so
I believed, once and for ever . . . I must go home again and
take up the burden I had tried to lay down; no one would
know more than that I was ill and needed home care, which
was true. Of course I would try to go on with music at
Frimhurst . . . but as well try to make water run up hill.
Well, renunciation meant that. . . .

Next day I telegraphed home to say I was ill and coming
back, and then dragged myself somehow to the Christmas
Morning Service in the little English Church. I stayed
there in a dark corner, weeping, weeping . . . stayed on
while others were communicating. I remember one or two
people glanced at me curiously, and that the officiant paused
a moment when all the communicants had returned to their
places and looked my way before turning again to the Altar.
I did not communicate myself, but went home full of a great

peace, though so ill that nothing but a long habit of organising my own journeys can have carried me automatically through the next twenty-four hours.

I have never quite known how I got home. There were no dining cars on that train, and I knew that as the hours wore on I might become too ill to get out and eat at the Buffet. So I bought, I forget on what principle, a piece of fillet of beef, cut it up raw into small cubes, and filled a soda-water bottle with weak brandy and water—strange fare for one in a raging fever! The only accommodation for dogs was a sort of square tunnel running under the luggage van. It was as long as the breadth of the van, but not high enough for Marco to stand up, nor wide enough for him to turn round in, and I shall never forget the anguish of shoving that huge frightened dog backwards into the horrible place and seeing the door locked on his poor white nose. I slept or dozed most of the way, occasionally chewing the juice out of a cube or two and putting up what remained in a bit of newspaper for Marco, together with some broken biscuit; and whenever I could during that night and the next day, I staggered through the snow and storm to the torture chamber to have a little reassuring conversation with him through the ventilation holes, bribing the guard to bring water and let me feed him now and again. Throughout that journey I was too ill to read, but held the little red book in my hand all the way, and am as certain as of anything in life, that but for that amulet I could never have reached home. I have no recollection of the arrival except as usual of mother's welcome, but know I was a few days in bed, generally with fever and always in pain somewhere or other . . . and then executed the usual lightning recovery.

One incident of the convalescent period has remained in my mind because it struck me as comic, and so very characteristic of my mother. The occasion was the appearance at dessert of her tonic, solemnly handed on a silver tray by the footman; this reminding me that I had forgotten my own medicine I jumped up to fetch it, saying :

> ' For her grief so lovely [1] shown
> Made me think upon mine own.'

Seeing that Bishop's ' As it fell upon a day ' had once been in her own repertory I rather expected praise for what I considered an apt quotation; her only response however was to say very impressively : ' You know, dear, this is not *medicine,* it's a *tonic.'* But when I reproached her with lack of appreciation she exclaimed remorsefully : ' Well, it's a great shame, for no one makes me feel as *clever* as you do ! ' . . . How I cherished, and still cherish, that little compliment !

.   .   .   .   .   .

Early in the New Year Bob was gazetted to the 21st Hussars and sailed for India in March. Throughout those two months mother's bearing with him, a certain bigness about the way she abstained from giving advice or otherwise tampering with his freedom, impressed me deeply. But magnificently as she played up, his going cut her to the heart, and when a day or two after he had gone she said quietly : ' I shan't see Bob again,' I was more thankful than ever at having come home.

Meanwhile she had one pleasure to look forward to, for rather to my surprise Manns had at once accepted my Serenade and put it on one of his April programmes. This would be the first public performance of any orchestral work of mine, and indeed of any work at all in England. I was then new to the business of one more desk of violins being required at the last minute—of suddenly discovering that all the percussion was played by one man (or, if you had put it all in one part, by three men) and similar complications. And through it all Pauline burned like a steady light beside me, warm and quiet, helpful and practical.

When the great day came the excitement at home was immense, even Papa, who had never been at a real concert

---

[1] The word is really ' lively.'

in his life, insisting on being present. The Serenade was admirably rendered, and being a first work one could more or less count on a good reception; but regardless of how that might be, he had ready in his pocket a short telegram to Bob in India : ' Great success,' which no doubt would have been dispatched in any case.

I was not sitting in the Hall myself but afterwards learned what had occurred on the family benches.

No sooner was the first movement over than Papa rose to send off the telegram . . . and get away himself; pulled down by mother, he attempted the same thing after the second, and again after the third movement. But after the fourth and last, having given up all hope, he remained patiently sitting, and thus had the gratification of seeing his daughter warmly called to the platform by that most delightful of audiences. I went home by a later train than the family, and when I met him before dinner he was beaming with delight, and said : ' Well, you had quite a jobation.'

A strange thing had happened at that concert. When summoned to the front I naturally looked towards the seats where the family were installed, and to my amazement, sitting just behind my mother was a man with a long beard whom for half a moment I did not recognise; but there was no mistaking the face I had always known as clean shaven, but for a moustache—a face I had not looked upon for many years . . . it was H. B. He had been passing through London on his way to America, and seeing my name on a poster had run down to the Crystal Palace. I afterwards learned that when Mary was claiming her reserved seat at the ticket office a strange man had said to her : ' I beg your pardon, but surely you must be a sister of Ethel Smyth? ' And though the family likeness between us all was a by-word, this incident could but gratify one, at least, of the two sisters in question ! After the concert H. B. and I met in the corridor, had tea together, and that night he started for Liverpool.

The result of the production of the Serenade was that other works of mine were now accepted for performance without difficulty, and suddenly, to my delight, I found that the power of work had come back. For one thing at last I was at peace; the Munich mood was no passing one, and for the next eighteen months, in spite of arduous work, at the bottom of my soul was one thought only—Christ. Hatred and contempt of Lisl fell away from me never to return, and though her action was as incomprehensible to me as ever, at that time my own failings and shortcomings were enough for me. I never lost the sense of our fate being inter-linked, but if I perhaps hoped that some day things might alter, that hope played no part in the scheme. Never again was her peace troubled by useless remonstrances, and I steadily turned my thoughts in another direction, as one who dreads vertigo might force his eyes away from the precipice. . . . And I remember, too, another thought that was brushed aside as dangerous, or at least futile; it occurred to me one day that Thomas à Kempis would certainly have disapproved of Shakespeare. . . . ! All the same I went on reading the Plays, but not the Sonnets and other poems that too obviously base on what the author of the ' Imitation ' would have called the carnal affections.

Meanwhile life at home assumed a different aspect; things in my mother that used to drive me frantic seemed not only bearable but of little consequence. And now a sort of eventual fairness came into play; if an argument could be kept in smooth channels she would presently admit that she had been ' trying,' and one day she amused and touched me by recalling that her grandmother used to say of the family she had married into : ' The Straceys are the *Jingle* family, my dear, much brilliancy and no foundation.' But I could assure her, without flattery, that this was not her case !

As striking proof of the altered state of things I may mention that the old, old subject of economy was now discussed between the three of us without heat, and whereas six short months ago Bob and I had been informed it was d—d impertinent to put in our oar at all, I now found myself

privately invited by one parent to back up schemes of re-
trenchment devised against the other. I remember a drama
concerning a horse and a carpet that played for several
months. My father, who objected to reducing the stud, put
forth as excuse that ' your mother likes going out with the
pair,' which was quite true. Thereupon mother heroically
took to a one-horse brougham, and while she was breakfast-
ing in bed as usual, dipping pieces of thin bread and butter
into her tea (a horrid practice she defended by pointing out
that cream and butter both come from the cow) I would be
asked to hint to Papa that his excuse was no longer valid.
Meanwhile certain useless trees had been marked down and
valued at £90, but long before they were felled, mother, who
had a way of suddenly getting bored with perfectly sound
carpets and curtains, decided to spend the sum on a new
dining-room carpet—about as unnecessary a piece of extravagance as could have been thought of ! In this case it was
my father who beckoned me into his room after luncheon and
suggested I might bring influence to bear on ' your mother.'

I forget how this particular tug-of-war ended, but remember being asked to look into household expenses generally,
and finding that the yard dog, who notoriously would not
look at dog-biscuits, consumed eighty-four per month according to the bill. Also that however long it may take to
argue the hind leg off a donkey, it took me a week to argue
away a certain garden boy whose presence involved other
complications and expenses ; and a month later, in spite of
having been theoretically dismissed, he was still in our service, and, as before, sailing boats on the canal in working
hours. I had often managed in past days to command my
temper for about a week, and as neither of my elders ever
stuck to their resolutions of economy for more than seven
days, the problem now was to keep them up to the collar
without causing them to jib. Strange to say, as far as I
remember, though little may have been achieved there were
no rows of any kind, and the persistence of my lamb-like
mood certainly impressed them, for I have contemporary
evidence to the fact. It would indeed have been strange had

such a passionate desire for betterness borne no fruit, and from her last pathetic letter to me [1] I have the consolation of knowing that my presence in the house was a stay and comfort to mother.

That spring the invention of ladies' bicycles was to demonstrate her superiority to stupid prejudice. In the *Illustrated London News* were to be seen pictures of wild women of the usual unprepossessing pioneer type riding about Epping Forest, and I at once decided to buy a bicycle. Aunts, cousins, and friends were horrified . . . never has the word ' indelicate ' been bandied about with more righteous conviction. But my mother said this was perfect nonsense; ' When we are dead,' she would reply to objectors, ' she won't be able to keep horses, and I can think of nothing more sensible than her buying a bicycle.' And buy one I did—with bad paces too, for pneumatic tyres were not yet invented; I also took lessons at a place called Cycledom, and the scene of my first unaided attempts was, O wonder! the gravel sweep in front of Lambeth Palace, where I even had the honour of giving instruction to the Dean of Windsor. (This of course was during the brief period of favour with the Archbishop.)

Strange to say one then looked upon this very useful and sometimes pleasant way of getting from one place to another as a form of sport, and though for many a long day to come no ' nice ' women rode bicycles, I pursued my solitary course with enthusiasm. By degrees, as we know, the thing caught on, and one day, about eighteen months later, when I met Mrs. R., the arch-prude of the neighbourhood, wobbling along the high road, and beheld her fall off her machine at my feet to explain that she had taken to it in order to avoid having out the horses on Sunday, it was clear that the indelicacy ghost had been finally laid.

By this time the Primrose League was in full swing, and much to my father's satisfaction I threw myself into propaganda, with great zeal. I remember a Primrose League

[1] Appendix VI., ii. p. 282, No. 2.

concert at which we performed some of Tosti's ' Songs of the Abruzzi,' arranged by me for an odd assortment of instruments, selected with regard to the accomplishments of various neighbours. There were guitars, violins, a triangle, a zither, and so forth, and the result was charming; particularly so in the case of the folk-tune known, if I may indicate the Italian pronunciation, as ' *Mam*-ma, *Mam*-ma,' but which Papa, reading from the programme, his spectacles well shoved up on his forehead, hurriedly announced as ' *Mama Mama* by Posti.'

That little experiment in sonority was responsible for other unusual Chamber Music combinations I was to attempt later in life.

CHAPTER XLIII

Spring and Summer 1890

Among the pleasant things that befell early in that year was making the acquaintance of Sir Arthur Sullivan, who came up to me in the house we met in, introduced himself as ' colleague ' so delightfully, with such a perfect blend of chaff and seriousness (the exact perfection of cadence there is in his work) that my one idea ever after was to see him whenever I could. He told me to show him a specimen of orchestration and was pleased on the whole, but I remember his putting his finger on a rather low flute passage and saying : ' Now here's a very pretty little pattern *on paper,* but . . .' (here he pointed to some strenuous violins) ' what's the poor chap to do against *that?* ' And then he added : ' An artist has got to make a shilling's worth of goods out of a penn'orth of material, and here *you* go chucking away sovereigns for nothing ! '—a sound statement on Art, and also a well-deserved and kindly bit of criticism. One day he presented me with a copy of the full score of ' The Golden Legend,' adding : ' I think this is the best thing I've done, don't you? ' and when truth compelled me to say that in my opinion ' The Mikado ' is his masterpiece, he cried out : ' O you wretch ! ' But though he laughed I could see he was disappointed.

Later on, inasmuch as I lived in the neighbourhood where his boyhood had been passed and to which he always hoped to return, I became his informal house agent, as will be gathered from one or two letters of his given later ; but alas !

he never reached the old age which he counted on passing among the Camberley pinewoods. His friendship was a great musical stimulus, and one day I wrote to Mrs. Benson, not without intentionally grim emphasis : ' May evil befall me if I look back from music.'

During the spring months I saw a great deal of her, and our relations went through a curious phase. My conversion, as Evangelicals would have called it, could but give her great pleasure (if one may use the word in such a connection) but as regards methods we were not of one mind. When I was young, engrossed as we all were in the story of the Oxford Movement, I had been very High Church, and later, when belief passed, this aspect of Anglicanism had never lost its grip on my imagination; naturally therefore the new religious conviction that now welled up within me poured itself into the old channel. I may add that an aversion to Low Church views and ways, which as I tried to show elsewhere was instinctive and violent, had been confirmed by many a subsequent experience, the type, the attitude of mind towards sacred things being the same whether met with in England or Germany. For instance a certain Frau von Bohlen (a dear old lady whom one might call grandmother of Big Bertha for her son married Krupp's heiress), once informed me that while nursing a niece she suddenly saw the patient was sinking, and being at her wits' end knelt down and prayed as she had never prayed in her life for guidance. ' And suddenly,' she said ' from behind that screen, as plainly as I am speaking to you now, an unearthly voice uttered the words : " *Give her a glass of old brandy.*" ' . . . Now Mrs. Benson might possibly have found this remark rather crude, but it certainly would not have sent her into paroxysms of amused disgust as it did me, for her own sympathies were at that time strongly evangelical.

Among other things she was an upholder, and sometimes a holder, of informal prayer meetings. Extemporary prayer is, as we know, part of the Presbyterian scheme; but firstly the ministers are trained to it, which takes away what I

cannot but feel as the offensiveness of the thing, and
secondly the training sometimes results in a Dr. MacGregor.
But it is quite another affair when the performer is an amateur—perhaps one of the many English ladies of high degree
who manage in some mysterious manner to combine saintliness with the social whirl. I remember an occasion when
one of these wound up her address with the gentle question :
' Do you think, dear friends, we shall smile in Heaven? . . .
I . . . do! '—whereupon she favoured us with the identical
saccharin smile that did so much execution in society. And
as Lucy Tait tramped out of that meeting I heard her mutter
low and thunderously : ' If people are going to smile like
that in Heaven, I don't think I want to go there.' These
and other Low Church practices affected me like ' foolish
basses,' and not even for the sake of her who had been my
sole support during the evil years could I disguise the fact.

And yet she saw—how could a woman of that type fail to
see?—the humours of Evangelicism. Once when I was at
Addington, Nelly, on practical information bent, asked a
certain rector's wife what they were doing about getting a
new curate; the answer, delivered with a broad, beaming
smile, was : ' We are praying for one,' and Mrs. Benson
was delighted to hear that Nelly had merely remarked : ' I
should have thought advertising would be a better plan.' I
remember too that when Mrs. Benson herself asked this lady
if they meant to choose a ' converted ' man and risk his
being a gentleman, or *vice versâ,* the eager reply was that
above all he must be ' converted.' But here the Rector
broke in with : ' No, no, converted or not I mean to have a
gentleman,' . . . and my enthusiastic endorsement of this
point of view ' jarred ' a little on Mrs. Benson. In fact,
strange to relate, we were now farther apart than in the days
of my unbelief.

There had of course been a moment when, unknown to
anyone, especially the Trevelyans, I had looked longingly
Romewards and read every available book on the question,
but the mood had passed. Everything narrows of course to
the supreme question : how can you best save your soul?

But without going so far as the old Duke of Cambridge who once said : ' Believe me, *every change is for the worse* ' I was a Conservative, and the idea of leaving the Church you were born in, and rejecting a formula to which you had never given a fair trial because another attracts you more potently, seemed contemptible and never really struck root. None the less I felt that the type of saintliness of Newman, whose ' Apologia ' I read in one sitting between Edinburgh and London, was only thinkable in a celibate priesthood, and so strongly did his personality draw me that in the August of that year, when staying in Norfolk, I was contemplating the difficult feat of returning home across country *viâ* Birmingham, in order to ask his blessing; not in the least as a first step towards Rome—that phase was behind me—but merely to carry his benediction about with me like a relic. Two days before my departure, when, immersed in Bradshaw, I was dizzily planning the journey, my host who had just opened his newspaper exclaimed : ' Hullo, Cardinal Newman is dead.'

The Hunters then lived near Durham, and while staying with them in September I saw a good deal of Uncle Charles's old friend Dean Lake, who showed me many of Newman's letters and talked to me by the hour of their common youth and the differences that parted them in the end. Rather pompous and unapproachable at a distance, I found him another man at close quarters, and remember his saying how often in his career as Churchman he had seen men of lofty character, fervent piety, and unequalled scholarship such as my uncle, go to the wall for lack of some little gift—possibly worthless in itself—that opens the door to preferment. ' Why in God's name,' he cried, ' should I be Dean of Durham, and Charles Scott hob-nobbing with pious old women at Bournemouth? '

If I mention what appears to be an irrelevant fact—that I played lawn tennis incessantly at Durham—it is because among my confederates were two jolly boys, nephews of a shy celibate Canon who, we were informed, used to watch

the games from his window, the court being in the Quad-
rangle. Twenty years later, women being eligible at the
Durham University for honours, the degree of *Mus. Doc.
Dunelm.* was offered me, and scanning the list of backers I
discovered that my name had been proposed by a person
whose face I had never seen—the celibate Canon behind the
window curtain ! Thus it was not to music but to lawn tennis
that I owe a title which compensates in some measure for the
non-realisation of my youthful ambition—' to be made a
Peeress in my Own Right because of Music.'

From Durham I went to stay with some people (I can't
remember their name) who had scandalised the world a few
months previously by having a ' pink wedding,' the breakfast being followed by a lawn meet and a rattling run—proceedings that I daresay would leave reporters cold nowadays.
And finally, after that, I paid a memorable visit to Addington.

Mainly from curiosity, certainly not from sentimental
reasons, an experiment that always tempts me is the bringing together of new and old friends. My mother being
favourable both to Nelly and Pauline they had already met
at Frimhurst, and liked each other so much that Mrs. Benson had begged me to find out if so devout a Catholic would
condescend to stay at the house of an heretical Archbishop.
I now had the delight of seeing all the family, including His
Grace, go down before Pauline, and of hearing Mrs. Benson
remark : ' If *she* hasn't made a Roman of you, you must
indeed be a good Anglican ! '

I was ; and this fact became the basis of a precarious
favour with the Archbishop already spoken of. He actually
went so far as to inform me one day at luncheon, by way of
a stately joke, that I was a better Churchwoman than his
wife—which according to my ideas was not saying much, for
often and often in the heat of controversy I would accuse
Mrs. Benson of being a Dissenter; to which she would reply,
in the same key : ' By all means ! if not caring two straws
about the Apostolic Succession ' (my special subject) ' spells
Dissent.' And eventually, with the approval of both parties,

though not in the same spirit, a long dreary border of spiky flowers at Lambeth was called ' The Apostolic Succession.'

Another point which won me for the time being the approval of the Archbishop was my interest in the Mission to the Assyrian Church, the only Mission of which I could say as much.

Few people have ever heard of this Church, an offshoot of Nestorianism that is still defying the Turk somewhere near Urmi, and had appealed some years back to Archbishop Tait for help. Driven from one rocky fastness to another, these few thousand Christians had suffered and survived for hundreds of years, resisting not only the sword of the Mahomedan but the more insidious persuasive methods of Roman Catholics and American Unitarians—meanwhile handing down by oral tradition a Liturgy, the significance of many details in which had been forgotten. With less written word to go on than the British Constitution itself, this Liturgy was eventually printed at Oxford (for the first time in history) in the middle of the nineteenth century, and Oxford men, attached to the Mission, expounded to Assyrian priests the meaning of their own rites ! In all this there was a strong imaginative appeal ; I loved too to think that the one Church to which this ancient community could turn without fear of being devoured in the warmth of welcome was the Anglican Church ; and though my support could have been counted in shillings it was unfailing. Indeed such was my zeal that I not only got up entertainments for the benefit of the Fund, but impartially pestered everyone I knew for subscriptions ; on which principle kind Mr. Jack Tennant once found his Monte Carlo winnings diverted into quite an unexpected channel.

And yet a third point in my favour was my being so greatly taken up with the trial of the saintly and celibate Bishop of Lincoln. I found the whole proceedings most impressive, the Archbishop absolutely in his element and his judgment very fine both as to matter and manner ; . . . in fact there was only one flaw, the thought of the beloved family dotted about the Palace in suitably upholstered bed-rooms, and now waiting to congratulate husband and father ! . . .

Thus then, for a while, things went so well with me under the shadow of the Anglican and Assyrian Churches, that one day Arthur Benson told me he thought I had won his father's heart at last ! Alas, if so I did not keep my winnings much longer than Mr. Jack Tennant kept his, for as time went on he reverted with increased emphasis to his first instinct of strong antipathy. Eventually I got so terribly on his nerves that it was found expedient to smuggle me into Lambeth by back entrances and hastily herd me into side rooms; in short the scenes of the memorable sojourn in Venice with Frau von Stockhausen were enacted on sacred English soil. It appeared that even the mere sight of me from a window, strolling with Mrs. Benson along ' the Apostolic Succession,' would infallibly wreck whatever work the Archbishop might happen to be engaged on at the moment; and though I was assured that some of the boys' friends were in the same case, and though it is rather flattering in a way to inspire so intense an aversion, the situation was more exciting than agreeable. Yet such was my veneration for Dr. Benson, my intense appreciation for all he said, and wrote, and did as priest, that I bore him no ill-will, and often think, among other sympathetic memories, of a little scene at Addington that touched and impressed me—the Head of the Church sitting at the feet of his guest, Mr. Spurgeon, and humbly soliciting information as to the spiritual needs of the London poor. In short he dwells in my memory as one of the loftiest-souled men I have known.

Mrs. Benson once said it was rather hard that any resentment I might feel on the subject of the Archbishop's really outrageous rudeness seemed cherished against her. This was quite true; if the men of the family are insupportable it is generally the fault of the women for not standing up to them—and *vice versâ* . . . as we so often remarked to each other at home !

In order to round off the story of this phase of intense belief—belief in the strictest sense of the word—I ought to say that during this and the ensuing year, in short for some time after these Memoirs close, I was composing a Mass, which was eventually produced in London in 1893. Into that work I tried to put all there was in my heart, but no sooner was it finished than, strange to say, orthodox belief fell away from me, never to return; and ridiculous as it seems, the fact that Thomas à Kempis would have condemned Shakespeare's Sonnets had a great deal to do with it. True, I remembered wise Lady Trevelyan once commenting on the ease with which one brushes aside exaggerations of specialists (such as abound in this book written by a monk for monks) and asking who would take literally the command to hate your father and mother for Christ's sake? Nevertheless I held, and still hold, that it is impossible to reconcile the teaching of the ' Imitation ' with many of the circumstances of an artist's life . . .or with many of the movements of his soul. Further, it is not given to everyone to accept dogma, and I for one had evidently not the gift. H. B., the most deeply religious spirit and the most inveterate enemy of creeds I ever met, used to infuriate me in after life by attributing this particular development to influenza; but if that be the explanation what matter? Who shall fathom the Divine plan? Only this will I say, that at no period of my life have I had the feeling of being saner, wiser, nearer truth. Never has this phase, as compared to others that were to succeed it, seemed over-wrought, unnatural, or hysterical; it was simply a religious experience that in my case could not be an abiding one.

.   .   .   .   .   .

One of the drawbacks of writing about a comparatively recent epoch is that you cannot speak freely of the living. To those who love human nature the faults of people you are fond of are as precious as their virtues; but this is delicate ground, and those who do not care about executing fancy portraits had better leave contemporaries alone—a consideration which will explain my reticence as to members of my own dear family, once they had been piloted in these pages out of almost prehistoric days. Again, for other reasons, much cannot be said on a subject that is now in the very forefront of my mind, inasmuch as by this time we had become standard guests in the household of the Empress Eugénie.

What this admission to a world in which French was habitually spoken meant to my mother can be imagined, and as the Empress and some of the household spoke English, it was no bar to my father's gratification when bidden to dine at Farnboro' Hill that he had no French. At that time the Empress wore gorgeously long trains of an evening; perhaps nine feet of heavy black silk trailed behind her as she walked down the corridor to the dining-room; and on one occasion, following in her wake, engaged in affable conversation with the lady on his arm, my father gradually marched up the whole length of that train. Being very short-sighted, and its wearer far too kind to remonstrate, he was quite unconscious of what was happening till she was bent backwards in an arc.

My mother's special ally was Madame le Breton, Dame d'Honneur, formerly the Empress's 'Lectrice,' a witty, fiery Greek whose legendary beauty was still eloquent though at that time she was over seventy. In spite of the chastening influence of Court life I never met with a temperament of greater violence, and in later years she used to say to me regretfully : ' Ah ! comme vous me plaisiez mieux dans le temps où vous disiez tout ce qui vous passait par la tête—à tors et à travers ! ' . . . Having lived only twenty years in England she knew not a single word of English, and as my father greatly desired to be civil to this good friend of my mother's, especially as she was General Bourbaki's sister, the intercourse between them was remarkable to watch. Many years older than the Empress, she was nearly stone blind and walked with a stick, and on their travels together sympathetic journalists were often led astray. References to the 'bowed and infirm Sovereign' rather amused the Empress, who in 1890 was straight as a dart, equal to a ten-mile walk, and has always looked at least twenty years younger than her age; but driven home in the right quarter by her secretary, M. Pietri, who was fond of teasing, they greatly irritated his venerable colleague, whose passionate vitality resented the imputation of age and infirmity.

I remember when I was well over thirty incautiously remarking that some view I had just expressed would probably not commend itself to a woman of her years, and the retort was : ' Et vous, ma chère, *malgré votre extrême jeunesse* vous savez très bien que ce que vous dites là sont des bêtises.' No cne had less patience with 'bêtises' than Madame le Breton. At one time there was a monk at the Farnboro' Priory whose ineptitudes in the pulpit got on her nerves to such an extent that she implored the ever-tolerant Empress to suggest he had better not be allowed to preach. One Sunday I persuaded a clergyman-cousin of mine, one of the J. clan, to attend afternoon service at the Mausoleum Church, and during the sermon the monk's remark, ' La Sainte Vierge a toujours aimé Paris,' was followed by such a crash from the Farnboro' Hill pew that everyone jumped; it was Madame le Breton who in her fury had aimed a violent kick at the wooden partition. We all know that because our serious-minded Victorian Court, which Parisians would not have put up with for a month, had not been faithfully reproduced across the Channel, certain foolish people charged the Imperial *régime* with going too far in the other direction. Hence my cousin demurred to this account of B.V.'s preferences and muttered in his beard : ' I don't think she can have liked Paris much during the Empire.'

As for M. Pietri, the subtlest, wittiest, hottest-tempered, and kindliest of typical Corsicans, whose existence was one burning flame of chivalrous devotion to his Sovereign Lady, when he died everyone who knew him felt not only grief at her irreparable loss but a sense of personal impoverishment. He was one of those pure golden people who nevertheless see things as they are, and, to me at least, his opinion on almost any subject was of value. I remember once expressing surprise that a certain exceptionally kind-hearted woman we knew so often failed in kindliness of judgment when to take the other line demanded some moral courage, and Pietri replied : ' Être foncièrement bonne et avoir du caractère, voilà deux choses différentes.' I daresay it was a truism, but it struck me a good deal and has often modified the severity of subsequent appreciations. There are two incidents trembling on the point of my pen, after relating which one might confidently add : ' Such was Pietri, such is the Empress ! '—so characteristic and exquisite an impression do they give of both. Alas ! both these stories have to be rejected as possibly too intimate. . . .

In the years immediately following the date at which these Memoirs close I was to owe to the Empress, one way and another, the demolishment of some of the barriers that block an unknown artist's road into the open, not to speak of the blessed certainty of contact, almost at my own doors, with an original and remarkable mind. I still enjoy that privilege, and the discretion observed as regards the living is more than ever incumbent in this instance. But one point which is of psychological interest may perhaps be mentioned without offence.

During all these years, strongly as she is attracted by beauty in others, I have never heard the Empress refer to the loveliness that once turned the head of the world. . . . Yet maybe some obscure reaction of this supreme record accounts for her impatience, not to say exasperation, if physical charms are spoken of in connection with the old. I quoted elsewhere something the Duchesse de Mouchy once said about time revealing the essentials of beauty, and can well imagine what the comment would have been had the Empress overheard that remark !

But if it was true of her in the sense intended in 1883, there is another sense in which it is true to-day. The lines of a character nobly planned, qualities such as courage, chivalry, sincerity, magnanimity to others, pitilessness to self, and above all unutterable and unwearying kindness to,

and thought for, all—these are essentials that may well become more manifest with years; especially if the mind and
sympathies have been kept young by an amazing interest in
life itself, whether as regards politics, the march of science,
or the birth of new ideas. . . . The Empress is no longer a
reigning Sovereign, none has an interest in laying exaggerated tributes at her feet; for this reason there is some point
in adding that every soul who has the privilege of really
knowing her would agree, reading the above words, that
they represent less than the truth.   But to say more here
would not be seemly.

Yet there is one drawback to this particular frequentation;
history is found to have lost part of its interest, in that your
faith in ‘ the Legend ’ has departed for good.   To mention
one detail only; if the word ‘ frivolous ’ has been applied to
the most fundamentally serious spirit you have known—and
time cannot alter the main lines of character—what of other
historical reputations? . . .

But one point can hardly escape the notice of posterity.
Nearly half a century has elapsed since the fall of the Second
Empire, and in all these years—betrayed, falsely accused,
vilified—the Empress has attacked no one, nor uttered one
single word in her own defence.   It was perhaps with this
and other facts in his mind that Lord Rosebery wrote in the
copy he sent her of his ‘ Napoleon : the last Phase,’ a dedication so beautiful that I pencilled it into my own copy :

‘ To the surviving Sovereign of Napoleon’s dynasty
The Empress,
who has lived on the summits of splendour, sorrow,
and catastrophe
with supreme dignity and courage.’

CHAPTER XLIV

Autumn 1890 to January 1891

LATE in the last autumn that will be re-lived in these pages I went down to stay with the Trevelyans at Nettlecombe, and much upset the aged local clergyman by urging him to hold Early Celebrations daily in the Parish Church. Perhaps it is because I was so peacefully happy there that I remember little about that one and only visit to the home so soon lost to my friends—for dear Sir Alfred died in the following year. But one typical instance of his commonsense and dislike of exaggeration I well recollect. A Catholic friend of theirs, of the strenuous aggressive type he had scant sympathy with, was relating in admiration how the Prior of a newly founded monastery obliged his priests to sit on the floor. Sir Alfred snorted; ' I suppose,' he said, ' the next thing will be to make them try and sit on the ceiling.' . . . Of course there were endless discussions on religion with Pauline, discussions invariably started by me, and one night I had such a completely absurd dream on the same lines, that I instantly wrote it down, and eventually copied it on a spare page of my terrible old collection of youthful dramas and poems. I believe the stage of relating dreams is one degree below anecdotage, but this particular one was so characteristic of all the people concerned that I cannot refrain from giving it—especially as its core might well be a genuine hagiological extract.

The entry in the book is thus :

' I, Ethel Smyth, who never improve upon anecdotes at the expense of truth, dreamed the following dream, at the termination of which I rushed into the room of my R.C. friend, Pauline Trevelyan, and related it.

The Dream

' I had successfully persuaded Lady Trevelyan and Pauline to go to a Celebration at a rather High Church. The Altar was beautifully got up, and the Celebrant in white vestments. It distressed me however a good deal that on this particular occasion tea and bread and butter should be handed round before the Service; I feared these R.C.'s would think it irreverent. The priest went up to the Altar, turned round, and said: " ' Now I will tell you an anecdote; when St. Augustine bade St. Patrick goodbye he said : ' The thing that touched me most was, that as I was saying farewell to you I found one of your tears in my eye.' " At this point I observed Lady Trevelyan lean over towards Pauline, evidently casting doubt, rapidly and in an undertone, on the authenticity of the anecdote. The Priest, noticing this, stepped down from the Altar and said : " May I ask if you have any objections to make? "—" O no, Sir," hastily replied the ever-polite Pauline, " no objection—we were only . . ." At this point I broke in with " You must not mind what these ladies say; they are Roman Catholics and unaccustomed to weigh historic evidence. But I have often had the pleasure of proving them to be in the wrong and no doubt shall be able to do it on this occasion." . . . (Here the housemaid entered.)
  ' Frimhurst. Copied into this book Dec. 1890.'

When I got home again I went off a long bicycle ride into the next county, in order, at the request of Nelly (who was coming to us that week), to make discreet enquiries concerning a young lady reported by her parents to be going off her head. The result was baffling ; harmony prevailed, the daughter seemed in high favour, and one could learn nothing; but the expedition was far from fruitless, for on it I made a chance discovery that gave rise to many a moral reflection in the vein of Dr. Watts. In that same county was a Rectory inhabited by what Mrs. Benson, who had known them in her Wellington College days, declared to be the ideal of a stupid family—and I, who had known them slightly for ages myself, considered that if anything she understated the case. Well; I now learned that all day long the women of that household sat together in dead silence, working tapestry so exquisite that some day specimens will doubtless be a cherished feature of the South Kensington Museum—further, that for years and years the mother's spare hours had been devoted to painting the ceiling of the church! . . . On our Cornish tour four years ago we had raved about an old clergyman who had spent his life in similar fashion, and here was the same thing going on un-heeded at our very doors! As a matter of fact I never was inside that house in my life, but why were their neighbours so silent? Why was their fame not bruited abroad? Was it that they were too dull to talk about at all? . . . But there are compensations. One day that family inherited half a million, and the many daughters at once selected and mar-ried an equivalent number of clergymen.

.　　　.　　　.　　　.　　　.　　　.

A day or two after that expedition of mine Maggie Benson wrote to say that Nelly was ill in bed. A few posts later I learned it was diphtheria, and almost immediately came the news that all was over.. . . . I remember walking dazed into my mother's room and saying: ' Nelly is dead.' She put aside her breakfast tray, burst into tears, and held out her arms. . . . Very fond of Nelly, miserable for me, her first words were, ' O poor, poor Mrs. Benson! '

.　　　.　　　.　　　.　　　.　　　.

The damp cold of autumn always told upon her, and though this year she had tried hard to make the best of her ailments—which were increasing fast—and as usual cheered

up between whiles, it was evident that in the depths of her
heart she was very unhappy. The worst thing was the deafness, for though by no means marked, it bred a constant
idea that people were slighting her. What with one's help-
less pity—and the endeavour to combat this illusion (which
mercifully she never entertained with regard to me) life at
home became even a greater strain than in the days of perpetual storm. To manage a proud, morbidly sensitive
nature like hers, to pilot her through a dinner or tea party
without her feeling herself neglected or pained, to do all this
in such a way that she, the cleverest of women, should not
see it—all this told on one's vital force. My father never
noticed these efforts of mine ; merely saw that some visitors
preferred talking to me rather than to her, and resented it
bitterly. Yet I think she understood, for a few months previously she had told Alice she felt more *certain* of my affection for her than that of any of us, except of course Alice ;
but she never fully realised what a grip she had on the hearts
and imaginations of most of her children.

Having suffered such agonising remorse about my mother,
it was the greatest comfort to me only the other day to find
the following passage in one of my letters to H. B., written
just after her death : ' Hardly three weeks ago, Pauline
Trevelyan, who has been much here, and was adorable with
mother, suddenly said to me as we were walking across a
London square : " Ethel, you are good to your mother."
Then I knew that she had seen what others did not see, how
the whole thing was cutting into my flesh, sapping my
strength, making me *have* to be untrue to my music—that
she guessed how all my strongest prayers and endeavours
were about that. . . . And when she said those words it
touched me so frightfully and I was so grateful that I broke
down and wept in the middle of the square ! '

One thing had made a very deep impression on mother,
a visit paid with me in September to Lambeth. The incredible loving kindness, the magic intuition of Mrs. Benson
never struck me more forcibly than on that occasion. Knowing all about my home life she had once said to me : ' If ever

I can do anything tell me,' and I had suggested this visit.
That there could be such a person in the world as Mrs. Benson, caught up in a ceaseless round of activities and yet able
to give to a stranger what she gave that day, was a revelation to mother, and I think the tears she shed on that
November morning were at least as much for another as for
me.   She wrote—she told me she could not help writing—to
Mrs. Benson, and received in reply surely the most wonderful letter ever penned by bereaved mother.   It absolutely
awed her to whom it was addressed, and she kept it close at
hand, reading it again and again; it must have been near
her to the end, and for that reason I have not found it among
her cherished papers.

Soon after Nelly's death Mrs. Benson wrote to me : ' All
is well here; our three sons have been so infinitely beautiful,
and have grasped the further communion of death (which
you speak of) so wonderfully.   " It is expedient for you that
I go away " is a human truth, I verily believe—if there is a
line, which I don't think, between human and divine.   Only
selfishness or dreariness or repining would really separate us.
Maggie is wonderful.   I could break my heart about her, but
loving is better—and God knows, as he does . . . all.'

Later on she told me that the only book she read throughout that time, reading it again and again, was ' The Prison,'
and no tribute that ever reached H. B.'s ears gave him such
intense pleasure.

Going through my mother's last letters to me it struck me
with a pang how uncomplainingly she bore what must inevitably have grieved her during the last months of her life, my
preoccupation with the Trevelyans—although as regards
Pauline she absolutely understood it, being as fond of her as
even I could desire.   I suppose too it is inevitable that growing spirits should look elsewhere than to home for nourishment and that every mother must face the fact; but what
touches me so deeply is realising that this mother, whose
child's gaze was always fixed otherwhere—always, always,
and with such extreme ardour—was facing it at last ! . . .

Meanwhile it was my privilege to give her two more great pleasures. That autumn two other works of mine were performed in London, one being the Overture to Anthony and Cleopatra; and on this occasion my wonderful father again decided to be present. I did not go back with them to Frimhurst, and next day my mother wrote me the sort of letter a mother would write under the circumstances, adding : ' In the train Papa said, '' Well, I thought the music very pretty and listened to it with pleasure '' ' ! Whether she was seriously gratified that this very stormy composition should have produced such a pleasing impression on one who appreciated music mainly as a soporific, or whether the remark amused her as intensely as it did me and was passed on in that spirit, I never learned. Perhaps she guessed that at such moments all tributes, even the most fantastic, are welcome.

It was in the November of this year, soon after Nelly's death, that the first stone was laid at Windsor of my long close friendship with her whose name stands on the dedication leaf of these Memoirs—of whom I have so often thought while writing them, smiling as I imagined to myself the caustic comment that would have been lavished here and there. I had occasionally met Betty and Maggie Ponsonby at the Deanery, and a year or two previously, she being in attendance on one of the Princesses, had even been introduced to their mother at some Sports at Aldershot. A short determined looking figure, the face very striking, the speaking voice and enunciation of an exquisite quality that was to be among other things my enchantment for a quarter of a century. The Empress had said she was considered very ' clever ' at Court, but Lady Ponsonby always maintained that was because she read the leading articles in *The Times*. It appears she had not been attracted by her daughters' description of ' the Contrapuntalist ' as they called me, saying it was bad enough if, like Mary in ' Pride and Prejudice,' people were ' occupied with the study of human nature and thoroughbass,' but Counterpoint *doublé* with Fred Archer (this in allusion to my love of riding) must be still more provoking. On the day I was requested by them to come to Norman Tower she withdrew, therefore, into her sanctuary, the Prisons; but after having been dragged forth by Betty to hear me sing ' Come o'er the Sea ' the ice was broken, and needless to say she instantly exercised the powerful attraction that even those whom she terrified could not resist. But it was not till some months later, thanks to my forcing her against her will (no mean achievement) to read Anatole France's works, that we really made friends.

.   .   .   .   .   .

It is a grief to me that in these pages I can only record the dawn of what was the longest, happiest, and best proven of all my friendships with women, but the only alliance that transcends it is in the same case. In December came the bend in a lane that seemed to promise no turning, and a correspondence, as between two great friends—the only matter that had been under discussion five years previously —now began between H. B. and myself. What once had been impossible now became possible, the striking of what exact hour set me free to leave the Desert for ever. . . these are things that cannot be told here; the explanation roots in a silent section of the past. I will only add that from now onwards our friendship became the pivot of my life—as it is to-day though my friend died ten years ago. All that story falls beyond the term of years set in these Memoirs, but what has already been said will explain why I date from December 1890 the beginning of a new life.

H. B., holder of views unworkable in the social scheme as we know it, writer of books which, though full of passages and pages of strange, incorruptible beauty, can only appeal to the few; H. B., able at a touch to ease even a stranger's burden; . . . H. B., one of the Wise Men of the World! . . . His life, an uneventful one, will never be written, but some day, through what agency I know not, his letters— letters unlike any others—will surely be edited. And I

think, too, that in fulness of time, maybe many, many years
hence, someone will stumble across the mine of his thought
and work it—perhaps make it accessible to the many . . . in
any case bring up rare treasures to the surface. And thus,
like Lâo Tsze, he may endure through the ages by virtue of
a few fragments that contain the essence of all we know or
need to know.[1]

We had a very jolly Christmas that year, the Henschels
to whom my mother was much attached being for the first
time our guests; and my father, whose prejudice against
artists had long since yielded to the irresistible ' good
fellow ' quality of Henschel, instantly took a great fancy to
his wife. By no means addicted to reminiscences as a rule
—and his family were far too engrossed in their own concerns, alas! to draw him out—under genial influence such as
that of our visitors he sometimes launched forth in astonishing fashion, and one evening related an Indian experience
so complete artistically, and of a character so dramatic, that
Lili Henschel begged me to write it out for her, as near
as possible in his own words; which I did, keeping a copy
myself. And I must preface by saying that to draw the long
bow was not among his weaknesses.

' Yes, Mrs. Henschel,' said my father, ' I assure you it
astonishes me sometimes to think what a lot of scamps I
have had to do with in my time. For instance there was a
fellow called Pattle whom I knew very well when I was on
the Governor-General's staff—Jim Pattle . . . as big a
scamp as ever you saw, and a bad fellow in every way.
Behaved very ill to his wife too, but she was devoted to him,
and when . . . well, when anything went wrong, he used to

---

[1] Henry Brewster's published works are : *Theories of Anarchy and
Law; The Prison; The Statuette and the Background* (Williams and
Norgate); *L'Ame Païenne* (Mercure de France); *Les Naufrageurs;
Drame en vers* (Perrin et Cie.).

say that it *couldn't be helped now,* and she was quite satisfied and forgave him again and again. Well, at last he drank himself to death, and they found to their astonishment he had left directions that he should be embalmed, and buried next his old mother in the family vault at Marylebone Church. Some of us were a good deal amused at this, but his widow said that it must be done, so they put him in a cask ready to be shipped off to England, and she insisted on having it placed in a spare room next her bedroom till the vessel was ready to carry him off. Well, in the middle of the night there was a loud explosion; she rushed into the room and found the cask had burst . . . and there was her husband half out of it! The shock sent her off her head then and there, poor thing, and she died raving.'

Thinking this was the end of the story we broke in with ejaculations, but my father lifted his hand and went on; ' All the same his friends thought they'd better carry out his last wishes, so they had him put up again and taken down the Ganges. The sailors hadn't the most distant idea what they'd got on board, and thinking the cask was full of rum, which was the case, they tapped it and got drunk; and, by Jove, the rum ran out and got alight and set the ship on fire! And while they were trying to extinguish the flames she ran on a rock, blew up, and drifted ashore just below Hooghly. And what do you think the sailors said? that Pattle had been such a scamp that the Devil wouldn't let him go out of India!'

This story had of course an immense success; my father leant back in his chair, a gleam of quiet triumph in his eye, and when we had quite done laughing he added: ' The end of it was that a letter came from the rector of Marylebone saying *the Pattles had never had a vault in the Church at all.'*

On another occasion, Christmas Eve it was, we were discussing who should drive, who walk, to Church next day, and Mrs. Henschel in an access of candour remarked to her neighbour: ' I'm going to your Church to-morrow, General, but I think I ought to let you know I am a Unitarian.'

Whereupon, bending forward with the geniality that was so characteristic of him, my father replied in a burst of confidence : ' Well, Mrs. Henschel, I've often said, and I daresay they are all tired of hearing me say it, that some of the best fellows I have known in my long life were Mahomedans.' And why everybody laughed, more particularly the lady to whom the remark was addressed, he was far too simple to understand.

I have said elsewhere that in later years, whether she liked them or no, resident visitors were seldom a success with my mother, the chief reason being that, owing to that fatal deafness, general conversation escaped her ; and as there was always plenty of it across our dinner table the attention of the guest engaged in a *tête-à-tête* with her would sometimes wander ; or perhaps after dinner he would join the younger group with too much eagerness. In short she felt out of it, neglected—as she often put it, a cypher in her own house. Thus all elderly mothers who have not learned certain lessons are likely to feel as the years roll by. On this particular occasion, however, I was thunderstruck at the way she pulled herself together, at her evident determination not to be a kill-joy, and in writing to Mrs. Benson about it attributed this wonderful change to the obscure working of her influence. But nothing is more common than reaction after a great moral effort, and it was on the following New Year's Day that she suddenly announced, as related elsewhere, that she could not go on living at Frimhurst.

This strange symptom of deep inward distress greatly upset my father ; indeed for some time past, though he said little, we knew he was as profoundly troubled about her future as we all were. Presently, though the London idea was given up, she got quite cheerful again, and one day in the first week of January after going to an afternoon party, she told us, evidently much pleased, that someone had complimented her on looking so well and young. (She was sixty-six, but at times one would not have guessed it.) I have said she had always suffered from an internal weakness; that night she was suddenly seized with what proved to be her last illness and died on January 12, 1891.

Almost all I could bear to say about her end has already been said, but one personal experience connected with her last moment on earth I must add. She had been operated on on the Sunday and on the Monday was going on well, but the surgeon had warned us there was cause for great anxiety. Towards 5 o'clock she became terribly restless, and though she presently quieted down and declared she could now get some sleep, we did not like her looks and it was decided to fetch the doctor. The coachman was ill in bed; someone helped me to put one of our irresponsible horses into the two-wheeled cart, and I set forth alone on the five-mile drive to Blackwater. It was a bitter star-lit night, the road was in places a sheet of ice, the horse not roughed, and the anguish of being unable to push along fast almost unbearable. . . . Suddenly a faint flash of light shot across the sky and I said to myself : ' She is dead.' As far as could be calculated it must have been about that moment that her soul passed. . . .

During my youth I had a mania for illuminating texts, and one of these, done specially for her, had been pinned by mother over her bed years and years ago. Once she told me I would hardly believe how often the sight of those words, ' Let not your heart be troubled,' had helped her. Just before the coffin was nailed down I laid the poor gaudy old scroll across her breast.

After the funeral I told Alice about her wonderful good temper and self-control during Christmas week. From my reports and her own observation she had known that during the whole of the past year there had been a continuous moral effort, which, in spite of occasional relapses, had completely changed the aspect of home life ; and we agreed it was as though, having at last really tried to accomplish it, she had been released from a task that was perhaps beyond her strength. For my own part I confess that a deep sense of relief was mingled with my sorrow. And I know it was the same with my father at the bottom of his heart . . . just because he loved her so dearly.

Meditating the events that ended in that nightmare return of mine to England at the close of 1889, I count it is the greatest mercy ever vouchsafed me that we thus were together during the last year of her life. And when I summon up the vision of her seated at her writing-table, eagerly cutting out all the favourable criticisms she could collect of those unripe productions of mine to send to Bob in India, it is good to know she believed, without shadow of doubt, that her faith, or rather her unfailing, most loving sympathy and support, had been justified by the event.

CHAPTER XLV.

Epilogue

I HAVE now reached Chapter the Last and have only to gather up a few threads concerning those who have figured prominently in my story, beginning with my father.

After my mother's death, perceiving ever more clearly the uniqueness of his personality, my admiration for him increased. Even the fact of not enjoying his unreserved approval was scarcely a subject for regret; one would have hated to see his character and instincts weakening. There was a moment when I feared this was happening, namely when we were allowed to play golf on the home course on Sunday, though lawn tennis had always been forbidden! Later on I came across Dr. Johnson's remark, that ' relaxation ' is permissible on Sunday but not ' levity '; ' people may walk,' he says, ' but not throw stones at birds.' This cleared the matter up satisfactorily. We had plenty of subjects in common, and as a kindlier and less exacting companion could not have been imagined we got on excellently, and I had looked forward to our living together at Frimhurst for many years; but he died in 1894.

Those who believe in ' judgments ' in the nursery sense of the word, might almost think a certain childish folly had been scored up against me, for of the five friends of my youth whose lives were most closely linked to mine—Lisl, Lili Wach, Rhoda, Nellie Benson, and Pauline—two died young, and two on the very threshold of middle life—

and of these deaths three were sudden! Even the last to go, Lili Wach, did not live to be an old woman.

Late in 1891 Pauline Trevelyan married a distant cousin of hers, Gilbert Heathcote of the Cameronians. After their marriage they followed the drum, and as I was much abroad and my life very strenuous, Pauline and I did not meet as often as formerly. In 1897, hearing she was ill and that they had taken a house in London so as to be near competent doctors, I went to see her and understood at a glance, though she was perfectly cheerful and full of plans for the future, that there was no hope. A country practitioner had mistaken certain symptoms, galloping consumption set in, and three weeks later she died peacefully. As I said it was always evident that she was not to be lent to this world for long.

To pass to my German friends; two of these died in the same year as my mother, Consul Limburger and beloved Frau Livia Frege—the latter after a painful illness borne with heroic fortitude and patience. Like my mother she was her best, and more than her best, self at the last.

Of Lili Wach I saw much in after life on various scattered occasions, but what would have been an enchanting surprise meeting was missed by a hair's breadth. After my mother's death I was much run down and Mary carried me off on a trip to Algiers (where I had another severe illness). This was followed by a dream-like tour along the East coast of the Adriatic in the Empress Eugénie's yacht, but unfortunately both these experiences lie beyond the limit I have set myself. On the way home *viâ* Italy we found ourselves as chance would have it at Interlaken, and knowing what such an event would mean for my old friends, apart from the delight of seeing them again myself, I persuaded H.M. to drive up to the Ried. Alas! the family were not expected till the following week, and while I was deliriously shaking hands with the old peasant-in-charge and his daughters, the big dog, reassured as to my respectability, advanced with stiff tail and low growls on the Empress and

Count Primoli. The excitement of the family when they heard of this visit, their pride and joy at H.M. having betrodden their meadows, their despair at not having been there to do her honour . . all these things can be read in two letters from Lili.[1]

But another meeting of ours was a great success. In 1892 she came to England and I had the delight of showing her Lambeth and introducing her to Mrs. Benson, whom she had loved and venerated from afar for many years, knowing what a friend she had been to me. The presence of the daughter of Mendelssohn . . . composer of ' The Elijah,' cast a vicarious glamour on Lili's unsympathetic friends, and the Archbishop, who was adorable with her, was more than gracious to me . . . so much so that Mrs. Benson and I agreed we had better leave it at that and not risk further experiments. The last time I saw Lili was in 1906, when I went to Leipzig for the first production of ' The Wreckers,' and not long afterwards, never even having heard she was ill, they wrote to tell me she was dead. . . . Such are the penalties of striking roots in far-off countries.

Wach I met again in comparatively recent years—1911 I think it was—at a concert in London, on which occasion, called to the platform after the performance of some Chamber work of mine, I nearly fell into the stalls with surprise at seeing him and two of the girls sitting in the front row. He had suddenly dashed over to London for some Juristical Conference, and seeing my name on a poster, like true Germans they all went to the concert. We had a glorious meeting in the tearoom afterwards, and they were amazed to hear my quiet, exceedingly feminine-looking companion was the redoubtable Mrs. Pankhurst. Needless to say this chance of hurling together new and old friends was taken, and a thrilling conversation, carried on in French, ensued between Wach and Mrs. Pankhurst, in the course of which he told her that he had attended a sitting of the House of

[1] *See* ii. p. 289, No. 2 ; p. 290, No. 3.

Early in January 1892 came further news. My old enemy, having done as much mischief as could reasonably be expected of one individual in a lifetime, had really quitted the earthly scene at last; but before I had even answered the letter[1] which gave me these glad tidings, a telegram was put into my hand. The sender may have fancied that I had heard from others what she herself had shrunk from telling me; but doctors are fallible, and no one had cared to speak. Thus it came that without the faintest preparation, without even knowing that she was in other than perfect health, I read the words : ' Lisl is dead—Lili.'

The letter[2] that followed this telegram, haunted, so it seems to me, by Lisl's ghost, conveys some idea of the irresistible appeal there was about her, since even one who judged her could mourn her in this fashion. I learned later that an old Leipzig friend of theirs, Helene Hauptmann, who had nursed her through her last illness, was going to live with and keep house for poor Herzogenberg ; then the curtain fell, and life went on as before. . . .

And now I realised that, apart from my work, what I had chiefly been living for all these years was to see my lost friend again. There is a sensation of bleeding to death inwardly that has ever since been associated in my mind with no other form of sorrow, however bitter, but only with the flickering out of a secret and passionately cherished hope. . . .

> ' . . . the night at length when thou,
> O prayer found vain, didst fall from out my prayers.'

Later on came the packet of my own letters; this part of our friendship, then, she had not had the heart to destroy . . . Mercifully I was in the midst of pressing work just then, borne along by something outside myself—as a mother might be by the needs of one of her children. . . .

. . . . . .

[1] App. VI., ii. p. 300, No. 6. [2] App. VI., ii. p. 292, No. 5.

The years passed, becoming more and more full. I was pushing difficult enterprises, and in possession of the greatest personal happiness that can fall to the lot of any woman. Then came one day a rumour that Herzogenberg's mysterious illness had returned, though not in acute form. He was still carrying on his work at the Hochschule with unabated zeal, but his limbs were gradually stiffening. I had always loved him and knew he had been fond of me, but as Lisl's life had doubtless been shortened by the troubles our friendship had indirectly begotten, I imagined he might well think of me now with nothing but bitterness. Nevertheless, one spring in the late nineties, some business seeming likely to take me to Berlin, I wrote to Joachim, asking if he thought Herzogenberg would like to see me. If the answer should be ' no ' it would change nothing—if ' yes ' it must surely be that he had comfort for me; and presently I got a message that he would be very glad to see me again. Alas ! the Berlin plan fell through, and soon after I heard that he had thrown up his post, Berlin being considered the worst possible climate for his malady, and gone, with Helene, to live permanently at the house he and Lisl had built for themselves at Heiden on the Lake of Constance. But for his immobility he was said to be well, cheerful, and musically as productive as ever. For a while it was impossible for me to leave England, but the following winter, which I spent in Rome, I wrote to him again, and it was settled I was to go to Heiden on my way back to England. . . . While I was yet in Italy the end came suddenly and peacefully.

I remember feeling this was the appointed consummation of an incomprehensible story ; apparently I was to go to my grave without the solace, as far as Lisl was concerned, of that strange commerce with the dead that plays so great a part in the lives of some people. Every deepening of life brought, in certain hours, increased nearness with some of these, above all with my mother . . . but between Lisl and me a gulf was fixed that nothing could span. Often and often in the twenty-four years that lay between her death and the outbreak of the War, I have been at or near St.

Remo, where she lies under cypress trees, and have sometimes wished my feet would take me to that spot . . . but it
seemed impossible. Again at Vienna, in 1914, turning over
some photographs of modern sculpture, I suddenly came
upon something that I laid aside quickly without examining
it; it was the portrait-medallion Hildebrand had carved for
the headstone of her grave. . . . Thus I thought to feel
about her and all that concerns her to the end of my life.

.   .   .   .

And now comes what is for me the strangest part of our
unusual history. Opening that locked door and staring into
the darkness behind it, little by little I have come to see
light, and as final word of my story can say what I never
thought to say in this world—that her death has lost its
sting for me . . . at last I understand.

This is how I see our story now. Commanded by her
mother to choose between us, I cannot doubt that, under the
psychological necessity I spoke of, she at first threw me
overboard not only actually but in a certain sense morally.
In one of her early letters is a confession that now seems
pregnant : ' I fear I rather lose the feeling of people when
they are far away.' Perhaps this helped her to let go of me.
Though I do not believe the faithless mood lasted long, it
lasted long enough, combined with the frenzied activities of
her relations and friends, to precipitate for the time being
the catastrophe they all wished to avoid. And though the
deadlock between the Brewsters soon came to an end, it was
then too late to deflect from the line taken.

Perhaps she had no wish to deflect; ' Action must be
simple,' she once said, ' in order to be intelligible '; but
supposing it were otherwise, and that she had determined to
convey to me some indirect assurance of unchanged faith
and affection, her great integrity would have forced her to
make confession to those whose will was her law. And if
the terrible scenes which would have followed were more
than she could face, it is not for people the valves of whose

hearts are sound to judge her harshly.—Alas! in those days I knew nothing about heart disease and had always found her dread of conflicts rather absurd. . . .

I am not trying to force the case in her favour. The instinct to belittle someone you have loved, in order to find strength to uproot that person from your life, is a mean cowardly instinct it is impossible to defend. On the other hand, given Austrian family traditions, it was as natural to her to divest herself of all responsibility towards me at their command, as it seemed—and still seems—monstrous to me. And once she saw her duty, consequences were not her business; the city, given over to fire and brimstone, must perish —the divine command was . . . not to look back.

But where I did her grievous injustice . . . how this was borne in upon me when, for the first time since youth was left behind me, I re-read her letters! . . . was in believing, that because my unassuageable grief wrung no sign from her, our parting caused her little or no pain.

It would be impossible to reproduce those letters as they stand. Even in the original German—a language better fitted than any I know to convey multiple shades of emotion without falling into sentimentality—one could neither lay bare nor inflict upon others this tenderness lavished on one whom she looked on as her own child, this constant, touching dread lest essentials should be neglected in what seemed to her a fantastic progress through an eternal transformation scene. But one thing is certain; all this is not mere froth and foam on a picturesque but shallow stream. A deep nature is involved.

It certainly was not an easy one to read. For instance, among her gifts was a rare intellectual imaginativeness, traces of which can be found in my poor translations of her letters—witness that phrase about the Brahms theme which reminded her of a giant holding his breath for fear of waking a sleeping child. Yet imagination of the heart she had none; and as, excepting her unsatisfied mother-instinct, she had never known sorrow, many things were hidden from her. In reality it was a stiff nature undeveloped by life, though

bafflingly suppled and disguised on the surface by a volup-
tuous ease of moods and rhetoric—a combination which
accounted for the abrupt, cruel transition from mid-summer
to winter.   When all was well between us it was natural to
her to give an almost bewilderingly rich, tender form to
affection; but the rock below, the possibility of seeing in one
thing—and one only—her duty, the consequent ruthless sacrifice of all the rest, in a word the nameless something that
chilled her music for me . . . this was equally Lisl.   The
one element that fuses all other elements was denied her,
and perhaps only passionate temperaments can stand erect
in elemental storms.   When Conrad Fiedler said she was
deficient in depth of feeling, possibly this is what he meant,
but I think with these letters before him he would have put
it differently.

I think, too, Lili Wach was right in saying, as she once
did, that Lisl's was a too ' simple ' affection, a mere matter
of personal inclination, lacking the subtle, tenacious web of
moral issues that is woven unconsciously into all perfect
human bonds.   But Lili never wearied in trying to persuade
me that, be that as it might, she suffered cruelly.   And it
was *I* who refused to believe this, I who alone among all her
friends knew of her ever-recurring grief at her childlessness,
who admired her effort to accept the inevitable cheerfully
and hide her pain in the depths of her heart !   In one of her
letters [1] she once spoke of this attitude towards harsh necessity as part of human dignity; if such was her instinct where
no loyalty to others was involved, how much more in this
case? . . . It is hard for people who are apt to translate
feeling into action to admit any other test of sincerity;
but . . . there are other tests, and to-day it is I who am
crying into the void : ' Credo, credo in te ! ' . . .

One more thing became clear to me as I re-travelled our
road.   It looks as if those at whose demand she cancelled
her past accepted the sacrifice with something very like indifference—perhaps, who knows? with a touch of a still

[1] Appendix III., ii. p. 23, No 5.

colder feeling. From a letter written after her death by H. B.[1] it is evident that the devoted couple were Julia and her mother, Lisl being relatively of little account . . . if so what pain for her! In this light one phrase in her final letter to me acquires a pathetic significance : ' Heinrich, the only being I possess in this world ! ' . . .

Meanwhile neither she nor her doctors saw any reason why she should not live to be an old woman. We were both young, and some day, in the natural course of things, the blind, passionate will that stood between us would disappear. And so she made no plans, but lived, as was her wont, in the present, till the day death fell upon her unawares.

Such I believe is the explanation of what has been for the greater part of my life a tragic inexplicable mystery. And as I lay down my pen it is stranger than any dream to find that the ice-bound years have melted, that there is still a debt to be paid—a debt which, across the faint line that divides the living from the dead, I can go on paying to the end.

October, 1918.

[1] Appendix, ii. p. 302.

APPENDIX VI

(THE LAST)

(a)

FROM TSCHAÏKOWSKY

London : April 11, 1889.

Chère, bonne, et très respectée Miss Smyth,—Je voudrais bien profiter de votre si aimable invitation, mais, chère Mademoiselle, je pars demain Vendredi à 8h. 20m., et il m'est tout à fait impossible de venir vous trouver chez vous. Espérons que j'aurai plus de chance la fois prochaine quand je viendrai à Londres. Quoique, à vrai dire, je doute fort que je reviendrai, vu qu'il n'y a pas moyen de faire bien les choses quand on n'a que deux répétitions, et quand le chef d'orchestre a à peine le temps de faire son devoir pour les autres morceaux du programme ! . . . Enfin, espérons que je reviendrai, et alors mon plus cher vœu sera celui d'aller vous trouver chez vous. Je pars demain pour Marseilles, où je prends le bateau à vapeur qui va directement au Caucase ; ce sera une traversée de 15 jours ! !

Il y a un mois j'ai vu M. Brodsky et sa chère femme, et cela va sans dire nous avons beaucoup parlé de vous. A Homburg j'ai passé une journée entière avec *votre Idole* . . . JOHANNES BRAHMS ! ! ! Il a été charmant pour moi. C'est un homme bien sympathique, quoique mon appréciation de son talent ne corresponde pas à la vôtre. . . .

Au revoir, chère Mademoiselle ; j'espère que vous avez composé de bien belles choses, et je vous souhaite tout espèce de prospérité.

P. TSCHAÏKOWSKY.

J'espère que votre *cher chien* va bien ! !

(b)

FROM MY MOTHER

(I)

[During the Paris Exhibition]

Frimhurst : October 15, 1889.

My darling,—What a dear you were to make time to send me those cards and almost a letter, in the midst of all that going and doing in Paris, and it is too sweet and dear of you to devote part of that rarity, a presented fiver, to get me ' a little something.' I only hope it will be a very *little* something; however, big or little, I shall receive it with unmixed pleasure, for I do love a remembrance from one I love, and am afraid with me it is even more blessed to receive than to give a ' little nonsense ' of the sort I hope yours is to me. I only trust Nina has not lost it on the way. . . .

The letting of this land is at a standstill, as Walter B. came to look at it without telling us and went round the place with *Allen,* who is in dire terror of losing his comfortable berth with coals, milk, eggs, chickens, rabbits, and vegetables for his family, and who of course gave the worst account of all the produce! However I am going to see Mrs. B. to-day and will report progress. Herbert too is going over the place and we'll see what *he* says. . . . He seems to have loved the trip to Paris; no one knows what I would have given to be with you! . . .

I went up yesterday to the oculist and lunched with E. There I met that odious W. S., whose one good point in my eyes is having married me to Papa! How I miss you and Marco no words can say. God bless you my own darling Phœnix.

Your ever devoted Mother and Admirer,

NINA SMYTH.

P.S.—I looked in for a moment at St. James's Hall; how well that Borwick bangs about!

(2)

[Written to Nettlecombe]

Autumn, 1890.

My darling,—I must send you a return line to tell you I don't know which delighted me more, your interesting letter, or to hear you are really coming back on the 6th. I have so wanted you for the last few weeks but have never said anything about it as I did not like to interfere with your work or your pleasures. But I am better now since that dear child Nina has taken L. and the fascinating B. off my hands! I was afraid they were bored and tormented myself so that I really couldn't sleep at night. And then a disappointment with the cook, etc., etc.—stupid things to make one actually ill, but I suppose I am become nervous, and a nuisance to myself and everyone else in consequence. . . .

How kind of dear Lady Trevelyan! and how I should enjoy all the delights of art and nature at Nettlecombe . . . but I am only fit for home. Give her my kindest regards and very warm thanks for proposing it.

Your devoted, truly loving
MOTHER.

(c)

FROM SIR ARTHUR SULLIVAN

(1)

Grove House, Weybridge: June 14, 1890.

Dear Miss Smyth,—*Me voilà.* In the same house I occupied last year. Not very far from you, only two stations. When you want some tea come and have it with me; I generally strike work about 5. Had I not been ill and in pain on that eventful Saturday [1] I should have been a gratified witness of your success. I had made all arrangements to go but I had a combined attack that day, my old physical trouble and . . . Gilbert! Nevertheless I was really pleased to read such nice things about the work of the *gracieuse jeune fille,* and I hope that you are beginning a brilliant and dignified musical career.

Ever yours sincerely,
ARTHUR SULLIVAN.

[1] The performance of my Serenade at the Crystal Palace.

(2)

Etablissement Contrexéville : Aug. 10, 1891.

Dear Miss Smyth,—In answer to your questions :
(1) I am not in London, and consequently
(2) You cannot find me any morning.
But if you pack up a small portmanteau at once and jump
into the next train leaving for Paris you will be here 21 hours
afterwards, and I need not tell you how really delighted I
shall be to see you.   There is a constant delirious whirl of
dullness here, the counterpart of which is only to be found
in England at a Young Men's Christian Association Weekly
Evening Recreation.   I am up at 6, am *massé'd* and
douched, and drink 6 pints of the mineral water, walking
all the time until breakfast at 10.   Nothing more to eat or
drink till 6 when we dine—then to bed at 10, to resume the
same existence at 6 next morning.   I need scarcely tell you
that the two meals are the two great events of the day. . . .
I still want a house in your neighbourhood and am likely to
want it, as I shall never get one to satisfy me.   I want one
unfurnished, so that I máy always have it to myself, to live
there when I like.   What has become of you that you have
never given me a sign of life for so long?   Absorbed in some
great work I suppose.   May an old man's blessing rest on
you.

Yours sincerely,
ARTHUR SULLIVAN.

(3)

[*Note.*—*I had told Sir Arthur of a friend of ours who had
five daughters and wanted to let his house, Fernhill near
Camberley.*]

Contrexéville : Aug. 16, 1891.

Dear Miss Smythe (oh that accursed ' e ' will slip in !)—
Your parable of ' a certain man had five daughters ' would
do admirably for one of the Three Choirs Festivals ; you
might do it.   I can't because it begins like ' The Prodigal
Son.'

Fernhill I believe to be the very house I have always longed for. It is near Minley, isn't it, and standing on a hill facing towards Cove? Oh dear how odd it would be if I went to live there—having longed for that house ever since I was a ' little human boy.' Can you and will you find out some particulars for me, such as rent, or price (if to buy), size of house, number of rooms, garden and extent of grounds etc.? Do, there's a dear (young lady I must add for *les convenances*) and write to me addressed to Queen's Mansions—only put ' private to be forwarded.' I will come down and see you and the house directly I return to England. . . .

Everyone seems to get well here but myself—it is most ' aggravating ' with as many ' g's ' as you like.[1] If you see the Empress will you convey to her my most respectful devotion—will you also let me say in all earnestness how grieved I was to learn (from your letter) of the loss you suffered in January. It was the first I heard of it. I lost my own dear mother not so very long ago, and therefore it is needless to say how very deeply I feel for you.

Ever yours sincerely,
ARTHUR SULLIVAN.

(4)

Contrexéville, Thursday Night : Aug. 20, 1891.

Dear Miss Smyth,—You are an angel, and what a house agent you would make ! I can't conceive a house ever remaining unlet if placed in your hands to describe.

My mouth waters at your description of Fernhill. It is just what I want and if I were in England I would come down by the next train to see it, but alas ! I am here and although I am leaving at 8.50 to-morrow morning I am not coming home yet, as I want to get a fortnight's mountain air first. I am alarmed at the prospect of someone stepping in before me. Do you think you could induce Mr. Burnett to delay any negotiations with others until my return? It would not make very much difference to him and it *might* (I say it *might*) be of great consequence to me. Use your

---

[1] This was a word I never could spell.

most diplomatic power, charm him with your manner and your music. I should at all events like to look at the place before others bar the way. If you write to me on Saturday (how coolly I presume on your good nature!) address to me

Hôtel de l'Europe,

Aix les Bains,

after that to Queen's Mansions (to be forwarded) as my movements are uncertain—Good-night.

Ever yours sincerely,

ARTHUR SULLIVAN.

P.S.—Having written this on Thursday so as to catch the post out, I put it carefully away in my pocket to take to the post and have kept it carefully in my pocket ever since. It is now hardly necessary to ask you *not* to write to me yesterday. It is pouring in that dismal hopeless fashion that is peculiar to Alpine or other mountain valleys. Please address to Queen's Mansions if you write.

I said *five* daughters, not fine.

(5)

1 Queen's Mansions : September 27, 1891.

Dear Miss Smyth,—No—I do not misunderstand you nor think you spoke foolishly. If you do not appreciate what you have done well and know that it is good, you cannot properly criticise your weak points. You must give me a few days before I look carefully at your Mass as I am going out of town on Tuesday till Friday.

I am at a standstill about Fernhill. I do not know Mr. Randall, his name, address, nor anything that is his. And I don't like to ask Mr. Burnett to assist me in turning himself out of his house. I am also shy of writing to Mrs. Hippisley, who although she is your sister, may not regard me with the same lenient indulgence. I must wait till you come back, unless *you* would ask Mrs. Hippisley to go and beard the Randall in his den. This is my 23rd letter; my secretary (Smythe with an ' e ') is away so I will finish.

Ever yours sincerely,
ARTHUR SULLIVAN.

(6)

[*Note.—This letter, written to me while I was staying at Cap Martin, is of later years, but I include it because of the reference to Fernhill, which by that time he had forgotten the name of!*]

1 Queen's Mansions : May 1, 1895.

My dear Ethel,—Surely Ethel must mean in old Saxon ' faithless.' I must look it up in Skeat. It was a grave disappointment to me not to see you last week for (I cannot explain why) I had a great longing to see you again—the longing one has to revisit a place where one has been very happy as a child. Although I am old enough to be your father you are connected in my mind with my childhood's days. I suppose it is because we visited all my old haunts together—Frimley, York Town, even Cove ! I wish I could have had that place we lunched at together; I forget the name of the house and its possessor but it was such a nice, comfortable house and had such a splendid view. The only drawback was the nunnery or monastery at the gates.

Well, as Dick Swiveller would say, ' I never loved a dear gazelle but what it was sure to spend the Spring at Cap Martin.' Let me know when you return and I will come over from my château at Walton to One Oak and see you— and your score. In the meantime believe that I have a true affection for you and the keenest interest in your work. Please give my humble duty to Her Majesty to whom I am devoted,

Ever yours sincerely,
ARTHUR SULLIVAN.

(d)

FROM FRAU LILI WACH

(*Translations*)

(1)

[*After my Mother's Death*]

Leipzig: February 6, 1891.

Dearest Ethel,—Last night my husband met Frau Consul Limburger at a party and learned the great loss you have sustained, that your beloved mother is dead, and I write at once to tell you how deeply I sympathise with you. I know how you loved and appreciated her, and freely confess that in days when I almost despaired of you, two redeeming features always appealed to me and warmed my heart towards you—the way you held aloft your relation to your mother and . . . your veneration for the Bible! In these two things I see comfort for you now. In spite of your being far from her, in spite of your development in foreign countries —possibly in directions that lay outside her path—you always clung faithfully and warmly to her and what she was to you; and it is good for those who love you to know you have the consolation of thinking how much joy and satisfaction you were able to give her in the last year of her life.

The letter in which you spoke of Mrs. Benson's wonderful resignation when her daughter died, and her close touch with things unseen, gives me confidence that you yourself will not let go the feeling that your path is directed by a guiding hand, hard though the ways have been through which it has led you. Do you remember how I always persisted in taking the sentence engraved in the bangle you gave me as a prophetic utterance for yourself ' there is a friend that sticketh closer than a brother '?—yes—closer even than a mother, and that support will not fail you. Adolf, the children, and Fräulein Jung all send you messages of sympathy, and I am, in faithful love,

Your
LILI.

(2)

[After the Empress Eugénie's visit to the Ried]

Ried : June 21, 1891.

My dearest Ethel,—You cannot imagine how your fairy-tale apparition here in the rôle of *demoiselle d'honneur* to such an interesting historical personage thrilled and amused the whole family; and how the unsuspecting Ulli [1] and his daughters are being cross questioned ! It was dear, faithful, and like you, to take the old road up here in your new incarnation and you would hardly believe how it delighted Adolf. But I think it must have given you pleasure to see once more the quiet spot from which you went forth into the world to meet with such overwhelming adventures. I can see you now, arriving on that first visit to the Ried in a rough frieze dress and a mannish-looking hat, with only one idea in your head . . . Italy ! And now you come back, a much travelled lady, a composer whose works are seeing the light of day, . . . friends—ah ! I wonder how many?—and above all the Friend that never fails. I love to think of you thus—in spite of the Magic Lantern changes of your life with a security which for many years you believed to be unattainable. What happier thought can there be for those who love you?

This was the part of your letter that arrested me most, but husband and children were wholly taken up with the thought that the Empress Eugénie has actually walked our meadows, and alas ! that Leo (isn't he a Marco on a bigger scale?) whose temper has been severely tried, first by a bitter winter and now by a plague of insects, welcomed her with growls ! O that we had been here ! yet how strange it would have been meeting you again in the company of an Empress *incognita* and an Italian cavalier ! Mucki, who has lately been plunged in Napoleonic memoirs, is frantic at having missed H. M. and implores you if possible to beg her autograph for the Visitors' Book, also that of ' the gentleman with the top hat.' When I asked Ulli how you looked, he said : ' as young as nine years ago but still slimmer ! ' (this

---

[1] The peasant in charge at the Ried.

last I put down to a well-cut travelling costume). . . . When you can, write to Frau Livia; it gives her so much pleasure. She was rather depressed last time I saw her, having been ill for some time, but when I read her passages in your letter, those young blue eyes of hers lit up with amusement and warmth. So write to her, and rejoice her heart. . . as you know how to! There is a sad song of ours :

> ' O love as long as you can,
> O love as long as you may,
> There will come a time, there will come a time,
> When weeping you stand by graves ! '

I won't end on this note, but with a special greeting from our baby girl who has an odd passion for your really not flattering bicycle portrait, and is for ever saying ' Mein lieb Mammali, zeig mal Ada Wach (for thus she styles herself) die Ethel im Rosenlaube ' (Dear little Mama! show Ada Wach Ethel in the rose-arbour).

So farewell, my dearest, and remember now and again that no one is fonder of thee than

THY OLD LILI.

(3)

[After Frau Livia Frege's Death]

Ried : October 4, 1891.

Dearest Ethel,—How like human nature that I rushed into the children's room the moment your last letter with the autographs came, and then let two months elapse before writing to thank you for them! How kind it was of you— but you always were dear and good to ' the many children ' who were beside themselves with delight. The precious bit of paper has been stuck into the book, and also, as historical evidence, your letter describing the great event. And on the opposite page, Leo's interview with the Empress—the supreme moment of his life of course—has been sketched by Mirzl! All the children once more send grateful messages, accompanied by a chorus of recollections concerning various scenes in which you and they took part. . . .

Ah! how times change! When we go back to Leipzig on the 20th, what will it be like without Livia Frege? You had heard of course of her long illness, endured with splendid fortitude and the greatest sweetness and patience, and of her end in that gloomy town-house of theirs;—in the summer too, when hardly a friend or acquaintance was there to attend the funeral! . . . It was strange getting this news in a polite communication from her son and daughter-in-law! . . . One of the last times I saw her—she was well then, looking magnificent in her mourning, and so young—she spoke of you with warm affection, and had that characteristic radiant look on her face that you loved so. There was much ardour and charm about her, and a big, noble genuine line such as is rarely met with nowadays . . . ' Und mir war sie mehr ' [1]

Tell me how your Mass is progressing. What you said about Herzogenberg gave me much pleasure; I can imagine that now, when you are beginning to see the fruit of your labours, you must often think of what you owe to his subtle gift for teaching.

Adolf, who sends you his love, has had a wretched summer. He sprained his knee on his very first excursion (the Titlis) and has been lame ever since and plunged in despair —just like you on a similar occasion. Meanwhile my nephew from Carlsruhe came to stay, got typhus fever, and gave it to his mother and cousins—no joke up in the mountains and not an ideal summer holidays for any of us! But when it is over you are conscious of a sort of gratitude for trials overcome that is a sounder feeling than anything you can get out of easy days. Farewell, and think of me when things are well with thee—for that is the great wish of

THY FAITHFUL LILI.

(4)

[*After Consul Limburger's Death*]

Leipzig: Winter, 1891.

. . . What you write about Consul Limburger I well understand. In spite of lack of sympathy between us I was

---

[1] ' And more than all this she was to me '; referring to Livia's friend ship with Mendelssohn.

not blind to the social talent that was so greatly appreciated here; but above all I am sorry for her, for whom on the contrary I have always had sympathy and who as you know has had a good deal of trouble in late years. Since you left Leipzig (strange to say) I was for ever finding myself beside him in the world, and on such occasions always thought of you and what a good friend he had been to you. And that reflection induced a less critical attitude towards his remarks! Many and many a time last winter we sat lovingly side by side at the Tauchnitzes, the Freges, in the Gewandhaus, and elsewhere, and then suddenly I would see a vision of you—a look of surprise and amusement on your face! You can imagine better than anyone how my heart aches at the sight of that shut-up, forlorn old house opposite,[1] all the more since the present generation does not exactly carry on the tradition!

(5)

[After Lisl's Death]

Leipzig : January 23, 1892.

My poor dear Ethel,—How I have kept you waiting for the news you must be longing for! But we ourselves were in the same case; only by degrees have we been able to collect and piece together different impressions of different people so as to arrive even at bare facts. As to what you and I care for most, her state of mind in these latter days, a chance word or reference to the past that might give a clue to such as can read between the lines—on these points it is impossible to gather anything. I only know Fräulein Hauptmann[2] very slightly; the little she wrote to Frau von Holstein and Line Trebst deals only with exterior facts, and one cannot worry the poor husband with letters, touching as were his two to Adolf—so utterly characteristic of his unselfishness, his depth of nature, his courage and bigness of soul. At present, he writes, it is as though he were merely separated from her in some inexplicable way for the time being,

---

[1] Frau Frege's house.
[2] The old Leipzig friend who helped to nurse Lisl during her last illness and after her death went to live with Herzogenberg at Berlin.

but that it would be unworthy of her to let bitterness or despair overwhelm him at the thought of the lonely life which will now be his to the end.

From a letter to Heubner it is evident that he only realised the imminence of death when she was actually dying, and that neither he nor the doctor anticipated such a rapid dissolution. As you knew about the death of Frau von Stockhausen when you wrote, perhaps you may have learned from the same source what a terrible complication and anxiety it was for them having to prepare Lisl gradually for her mother's end. This had of course a bad effect on her condition and as it turned out was unnecessary, for she never learned in this world that her mother was dead.

As for my own impressions, all I can tell you is that I saw her eight months ago, that is in May last year, when, after a long spell of bad health in Berlin, she came here for the second performance of his Requiem in the Thomas Kirche. In some respects I thought her changed, shorter of breath and thinner; her eyes had a tired look and she was inclined to become agitated when there was too much movement round about her. But in between whiles she was as full of life, as young, even as child-like in appearance as in the old Humboldtstrasse days. Thus I found her the morning I took my youngest to see her at old Frau von Holstein's, for she was not allowed to climb our stairs. She was standing in the corner bay-window, looking out; in her hand a comb, and two streams of hair flowing over her dressing jacket. I shall never, never forget the transition from shyness to wondering confidence on the face of the child as he looked up at her, and she looked down, so eagerly and tenderly at him. . . .

That evening in the Church she sat opposite the pulpit with her aunt Frau von Wüllerstorf . . . and Frau X. who needless to say had contrived to tack herself on to them. Unfortunately I was far away, right up near the Altar, but she sent messengers to fetch the three girls in succession, and after it was over, when all the old friends came crowding round, she looked wonderfully well, full of animation and joyous excitement. In fact she protested indignantly when my husband carried her off by force and escorted her back in a cab to Frau von Holstein's, where he made her promise to lie down at once.

I did not see her again till next morning at the station. As ' Tante Léonie ' was with her one felt it would not be advisable to linger and time was short.   Very pale, moving with difficulty (it was a great effort to her getting into the railway carriage) wrapped in a grey dust cloak, a black lace veil over her face—thus it was I saw her last, and parted from her without any sort of presentiment, counting on many future meetings, whether in Switzerland, Berlin, here, or at Nauheim.   She was going to Nauheim almost at once and it appears to have suited her admirably—so at least she wrote me in August, for a long time had elapsed since I had had news of her.   In memory of her subsequent complete recovery at Heiden (where her mother had been with them and feeling particularly well) she had decided to build a little double house there, in order to be together in the summer.

By the time my congratulations on this excellent plan reached her, it had already, so she wrote, become dubious. On her way back to Berlin, as she then thought, she met Mrs. Brewster and the children—whether in Zurich or Geneva I am not certain—travelled thence to Munich where I fancy her mother was, and there became so seriously ill that the doctors urgently advised giving up Berlin and taking her to the South.   It appears there were grave symptoms of kidney disease and Doctor Schmidt did not believe she would ever come back from Italy ; but this I only learned from Hugo, who is studying at Munich and who saw and spoke to her for quite an hour at the Fiedlers on November 9, the day before they left for San Remo.   The boy said he had heard that this was the opinion of the doctors ; but as at the same time he told us how full of life she seemed, how young as to ways and appearance, I didn't believe it.

Then, quite at the end of December, came short bad reports from Helene Hauptmann ; she had been sleeping very badly, had next to no appetite, was very restless, and her feet were swelling.   But in the same letter she added that having had two good nights the patient was wonderfully better, had greatly enjoyed some food prepared by an Austrian cook, and was continually talking with greatest delight about her summer plans in Heiden (it appears she did so on the very morning of her death).   Thus it seemed impossible to believe the worst.   In this letter of December 29, Fräulein Hauptmann begged me in Lisl's name to write out for her the words of my father's song ' Fern und Ferner,' [1] the melody of which was constantly haunting her. I wrote them out at once, answering too a number of little questions on trivial matters, but my heart contracted when I remembered for how long a time there had only been this indirect kind of intercourse between us. ' Can it be as serious as all that? ' one asked oneself—and yet could not realise it.

Throughout all these later years, when for one reason or another our rare meetings always seemed fated either to be cruelly curtailed or postponed, I had hoped, longed for, counted on a Wiedersehen that should be neither interrupted nor cut short,—a real good long talk and mutual explanation. And now here I am, without even a word of farewell—in possession of not one deeper thought of hers—having received no message of affection. . . . Everything I hoped for, for you and myself, has perished miserably in the silence she has taken with her to her grave—a grave under beautiful old cypress trees at San Remo. It is bitter and seems incomprehensible, one of the many tragedies of life against which it is useless to rebel.

I want to know how it is with you, what is preoccupying you chiefly just now? To send you nothing but these few superficial indications cuts me to the heart, but it is all I have for you. I myself am suddenly and utterly bankrupt as regards my fondest hopes and feel very old and lonely. Perhaps I shall see you again in England, where it is not impossible I may be going for ten days or a fortnight in order to be with my sister ; and if so we'll meet somewhere ' for the sake of auld lang syne ' won't we?

Till then God be with thee and bring thee much good.

Thy
LILI.

---

[1] Fern und ferner verhallet der Reigen.
Wohl mir, um mich her ist Schweigen
Auf der Flur :
Dem bangen Herzen nur
Will nicht Ruh' sich neigen . . .

Far and farther . . . the music dies away,
Blessed silence has fallen

On the plain :
Only from my troubled heart
Does quiet hold aloof , , ,

(e)

FROM HENRY BREWSTER (' H. B.')

(1)

[*After my Mother's Death*]

January 14, 1891.

It grieves me not to be able to see you and to think how bereaved you must feel at moments. All I know of her is that she was your mother and loved you. That suffices. It is a cruel wrench at first—and the death bed gives the lie so directly to all our conventions! Perhaps you have never been before at that hour with one dear to you. A little later on—I tell you how it is with me at least—there is something noble in sorrow if one does not spoil it by trying to make it continuous; it is intermittent, and the fresher we are for other feelings, the fresher too for it. . . . I *do* regret not seeing you.

Yours

H.

(2)

January 16, 1891.

. . . Have I ever told you about my father's death? I was with him alone at Versailles, and our house, like all the others, was full of Prussians; 16 officers, 40 soldiers, and 20 horses. My mother and the rest of them had been sent off to England with the jewellery and the moneybag (not so needless a precaution as your German friends would tell you; I saw a good many houses sacked; what is perfectly true is that the soldiers never did it without orders from their officers). Nothing could induce my father to leave his house, so I had to stay with him and take care of him; he was seventy-one, and gouty, and hot-tempered, and he treated the Prussian officers outrageously. My time was spent in explaining ' spread eagle, and the land of the free and the home of the brave ' to them, and soothing their feelings; they were on the point of arresting him time and again.

But all the while I was burning inwardly with a sort of shame-fever at not being able to join my old schoolmates and enlist in the *franc-tireurs*. Often that seemed to me the higher duty; the commonwealth before the family. Then death came and struck my old father down and there was no one but me to hold his hand. That settled my opinion for life : first think of persons and then of ideas if you have leisure; ideas can wait. I don't know why I am telling you this. I wish so I could do something for you. . . .

(3)

January 20, 1891.

. . . I knew there was some trouble about your mother, but did not know it was so bad. I am glad you have told me; when things are mixed up in that way one has to be brutally sincere to have any genuine feeling at all, and one's sorrow is only true if one recognises honestly the relief. They go quite well together ; they don't agree on the stage but they do in life. The sorrow is for the beautiful traits that were there, and the unswerving affection, and for all that one owes, and for the terrible nearness that nothing can obliterate; and the relief is for something alien, hopelessly intertwined with all this, and which may drive us to the verge of despair or of madness. Think of it and you will find that there are harder cases than yours was, or at least more cruelly complicated ones. But I realise what you had to bear and am glad you bore it.

When you have got through your proof-correcting you must take your philosophical autobiography out of the nutshell into which you have packed it so tightly that I don't exactly know how to spread it out correctly. [*N.B.*—I had written : ' I agree with you about people coming before ideas. But sometimes the idea represents a person, viz. yourself ! And while you are apparently fighting for principle it is really your own life you are fighting for. Please mark this profound statement for it is my own philosophical autobiography in a nutshell.'] Of course there are cases in which ideas—if one can call them so—must take precedence over persons ; for instance in the case of a vocation. The vocation, as you say, really is a person, viz., the one who is called on to renounce it and who must not. But if it is only a question of the greater or lesser difficulties under which the vocation can be pursued—as for example a musician's career in an unmusical country or a thinker's work in the midst of a hostile community, *e.g.* Voltaire in New England, well, then I am inclined to think the world only needs the work of those who can work under difficulties; and persons must resume their precedence over ideas. The moral effort somehow tells on the quality of the work; not directly of course but in a roundabout way, as gymnastics might. You found it so yourself. This runs into the old question of morality and art which can be answered in a breath. A poet who can write better verses with the help of gin (like Byron?) had better remain sober and do as well as he can in that state. But if he cannot do anything at all in that state let him get drunk like Musset; it is part of his vocation and not a mere help to it; and he is not shirking difficulties, he is struggling with death all the time. The wrong thing is to shirk difficulties, and it is only because they generally present themselves under the form of persons that I say, first consider persons and then ideas. Do you agree? The man whose work is not wanted is the one who makes it easier for himself at any cost. That settles him.

Yesterday evening I went to see Much Ado about Nothing at the Lyceum, with our friend Irving as Benedict and the voiceless but genial Terry as Beatrix. Is the play supposed to be a genuine work of Shakespere's? I can hardly believe it; he may have arranged it a little, but it is a weak and silly thing. They all try to be witty the whole time in the most self-conscious manner, and don't succeed once even by chance. When I came out I thought I should never smile again. But I shall.

Tell me more when you have time to stretch and breathe.

H.

(4)

Dresden : December 14, 1891.

. . . Frau von Stockhausen is better, but getting near the end of her lease. I have forgiven her long ago, as one forgives people who have never in their life known what they were doing or where they were going but who glitter like beautiful fishes. I am acting very dutifully by her, taking her down to Florence, etc. We are on the best of terms and she is persuaded I am the devil; tells everybody so. . . .

Thank you for your letter.[1] Believe me it is not the author but the friend who is pleased though he only comes in under cover of the other. I find (don't you?) that after the first fortnight or so an author doesn't much care about his work, *quâ* author. It is cut off from his flesh and has gone forth on its own account. 'Dieu te mène à ton adresse!' said Musset. . . .

(5)

Rome : Christmas Eve, 1891.

. . . We dined with the Fiedlers the other day in Munich. She has a very pretty expression of countenance, something brave and nice in the eyes that is quite an invention. [2] He seemed to me to be looking younger than in former days; perhaps that is because he is not writing anything just now. I told him his book on the artistic Thätigkeit [3] ought to be translated into English to counteract some of Ruskin's poison. But would the English read it? I wish you could have heard Henry James's lamentations over the British brain the other day in the Dresden Gallery. Of course only as regards things intellectual, otherwise it is a powerful instrument. So don't be offended. What made it so very comic is that he doesn't like the Germans—is affronted at their meals and the hours of their meals, their beds and their bedclothes; and their stoves, and their sausages, and their faces and their beer; so that their power of following ideas, which he was comparing with amazement to English incapacity, seemed to come in as an extra grievance against them—a way of adding insult to injury. . . .

I am glad you have a Latin friend at last. It is an utterly unknown race in Gothdom, whether English or German, as I

---

[1] I had been angry with him, but had got over my anger re-reading *The Prison.*

[2] Used in the sense of ' trouvaille.'   [3] The function of art.

am sure you will find out in a few years—as unknown as
the Chinese, and as remote. I am never weary of watching
them and am always discovering things I had not suspected;
especially in the French who are strangest of the lot and
the hardest to read. . . .

. . . I am alone here; the others are in Florence till I
have chosen a dwelling. Looking at miles of painting and
statuary I ask myself why all this labour, unless the good
people enjoyed it? As soon as one fancies them having
toiled with love and got up cheerfully in the morning for the
day's work, their pictures and their statues become quite
pleasant to look at; but if they were simply struggling to
do something remarkable they might just as profitably for
themselves and for us have walked the treadmill. I think
most reputations seem stolen after a while because they were
not earned with enough joy. . . .

(6)

[*After Frau von Stockhausen's Death*]

Rome : January 4, 1892.

You must have been puzzled by my telegram a few days
since. I was called suddenly to Florence on account of my
mother-in-law's death. I think I had told you she was with
Julia in the Via de' Bardi. It is extraordinary how many
things there are to be done when a relative dies, especially
when the coffin is taken to a foreign land, and I have given
up going to Paris or London this month in favour of April.
I could not go far away just now. Stockhausen and his son
are in Florence; meanwhile I am getting things ready in the
apartment I have taken here—a nice old-fashioned one—and
Julia arrives as soon as all is in order.

You don't expect an *oraison funèbre* from me. Peace to
the dead. I never could give her my sincere affection, but I
honestly gave some admiration—and a great deal of kindness, which I hope will be counted to my credit in some
future life.

Do you recollect Rome? I think I shall be fond of it.
Perhaps the spirit will move me to write once more. After

all it is fun. And fun is a great god as you know. . . . My dear friend I wish you for this year, and always, the best that I can wish.

Your

H.

(7)

[After Lisl's Death]

Rome : January 30, 1892.

. . . Since I wrote to you Lisl is dead. Perhaps you have heard of it through the Fiedlers or Wachs. I wonder if it recalls past friendship to you, or if the breach was too wide even for memory? I could talk with you about it but am at a loss to soliloquise, because I don't know if enmity or goodwill prevails in your heart. For this reason I did not inform you at once; also because I thought I should get a letter from you. I often go to the Post Office to ask, and hate to go away disappointed. Have you seen a cat return to its saucer every five minutes to see if perchance milk has not grown there again? And fancy if it waits a week between each trip and still finds nothing ! . . .

(8)

Rome : February 8, 1892.

. . . I am glad to hear you speak of Lisl as you do. Very glad. With your Celtic exuberance of expression you once spoke, or rather wrote, about her in a way that grieved me and shut me up on that subject, though I hoped, as it has turned out, that sometimes you felt otherwise. It was about having wasted your time and your treasures on her. No, you certainly did not waste your time, as your sorrow for her now proves. You really did love her, and that in itself is enough. Perhaps she returned less than you gave; if so the loss was chiefly hers; but *as far as I know* I don't think the word traitor applies to her. It may be that I have not all the facts (you speak sometimes as though I had not) but I doubt if you have them either or have ever quite realised the cruel position she was in. Yes, we were on quite friendly terms, she and I; never intimate of course—firstly because there was a big silence between us about you and the ——s,[1] and then because of something so German about her that all my Latin colours glowed at once with redoubled fury as soon as we met. But she had a wonderful grace of moods which I could not look at without admiration, and I suppose she had the penetration of her sex in finding this out, and so liked me well enough, as an unclassable curiosity of a brother-in-law. Julia was fond of her in the usual proper, sisterly fashion but nothing out of the way, whereas she worshipped her mother, to whose shortcomings her eyes were lovingly blind; and the minor loss has been swamped in the greater one. Love is good no matter whom it goes to; and if perchance to one's mother, who would protest or breathe a word?

I am glad you grieve over Lisl, because a great affection ending in total indifference is inexpressibly sad to me. Why go on with one's self, with the same body and the same name, why not blow one's brains out and make a fresh start if such things can be forgotten? Times may change and trouble may come, even strife and separation; but something must surely remain as long as those who have loved one another remain alive—respect for the feelings they wrought together, and gratitude therefore to one another. You cannot at all be sure, I should fancy, that because Lisl turned away from you and held aloof, or was hard or unjust on some point or other, she had forgotten. I imagine not. She was too musical to forget, and her eyes were too deep and pure. The strife and separation were necessities of the foreground, one of the tragedies we are called on to play without knowing why. I wish you could have been sure of this, and, as you say, have joined hands for a minute; but unless you have very strong proof to the contrary—something of which I am quite ignorant—judge her by yourself, and what she felt by what you feel.

I have not spoken to you yet about the Mass and Levi's verdict. . . . You happy, clever one to have made yourself intelligible! I envy you, with affectionate pride and joy. I never shall have that luck, or skill . . . or goodness?

[1] The couple who had done so much mischief seven years previously.

Perhaps it is goodness, warmth of feeling for others, that makes one clear to them. If it were not for the thought that perhaps it is goodness that does it I would go to sleep comfortably in my obscureness. You see we have two *rôles* in the world; one as human beings, and the other as cosmic atoms, grains of dust filtering eternally through space. As human being I don't seem to have got on very far somehow, but as cosmic atom *je suis très réussi*, I assure you! Of course the question may arise : ' was kann ich mir dafür kaufen?'[1] but such mercantile meditations must be instantly repressed. Only the other thought remains : perhaps it is a lack of love for others that makes what one has to say a hard saying for them. One tunes one's guitar for a great song, and nothing is heard save a sound of riddles. I will arise and go unto my Father and will say unto him : Give me a slate and a piece of chalk that I may work out the problem of life eternal. Funny and sad. But after all that is not such a bad mixture; a sort of gooseberry tart in morals. . . .

I don't tell you anything about Lisl's last months because you must have heard all from the Fiedlers. I am glad you feel in sympathy with them. I saw them again with a distinct feeling of pleasure.

Good-night to you.

H.

---

[1] What can be purchased with that?

INDEX

Printed in Great Britain by MACKAYS LTD., Chatham.